# PRAISE FOR *BANKING AS A SERVICE*

"Jason Mikula's experience as an operator in fintech and banking, combined with his incredible reporting on the banking-as-a-service space over the last few years makes him the best person to write the definitive book on the past, present, and future of BaaS. He's done just that."

**Alex Johnson, Founder, Fintech Takes**

"As a banker, investor and someone that's done upwards of 1000 deals in the fintech space, I can highly recommend this book for anyone in the industry or those trying to break into it. The book contains a treasure chest of insights, does an excellent job of capturing the nuances of a rapidly evolving space, and will be required reading for everyone I work with."

**Steve McLaughlin, Founder and CEO, FT Partners**

"Jason Mikula is one of my favorite sources of fintech news and analysis. He has his finger on the industry's pulse and is often first with breaking news. He stays with the story after it breaks, chasing down additional developments and exploring all the angles and he really understands and is able to explain the complex regulatory framework in which fintechs operate. This all adds up to Jason Mikula being a must-read for me and other industry professionals."

**Michele Alt, Co-Founder, Klaros Group**

"To understand the future, one must understand the past. Jason Mikula takes us on a thorough but delightful journey beginning with the predecessor models that laid the foundation for BaaS as we know it today. The book isn't just a history lesson, it is a practical guide to what the future holds."

**Jason Henrichs, CEO, Alloy Labs Alliance**

# Banking as a Service

*Opportunities, Challenges, and Risks
of New Banking Business Models*

Jason Mikula

KoganPage

First published in Great Britain and the United States in 2025 by Kogan Page Limited

2nd Floor, 45 Gee Street
London
EC1V 3RS
United Kingdom

8 W 38th Street, Suite 902
New York, NY 10018
USA

www.koganpage.com

Kogan Page books are printed on paper from sustainable forests.

**ISBNs**

Hardback    978 1 3986 1790 2
Paperback   978 1 3986 1788 9
Ebook       978 1 3986 1789 6

**British Library Cataloguing-in-Publication Data**

A CIP record for this book is available from the British Library.

**Library of Congress Control Number**

2024041482

Typeset by Integra Software Services, Pondicherry
Print production managed by Jellyfish
Printed and bound by CPI Group (UK) Ltd, Croydon, CR0 4YY

*To my entire family, especially Luis and Lito, for supporting (and putting up with) me while I tackled this project.*

# CONTENTS

# ABOUT THE AUTHOR

Jason Mikula is the publisher of *Fintech Business Weekly*, a newsletter going beyond the headlines to analyze the technology, regulatory, and business model trends driving the rapidly evolving financial services ecosystem at the intersection of traditional banking, payments, and fintech. He also advises and consults for and invests in early-stage startups. Previously, he spent over a decade building and scaling consumer finance businesses, including at Enova, LendUp, and Goldman Sachs.

# FOREWORD

*by Simon Taylor, author of* Fintech Brainfood

Today companies like Chime, Monzo, and Revolut are household names, but this first wave of consumer fintech companies launched cards and accounts powered by new providers like Marqeta and GPS (Thredd). Seeing this success, new providers emerged worldwide, like Solaris in Germany, Railsr in the United Kingdom, Swan in France, Synapse in the United States, and Audax in Singapore. Technology that used to be exclusive to banks was now openly available to developers to innovate. Suddenly, creating a card program and mobile app felt as easy as accepting payments online. With a few lines of code and a low upfront cost, almost anyone could launch a financial product or embed it into their technology platform.

It's no surprise then, that by 2021, fintech represented one in five of all venture capital dollars invested. The once sleepy world of financial services became the hottest thing in technology. This new generation of API-first technology providers, often called "Banking-as-a-Service" (BaaS), unlocked hundreds, if not thousands, of new consumer and business financial accounts and propositions. They could get to market faster for lower upfront costs, and the supplier would take care of all of the boring technical and compliance stuff.

These providers would connect with one or multiple banks with a compelling offer. Banks would attract new customers without having to invest heavily in technology or marketing. Entrepreneurs could solve problems for consumers and get their products to market, and the BaaS provider would help pull all of this together as a platform. This became so attractive that the early moving banks have shown this business model to be enormously lucrative, with return on equity in the 25 per cent + range, compared to 10 to 15 per cent for the top 10 banks.

This seems like the ultimate win/win/win.

There was just one issue. The banks, regulations, and investor ecosystem were never designed to handle this scale of new customers and fintech programs.

Banks primarily operated direct-to-consumer and didn't have the controls and processes to oversee the new BaaS providers. Some fintech programs and entrepreneurs lacked the experience to ensure they met all their compliance obligations. Inevitably it started to go wrong.

In the United Kingdom, regulators have discussed "putting grit in the system" to ensure anti-money laundering (AML) controls are in place, and Europe also saw the implosion of Wirecard, one of the first program managers and BaaS providers that was instrumental in helping companies like Monzo and Revolut get to market initially. The successful models in the UK are now banks with application programming interfaces (APIs), such as Clearbank and Audax.

Perhaps the culmination of regulator and market shifts in tone was the explosive bankruptcy of Synapse. Synapse was a first mover in BaaS but is now embroiled in a bankruptcy court case involving Evolve Bank, Lineage Bank, and a handful of fintech programs, where consumers cannot access their funds. Jason Mikula of *Fintech Business Weekly* chronicled all of this. His weekly newsletter became the entire fintech news for the year, critical reading that has led to citations from many mainstream media outlets. Jason has now compiled the most comprehensive set of case studies, challenges, and opportunities for any financial institution, investor, or entrepreneur looking to move into financial services.

The devil is in the details, and not all banks, providers, or fintech programs are created equal.

Financial services remain the world's largest profit pool, and embedded finance remains the single largest upside opportunity for banking. We've barely scratched the surface of what could be done, and the large banks are only just at the starting block. The banks that have successfully executed their embedded finance strategy remain incredibly profitable, but have gotten there through substantial investment in third party oversight, compliance, and fraud mitigation.

The nature of venture capital is to try things that might not work. The best time to invest is often when sentiment is at its lowest. Sentiment on BaaS is low, but the opportunity is staggering. Not everything in BaaS has worked, but the core business model remains lucrative. If we can learn how to move faster without breaking things for consumers.

# PREFACE

I began writing this book in earnest in January 2024, and it has been a bit of a surreal experience. In the course of writing this book, the topic itself, banking-as-a-service, has been rapidly evolving, at least in the US market. During the six months I worked on drafting these 15 chapters, several BaaS-focused banks, including Blue Ridge, Choice, Lineage, Thredd, and Evolve received enforcement actions, several BaaS middleware intermediaries pivoted their business models, the consolidation in consumer fintech continued, and Synapse, a pioneer of the BaaS model, collapsed into bankruptcy, leaving hundreds of thousands of users unable to access their funds. Even as I write this preface, at the end of June 2024, the Synapse situation remains unresolved, casting a long shadow over fintech and BaaS in the US, with more regulatory actions seemingly inevitable. And, in a truly shocking twist, Evolve Bank, likely the single largest banking-as-a-service provider in the United States, became the victim of a Russian ransomware attack, with repercussions that are likely to reverberate across the entire industry and for years.

But writing this book gave me a chance to take a closer look at fintech and BaaS models in other jurisdictions. The US, as is so often the case, is an outlier. In other regions, it's often simpler to apply for a new bank charter, and alternate charter types, like e-money institutions, exist—in many cases, reducing the need for the BaaS model and providing greater regulatory clarity, for banks, fintechs, and their users alike. While the prospect of such licensing regimes in the US seems dim, other countries' successes and failures offer valuable lessons that legislators, regulators, and banking and fintech practitioners would be well-served by taking advantage of.

I hope that this book can serve as a productive addition to the conversation by exploring both the opportunities and the risks in banking-as-a-service business models. There is no turning back the

clock, with ample evidence pointing to the continued decline of physical branch-based banking and, absent a change in strategy and
tactics, continued consolidation in the banking sector, if not globally,
certainly at least in the United States. I sincerely believe that BaaS and
the embedded finance use cases it enables still hold the potential to
expand access and inclusion for consumers and businesses, while
offering a lifeline to smaller and community banks that are facing
existential threats.

# ACKNOWLEDGEMENTS

I'd like to take a moment to acknowledge industry colleagues, who have been supportive and invaluable resources as I've written this book and more broadly as I've worked covering the banking and fintech space. There isn't enough space to thank everyone, but my heartfelt appreciation in no particular order goes out to: Alex Johnson, Jason Henrichs, Kiah Haslett, Jesse Silverman, Simon Taylor, Soups Ranjan, Phil Goldfeder, Matt Janiga, Sharon Olexy, Robert Keil, Brett King, Ron Shevlin, Jim Marous, Arcady Lapiro, Marcel van Oost, Hugh Son, Michael Roddan, Adwait Joshi, Jonathan Awad, Rory O'Reilly, Erin Bruehl, Jon Zanoff, and many, many others. It wouldn't be possible to do what I do without those that have come before me or without a strong, supportive community— so, thank you!

# 1

# What Is "Banking-as-a-Service," and Where Did It Come From?

CHAPTER OBJECTIVES

In this chapter, we will explore the history of non-banks partnering with chartered institutions and how the partnership model differs from and evolved into "banking-as-a-service" (BaaS) as we now know it. We will introduce some of the reasons why non-banks need to partner with banks. And we will unpack the forces that drove explosive demand from fintechs for bank partners and the forces driving more banks to explore banking-as-a-service business models.

## Applying a Software Mindset to Banking

The "as-a-service" moniker, popularized by the idea of software-as-a-service (SaaS), is used to describe a capability provided by a third party on a subscription or an on-demand basis, rather than owned outright by the organization making use of it. The movement toward "as-a-service" mirrors the transition in software architecture from monolithic, self-contained applications to flexible, microservice architecture and application programming interfaces, or APIs. Whether building a piece of software or building an entire business, an "as-a-service" approach potentially enables one to build more quickly and flexibly, thus spending less to get to market and being more adaptable once there.

But how does this "as-a-service" mentality, born in the world of software, apply to the highly regulated world of banking and financial services? While specifics vary by jurisdiction, the business of banking broadly consists of holding customer deposits, making loans, and processing payments. These activities come with unique responsibilities and risks not present in other businesses.

KEY LEARNING POINTS

The business of banking, at a high level, consists of holding customer deposits, making loans, and processing payments.

For example, holding customer deposits on a "demand" basis and using them to offer loans of a longer, fixed duration, known as maturity transformation, creates liquidity risks that banks must manage responsibly.[1] Given the history of "bank runs," or situations where depositors lose confidence in a bank and rush to demand their money back, an incredibly complex web of regulations and government supports has evolved to mitigate the risk of deposit runs and to protect depositors, up to a certain point, if a bank were to fail.

## The Privileges of Being a Bank

In addition to holding customer deposits, there are numerous other privileges chartered banks uniquely have. For example, in the United States, banks can belong to the Federal Reserve System, giving them access to the central bank's payment infrastructure, including a Fed master account.[2] This means that banks serve as the gateway to common money movement methods, including wire transfers and automated clearing house (ACH) transactions. While non-banks can secure state-issued money transmission licenses (MTLs), they would need to do so in each state they plan to operate and would still need to work with a bank to actually run their business.

In the United States, only banks can be principal members of card network schemes, like Visa and Mastercard, giving them the ability to issue credit and debit cards that operate on these networks.

While it is possible to secure state-issued licenses to lend without being a bank, chartered banks enjoy numerous advantages in lending, generally including the right to preempt state law, enabling them to offer a consistent lending product, across the entire country, without needing to obtain a license in each state.[3] Access to stable, low-cost deposit funding is also generally considered an advantage, compared to non-bank lenders that rely on other mechanisms to fund their balance sheets.

> KEY LEARNING POINTS
>
> In the United States, chartered banks enjoy key privileges by virtue of their charters, including the ability to hold insured customer deposits, direct access to payment rails, the ability to belong to the Federal Reserve System, and, generally, the right to preempt state law.

These privileges also come with risks and thus responsibilities. For instance, managing the liquidity risk of "borrowing short" (by holding deposits) and "lending long" is but one example of a risk banks must understand and mitigate. Other examples of risks that banks face include credit risk, market risk, model risk, operational risk, financial crime risk, supplier risk, and conduct risk—with each applicable category of risk coming with a complex mitigation framework and, often, strict legal and regulatory requirements.[4]

Companies in the United States that want to offer products or services that would be considered the business of banking—but *without* getting their own bank license—must work with a chartered bank to do so.

## Prepaid Debit Cards Are an Early Example of a Bank/Non-Bank Partnership

The idea of a non-bank company partnering with a chartered bank to offer regulated products is not new. One key example that paved the way for the neobanks we know today is the humble prepaid debit card.

The roots of prepaid debit actually date to Europe in the 1970s, where prepaid phone cards were developed as an alternative to using coins in payphones.[5] The concept was introduced in the United States in the 1980s, and expanded from payphones to include other merchant-specific use cases. These kinds of private-label stored value cards are still in use today, popularly known as "gift cards." By the early 1990s, the US Government began replacing paper "food stamps" with electronic benefit transfer (EBT) cards, which recipients could use to purchase qualifying goods at stores that accepted them.

Unlike merchant-specific stored value cards, prepaid debit cards are "open loop," meaning they can be used at numerous merchants. Most prepaid cards in the United States are issued on the Visa or Mastercard networks, meaning they can be used to make payments at almost any merchant that accepts Visa- or Mastercard-issued payment cards. General purpose reloadable debit cards began to grow in popularity in the late 1990s and early 2000s, particularly among lower-income, unbanked, and underbanked consumers.

> **KEY LEARNING POINTS**
>
> General purpose reloadable prepaid debit cards were an outgrowth of private-label stored valued cards, popularly known as "gift cards," that could only be used at a specific merchant. Popular companies in the space as it gained traction in the 1990s had to partner with banks to hold deposits and issue cards.

The major players in the prepaid card space at the time, however, typically were not banks. They included names like Blackhawk Network, AccountNow, and Green Dot (which eventually acquired a bank). In order to operate, these companies needed to partner with banks to handle critical, regulated, and restricted functions, including holding deposits and issuing payment cards on the widely accepted network schemes. This is just to say, the idea of a non-bank partnering with a chartered bank is, in and of itself, not new.

## The 1990s Rise and Fall of "Rent-A-Bank" Partnerships

Like prepaid debit partnerships, examples of non-bank lenders partnering with chartered banks also date to the 1990s, if not earlier. While many states have usury caps, which set the maximum permissible interest rate in the state, banks typically enjoy the right of "preemption," which allows for a bank in one state to export, or write loans into, another state, even at rates that exceed that target state's usury cap. This mechanism allows for banks based in states with higher or no rate limits to offer credit to borrowers in other states at interest rates that exceed the borrower's state's usury limit.

KEY LEARNING POINTS

Historically, payday lenders could only operate in select states in which they could obtain licenses. By partnering with chartered banks, payday lenders could preempt state laws by operating as agents or brokers on behalf of chartered banks. This so-called "rent-a-bank" model generated pushback from states that did not permit such loans and consumer advocates, leading to regulators effectively shutting down the practice in the early 2000s.[6]

Like the opportunity prepaid debit issuers identified in the 1990s, a segment of non-bank lenders known for sometimes aggressive regulatory strategies took advantage of banks' preemption and interest rate exportation rights. Deferred deposit transaction lenders, popularly known as payday lenders, expanded aggressively in the United States in the 1990s, operating under state licensing regimes. But not all states permitted the product category, where interest rates, on an annualized basis, reach into the triple digits. And for the states that did permit the product, loan amounts and terms varied state to state, creating logistical and administrative headaches. By partnering with banks and purportedly acting as agents or brokers to originate the loan on behalf of a bank, and then service the loan, payday lenders were able to circumvent state restrictions capping interest rates. Payday lenders leveraged such partnerships to operate in states where such products would have otherwise been illegal.

However, given the high interest rates and controversial nature of the loans they were offering, the payday lender-bank partnership model, often referred to as "rent-a-bank" by critics, came under increasing scrutiny from consumer advocates, legislators, and banking regulators. Ultimately, over the course of several years in the early 2000s, bank regulators issued various guidance and pursued enforcement actions that effectively put an end to these kinds of non-bank lender/bank partnerships when used to originate short-term, high-rate loans.[7]

## From Partner Banking to Banking-as-a-Service

So, what is the difference between the partnerships between prepaid debit companies and lenders in the 1990s and 2000s compared to "banking-as-a-service" relationships today? And what drove that change?

As with many aspects of American fintech, many of the underlying forces that shaped and support what became known as banking-as-a-service have their roots in the aftermath of the 2007–2008 financial crisis. The housing bubble and subsequent banking and financial crisis led to the most significant attempts at banking reform since the 1980s savings and loan meltdown. In the wake of the crisis, Congress passed the Dodd-Frank Wall Street Reform and Consumer Protection Act, popularly referred to merely as Dodd-Frank.

Dodd-Frank's reach and impact are significant. The bill itself is over 800 pages, and it calls for more than 10 regulators to promulgate rules and regulations—a process that, more than 13 years later, still is not complete.[8] Two components of Dodd-Frank that have contributed to the rise of banking-as-a-service are the creation of a new government agency to safeguard consumers' rights, the Consumer Financial Protection Bureau, and a cap regulating how much large banks could earn from processing customers' debit card transactions.

## It Always Goes Back to Durbin

Part of Dodd-Frank, popularly known as the Durbin amendment, instructed the Federal Reserve to calculate and implement a cap on the interchange rates, or "swipe fees," for debit cards issued by larger banks. One of the arguments to cap these fees was that doing so would save merchants on payment processing costs, with merchants then passing those savings along to shoppers in the form of lower prices. However, there is little evidence that this was actually the case, with studies suggesting merchants themselves ended up pocketing the lion's share of the savings.[9]

### KEY LEARNING POINTS

The Durbin amendment regulates how much larger banks, those with over $10 billion in assets, can earn from debit interchange. Passed as part of 2010's Dodd-Frank, the measure has had far-reaching consequences for banks, fintechs, merchants, and consumers.

The Durbin amendment only applies to debit cards issued by banks that have $10 billion or more in assets. The Federal Reserve calculated a cap of 0.05 per cent of a given debit transaction plus a fixed $0.21. The cap went into effect in October 2011. Once the cap went into effect, the average "swipe fee" for covered transactions dropped from about $0.60 per transaction to approximately $0.20. In late 2023, the Fed proposed an update to how this cap is calculated, which, if finalized, would reduce the cap to be 0.04 per cent of covered transactions plus a fixed fee of $0.144.[10]

The proximate effect of the Durbin amendment was that covered banks, those with $10 billion or more in assets, saw a significant drop in interchange income earned from debit transactions. It is generally accepted that, in an effort to make up for the revenue lost due to lower interchange rates, impacted banks began adding and increasing checking account-related fees, including minimum balance, non-sufficient funds, returned check, and overdraft fees. Given the nature of these fees, they were (and continue to be) disproportionately borne by lower-income consumers. The result for many lower-income consumers was an increasingly negative experience at larger banks.

Banks with *less* than $10 billion in assets are exempt from the interchange caps imposed by the Durbin amendment. As a result, the revenue generated as a share of the size of a given transaction on a debit card issued by a smaller bank can be more than twice what it would be for the same transaction at a larger bank. In 2022, the average interchange fee per transaction for exempt banks was $0.52, compared to just $0.23 on average for non-exempt banks.[11] This difference in revenue opportunity had the unintended consequence, years later, of positioning sub-$10 billion banks as having a competitive advantage versus larger ones when it comes to fintech and banking-as-a-service.

Together, the increasingly negative experience some consumers had at larger banks and smaller banks' advantage of not being bound by the Durbin amendment's cap on debit interchange would help power what would become a key driver of demand for banking-as-a-service providers: The neobanks. (We'll explore this in greater depth in Chapter 3.)

### The Creation of the Consumer Financial Protection Bureau

In addition to the Durbin amendment, Dodd-Frank also created the Consumer Financial Protection Bureau (CFPB). The impact of the creation of the CFPB on the US banking and financial services landscape has been far reaching. Unpacking it in full would require a book unto itself. But it is worth calling out an early area the CFPB developed regulations for, which, over time, helped contribute to the rise of fintech and the creation of demand for banking-as-a-service capabilities.

KEY LEARNING POINTS

The Consumer Financial Protection Bureau, or the CFPB, was created in the wake of the 2008 financial crisis as an independent federal agency focused on consumer protection matters. The CFPB's prepaid card rule altered the existing market dynamic and helped pave the way for the creation of neobanks.

One of the CFPB's earliest efforts was to introduce regulations governing the growing general purpose reloadable prepaid card market. The CFPB, which officially began operating in July 2011, introduced its proposed rule governing prepaid cards less than a year later. The rule sought to strengthen consumer protections and limit fees charged to consumers who used prepaid cards. Elements of the rule, which was finalized in 2016, include requiring providers to give consumers free access to account information, protections for lost cards and unauthorized transactions, error and dispute resolution rights, and mandatory "know before you owe" fee disclosures.[12]

The rule brought the rights and protections of prepaid cards closer to parity with traditional bank-offered checking accounts. But the rule also had the effect of tending to increase costs and decrease revenue for prepaid card providers, resulting in lower profitability. Combined with numerous other factors discussed here, this change helped contribute to a shift from prepaid cards to what would become known as neobanks—a key use case and source of demand for banking-as-a-service.

### Venture Capital Funding for Fintech Explodes

Against the backdrop of the unfolding impacts of Dodd-Frank, fintech was becoming a bona fide phenomenon. Although use of the term "fintech," a portmanteau of "financial" and "technology," didn't really begin to take off until 2015, entrepreneurs and founders began building companies in the emerging space by the late 2000s.

Simple, formerly known as BankSimple, was founded in 2009. Moven, formerly known as MovenBank, was founded in 2011. Both were early movers working to capitalize on the then-new ability to install third-party apps on smartphones. Apple's App Store and the Android Market, now part of Google Play, both launched in 2008, enabling companies to offer functionality through apps on mobile devices. Establishment banks, as they are wont to do, were slower to roll out native mobile apps. And, when they did so, their apps tended to have a barebones set of features and offer a design and user experience that left something to be desired. At the time, merely existing and offering a polished user interface was a competitive differentiator versus incumbent banks.

Fintechs focused on lending also began forming in the late 2000s. A pair of companies, LendingClub and Prosper, were the poster children of this early era of fintech. The two companies' business models were functionally identical. At the time, both operated "peer-to-peer" lending platforms, in which they operated a marketplace of sorts that sought to match borrowers with savers/investors. The promise to borrowers was expanded access to credit and lower interest rates, particularly compared to credit card borrowing. For investors, the appeal was the chance to earn significantly higher returns than a typical savings account, which more or less offered 0 per cent from the time of the 2008 housing crisis until about 2016.

KEY LEARNING POINTS

While there were some early movers in applying emerging technology to financial services, the term "fintech" did not really begin to take off until 2015. The amount of venture capital funding to fintech companies rose dramatically in the 2010s, peaking during the early phase of the Covid-19 pandemic.

Both LendingClub and Prosper offered unsecured personal loans, a product that many banks had ceased to offer following the 2008 crisis.[13] But, at the time, neither LendingClub nor Prosper were banks. In order to scale quickly and offer a consistent product across the US, both partnered with banks—the same bank actually, Utah-based WebBank.

With companies like Simple, Moven, LendingClub, and Prosper showing initial promise, venture capital firms became increasingly willing to invest in the category. Entrepreneurs' interest in founding companies in the space and talent's desire to work in the field began to grow. Less than $10 billion was invested in fintech startups globally in 2010, 2011, and 2012. But in 2013, the amount jumped to nearly $20 billion. And by 2015, nearly $70 billion flowed to fintech startups, accounting for about 13 per cent of all venture dollars that year.

*More Money, More Fintechs, More Demand for Bank Partners*

As the idea of fintech really began to take off and funding to startups in the space grew dramatically, companies began building and iterating on products and services. At the time, there were only a handful of banks that were interested and had a track record of working with third-party partners: Names like The Bancorp Bank and MetaBank (now Pathward), which had a history of serving as bank partners for prepaid card issuers and private-label stored value cards.

But whereas prepaid and private-label cards were fairly straightforward propositions, emerging fintech companies had greater ambitions. They were looking to create new products and features with polished, elegant, typically mobile-first experiences. Fintechs, tending to be engineering-led organizations, often blanched at banks' outdated technology stacks, typically running on legacy core providers. Much of the financial system, even in 2024, runs on COBOL, a programming language that dates to the 1960s. Integrating with a bank partner often meant passing batch files back and forth—anathema to technologists that were building their own applications with the latest API-first, microservices architecture.

KEY LEARNING POINTS

Because most fintechs sought to offer products or services that are regulated or need to access underlying bank infrastructure, the demand for bank partnerships began to increase dramatically in the early 2010s. As more fintechs began working with banks, pain points, including banks' antiquated technology and risk-averse cultures, began to emerge.

Bank culture could also be a shock to those used to Silicon Valley's engineering-driven culture, which emphasized building quickly, deploying "minimal viable products" to customers, learning what worked and what did not, and iterating. By contrast, banks, particularly in the late 2000s and early 2010s, were overwhelmingly not technology organizations. Technology was often viewed as a support function and something that vendors supplied—not something that banks created. This is particularly true of the smaller and community banks that would come to power many fintechs. Instead, most banks' core competency is risk management, which, often, lends itself to the opposite of "moving fast and breaking things."

The challenges for fintechs of working with banks—old tech, cumbersome risk and compliance procedures—would eventually give rise to a set of companies that specialize in facilitating bank-fintech partnerships: Middleware providers. The difficulties of working with established banks would also spur the creation of new banks whose primary business model focuses on supporting fintech partners. We'll discuss both further in Chapter 6.

### Community Banks Look to BaaS for Growth, Diversification

The increasing availability of venture capital (VC) funding and growing number of fintechs help explain the growing demand for banking capabilities, contributing to the rise of banking-as-a-service. But what about the supply side—the banks that actually hold the necessary charters to power these products and services?

While a full discussion of the forces reshaping the banks most likely to partner with fintechs, those with less than $10 billion in assets, is beyond the scope of this book, it is worth examining some of the trends driving smaller banks to explore new business models, like banking-as-a-service.

There are numerous things that make the US banking system unique, including its dual federal-state nature. Both the federal government and state governments can grant bank charters and thus have a role in regulating the banking system. One result of the country's historically balkanized banking system is the sheer number of chartered banks. As recently as the late 1980s, the US had over 14,000 insured depository institutions with some 44,000 branches. But in the 1980s and 1990s, federal and state governments relaxed a variety of rules that made it easier for banks to operate across state lines.[14] Regulatory changes and market forces have contributed to a steady consolidation and decline in the number of chartered banks, even though the number of bank branches continued rising into the early 2010s. By 2022, the number of chartered banks had declined by over 70 per cent from its peak in the mid-1980s to fewer than 4,200 insured commercial banks.

KEY LEARNING POINTS

Smaller and community banks face a multitude of challenges. The longer-term trend in the US has been toward consolidation. The rise of internet and mobile banking has eroded the importance of geographic location and physical branch networks. And the costs and scalability of tech infrastructure tend to favor larger banks over smaller ones.

Changes in regulation that enabled increasing consolidation are hardly the only forces buffeting smaller banks. Another key factor that has steadily eroded the community-banking business model: The rise of online banking, beginning in the mid-1990s, and especially the advent of smartphone-enabled mobile banking in the late 2000s. For millennia, banking has been a local business. Like the proverbial bank in *It's A Wonderful Life*, financial institutions were typically pillars of their local community, holding customers' deposits and making loans in the surrounding geographic area. If this model was already beginning to change as consolidation began to take off in the 1980s, the rise of the internet fundamentally changed the geographic constraints, or lack thereof, of banking.

The internet enabled users to do most everyday banking activities from home—signaling the decline in the importance of a physical branch network. Recognizing the potential benefits of operating nationwide without the expense of physical branches with tellers, in the late 1990s and early 2000s, direct-to-consumer, branchless banks entered the market. First Internet Bancorp launched in 1999, followed in 2000 by ING Direct, later acquired by Capital One. The introduction of the iPhone in 2007 and Apple's App Store the following year built on internet banking, enabling users to manage their account from anywhere. While web and mobile access have inarguably been a boon for consumers, they have steadily eroded what had been a defining characteristic of the community bank: Its geographic location. Local banks were no longer just competing with whoever had a branch down the street or across town, but every bank with a website or app. The impact of this revolution is still unfolding. The number of physical bank branches in the US did not peak until 2012, at 82,126. With proximity to a branch location increasingly irrelevant for many consumers, the number of branches had dropped to less than 70,000 a decade later and will almost certainly continue to decline.[15]

Beyond reducing the importance of branch networks, the amount of investment and skills necessary to build and operate digital banking infrastructure tend to favor larger versus smaller banks. Creating a robust digital banking experience, online and in app, can have significant upfront and ongoing costs—this was particularly the case when these technologies were first emerging and the modern tooling available today did not yet exist. While significant upfront investment in digital tech is typically necessary, the flipside is that such investments can pay off as they usually have low marginal costs—they scale well, to use a favorite Silicon Valley term. A small community bank with thousands of customers, historically, would have to make substantial investments to build out their own web and app banking infrastructure.

With many smaller banks reluctant to make such investments or lacking the expertise and talent to do so, they were and, in many cases, continue to be dependent on third-party vendors to meet these needs. Specifically, their "core banking" providers—companies like Fiserv, FIS, and Jack Henry, which have long dominated the banking software market. The combination of this long-standing core banking oligopoly and bankers' general aversion to risk has contributed to a lack of innovation, especially for all but the largest banks that have the budgets and talent in house. Over time, this created a gap in capabilities and experience between the large number of smaller community banks and a small number of mega-banks. This simultaneously fed into the trend toward banking concentration, encouraged smaller banks to explore new business models and sources of revenue, and created a lane for consumer fintechs to compete in.

## Costs of Rising Regulatory Burdens Fall Unevenly

Another factor making life difficult for smaller banks has been the increasing burden of regulation. While the long-term trend in the United States from the Reagan-era through the 2008 financial crisis was deregulation, in the wake of the housing crisis, significant reforms were made to banking regulation. Reforms were aimed primarily at the largest institutions, particularly those colloquially referred to as "too big to fail." The creation of the Financial Stability Oversight Council (FSOC) and designating certain institutions as Globally Systemically Important Banks (GSIBs) or Systemically Important Financial Institutions (SIFIs) impacted the global financial system in ways that continue to be felt today.

The process to update and implement the Basel Committee's framework for liquidity risk management and supervision, a process that began in the wake of the crisis, is still ongoing as of early 2024, with so-called "Basel III endgame" proposals slated to begin taking effect in July 2025. Regulations called for enhanced capital buffers, limitations on leverage, liquidity requirements, and annual "stress testing," among numerous other reforms, all of which had the impact of increasing the workload on bank compliance teams and decreasing banks' profitability. The creation of the Consumer Financial Protection Bureau added a new regulator to the mix. The US Congress consciously tried to shield smaller, less-complex banks from some of the impacts of various reforms passed after the crisis by exempting banks below $10 billion in assets from various requirements.

KEY LEARNING POINTS

In the wake of the 2008 crisis, the regulatory burden on the banking sector increased significantly. Although legislators and regulators sought to exempt smaller, less-complicated, and less-risky banks from some requirements, the overall regulatory burden has increased.

Post-crisis measures are hardly the only incremental legislation or regulation impacting bank business models and operations since 2008. Indeed, Dodd-Frank directed bank and securities regulators to undertake a wide variety of notice-and-comment administrative rule-making, which remained incomplete some 13 years later. And apart from Dodd-Frank, new or updated regulations touching on everything from anti-money laundering to cybersecurity and consumer privacy have impacted banks of all sizes. While the burden of regulatory compliance to some extent does scale with the size and complexity of an institution (asset size, number and types of customers it serves, and so on), dealing with regulatory complexity, like building technologies, does tend to have economies of scale. A small bank that serves geographically local customers with straightforward products will have a lower regulatory burden than a global bank serving a wide variety of customers with complex products. Nonetheless, that small, simple bank has seen its regulatory compliance burden increase significantly over time, even in cases where the nature of the underlying business has not substantially changed.

## Rate Environment Has Weighed on Banks' Profitability

At a high level, commercial banks have two kinds of revenue: Interest income and non-interest income. Interest income is the revenue derived from lending activities from products like credit cards, mortgages, small-business loans, and so forth. Banks can generate interest income from loans they originate as well as through purchasing participation stakes or whole loans originated by other institutions. The makeup of non-interest income is determined by a bank's lines of business, but would include things like service fees on deposit accounts, annual fees on credit cards, spread on foreign exchange transactions, safety deposit boxes—really, any revenue that is not interest income.

A key metric to assess banks' profitability is their net interest margin, or NIM. NIM is the difference between the average rate a bank charges on its loans less its average cost of funds. Banks have various sources of funding, which have different tradeoffs, including their cost. For the purpose of this example, when we discuss a bank's funding or cost of funds, we will be referring to customers' deposits at the bank, unless otherwise stated.

KEY LEARNING POINTS

The extended period of low interest rates following the 2008 housing crisis compressed banks' net interest margins, weighing on their profitability. Conversely, the aggressive rate-hiking cycle beginning in early 2022 helped drive a drop in deposits and significantly increase banks' cost of funds.

In the wake of the 2008 financial crisis, the US central bank, the Federal Reserve, cut interest rates to essentially 0 per cent, where they remained until 2016. Given the global nature of the crisis, and the tendency of some countries to move rates in tandem with the US, many central banks around the world cut rates to zero or, in some cases, below zero, and kept them low for an extended period of time. Central bank rates typically form the benchmark for deposit and lending rates. While near-zero rates flowed through to deposits, meaning banks' cost of funds declined, they also resulted in lower interest rates for lending. Typically, declining interest rates result in a compression of banks' net interest margin, reducing profitability, which was generally the case in the wake of the 2008 financial crisis.

The more recent past illustrates other challenges banks, especially smaller ones, can have in managing their balance sheet. In the initial stages of the global Covid-19 pandemic, central banks, many of which had started cautiously raising rates in the mid-2010s, quickly dropped rates, often all the way back to zero. Governments around the world quickly rolled out unprecedented levels of fiscal support for their economies, particularly focused on consumers and small businesses. Consumers, facing unprecedented economic uncertainty, dramatically cut back on spending, with household savings rates in the US spiking from about 7 per cent to over 30 per cent.[16] The result of the various government interventions and consumer behavior change was a deluge of cash flowing into the banking system. At first blush, this might sound like an unequivocally good thing—why wouldn't banks want more deposits? But deposits are a liability on a bank's balance sheet; they are only helpful to the extent a bank can deploy them in a way that generates revenue. Particularly in the early phase of the pandemic, when consumers and small businesses were deleveraging, many banks slowed credit origination, both as prudent risk management and owing to reduced demand for credit.

As the pandemic waned and supply chain and consumer habits normalized, a different problem emerged for banks and the economy: Inflation. As it became clear the post-pandemic inflation was not as transitory as conventional wisdom predicted, the Fed embarked on its most aggressive rate-hiking cycle since the early 1980s. The unexpected, rapid rate hikes posed a multitude of challenges for banks, including shrinking deposits.

What had been a deposit glut during the height of the pandemic abruptly reversed, as depositors sought out higher yields available from products like money market funds or short-term government bonds. Around the same time, the spring banking crisis of 2023, which saw Silicon Valley Bank Signature, and First Republic fail, drove a flight to safety, especially for depositors with funds above the Federal

Deposit Insurance Corporation (FDIC) insurance limit of $250,000. Skittish customers moved funds from smaller banks to "too big to fail" institutions like JPMorgan Chase, Wells Fargo, and Bank of America, draining deposits from some regional and community banks that were, rightly or wrongly, perceived as risky.

## What Counts as Banking-as-a-Service?

There is far from universal agreement about the definition of "banking-as-a-service." There is broad agreement that the term refers to non-bank companies partnering, directly or indirectly, with chartered banks or other licensed institutions, depending on geography, in order to make use of products and services that require a license.

For the purposes of this book, we will use the term banking-as-a-service to refer to relationships in which a non-bank partners with an underlying bank or other licensed entity, directly or through an intermediary, to offer regulated products to end users that they otherwise would not be able to. Examples of core capabilities banking-as-a-service can enable non-banks to offer include holding insured customer deposits, issuing debit and credit cards, lending, and payment processing. Categories made possible by banking-as-a-service include "neobanks," where many customer-facing functions are handled by a fintech, but deposits are held and cards are issued by a partner bank, and point-of-sale lending, where a bank partner leverages its license to originate a loan, but the consumer-facing fintech is responsible for customer acquisition, underwriting, and servicing.

KEY LEARNING POINTS

There is not universal agreement on the definition of "banking-as-a-service," but the term is generally understood to refer to arrangements where a non-bank partners with a chartered institution to make regulated bank products, like deposit accounts and debit cards, available to end users.

Merely being a customer of a bank usually would not typify a banking-as-a-service relationship. For example, a ride-sharing company has numerous, complex financial flows, including collecting payments from riders through a variety of payment mechanisms and disbursing funds to drivers. To do this, the ride-share company would likely make use of a number of financial and bank partnerships. By itself, these relationships would not typically be considered an example of banking-as-a-service. On the other hand, if the ride-share company wanted to offer its drivers a "wallet" that could hold their earnings and provide a branded debit card that allowed drivers to spend those funds, those capabilities would require a bank partner to hold the drivers' deposits and to issue Visa- or Mastercard-affiliated debit cards. That would generally be considered an example of a banking-as-a-service relationship.

Whether or not certain kinds of non-bank service providers are considered to enable banking-as-a-service is also a point of contention. The class of companies whose primary purpose is simplifying technological integration with banks—sometimes referred to as "middleware," "connectors," or "BaaS providers"—clearly fall within the definition of banking-as-a-service (we cover this in depth in Chapter 6). There is less agreement about where a category known as issuer-processors sit. Issuer-processors' core function is to connect card networks, like Visa or Mastercard, to the banks that issue cards. But some modern issuer-processors offer a wider breadth of capabilities, including aspects of program management, and could be considered to be BaaS providers.

There is no legislative or regulatory definition of what is or is not banking-as-a-service in the United States, though some jurisdictions do provide greater regulatory clarity. The market continues to evolve at a rapid pace, responding to shifting customer demands, increasing regulatory scrutiny, and developments in technology and business models. As the market and the players in it continue to develop, what is and is not considered to be an example of banking-as-a-service is likely to change as well.

While much of this initial chapter has focused on banking-as-a-service in the United States, the approach has caught on in jurisdictions around the world. And just as financial legal and regulatory requirements vary country to country, so too do BaaS legal frameworks and operating models. The demand for such partner banking services, the available supply of banks willing to engage, and the economic and business models can vary significantly country to country. We will explore some of these regional differences alongside case studies later in the book.

## Quickly Growing BaaS Business Models Remain Unproven

The model of a non-bank partnering with a chartered bank to offer regulated financial products is not new. The dawn of the "as-a-service" era of these arrangements broadly reflects technologists' impulse to make onboarding a vendor (in this case, a bank) to build a financial product as quick and seamless as making a few API calls. Of course, the reality of building and operating a financial product is far more complicated than, say, launching a dating app.

In this chapter, we have examined some of the forces that gave rise to banking-as-a-service. On the demand side, the rise of fintech, driven by technological developments, like ubiquitous smartphone adoption, and a growing flood of venture capital meant an explosion in the number of fintechs needing bank partners.

On the supply side, changing market and regulatory forces provided reasons for banks, especially smaller ones, to enter the banking-as-a-service space. Increasing consolidation in US banking markets, the decline of the importance of physical location and branch networks, the need for new channels to source deposits and write loans, and pressure to find new revenue sources all drove more banks to explore BaaS models.

These increases in demand for bank partnership capabilities and supply from the bank side were intertwined with the creation of a new category of service provider, BaaS middleware firms, which promised to streamline the process of fintechs onboarding, integrating with, and building on underlying bank partners.

But aspects of these evolving business and operating models, which exploded in popularity beginning in the mid-2010s, remain unproven. Whether or not banking-as-a-service approaches are sustainable, from economic, legal, and regulatory perspectives, are questions we will seek to answer throughout this book.

## Endnotes

**1**  Paul, P. (2022) Banks, Maturity Transformation, and Monetary Policy, Federal Reserve Bank of San Francisco Working Paper 2020-07, doi.org/10.24148/wp2020-07 (archived at https://perma.cc/2LP5-XPXA)

**2**  Labonte, M. (2022) Federal Reserve: Master Accounts and the Payment System, Congressional Research Service, crsreports.congress.gov/product/pdf/IN/IN12031 (archived at https://perma.cc/M6VN-GUTS)

**3**  Beam, D. et al. (2018) Federal Preemption of State Regulation of Banks—Current Developments, *Mayer Brown*, www.mayerbrown.com/-/media/files/perspectives-events/events/2018/09/consumer-finance-monthly-breakfast-briefing/files/view-slides/fileattachment/federalpreemptionofstateregulationofbankscurrentde.pdf (archived at https://perma.cc/ZNM5-MTV8)

**4**  Office of the Comptroller of the Currency (2019) Comptroller's Handbook—Corporate and Risk Governance, www.occ.treas.gov/publications-and-resources/publications/comptrollers-handbook/files/corporate-risk-governance/pub-ch-corporate-risk.pdf (archived at https://perma.cc/7WPE-WGU7)

**5**  Bennett, J. (2015) From Coins to Big Bucks: The Evolution of General-Purpose Reloadable Prepaid Cards, Federal Reserve Bank of St. Louis, research.stlouisfed.org/publications/page1-econ/2015/04/01/from-coins-to-big-bucks-the-evolution-of-general-purpose-reloadable-prepaid-cards/ (archived at https://perma.cc/3E5M-PKM9)

**6**  Fox, J. (2004) Unsafe and Unsound: Payday Lenders Hide Behind FDIC Bank Charters to Peddle Usury, Consumer Federation of America, consumerfed.org/pdfs/pdlrentabankreport.pdf (archived at https://perma.cc/ERU3-DJHY)

**7**  Levitin, A. (2021) Rent-a-Bank: Bank Partnerships and the Evasion of Usury Laws, *Duke Law Journal*, scholarship.law.duke.edu/cgi/viewcontent.cgi?article=4091&context=dlj (archived at https://perma.cc/7S82-L2CF)

**8**  Dodd-Frank Wall Street Reform and Consumer Protection Act (2010), Pub. L. No. 111-203, 124 Stat. 1376, www.govinfo.gov/content/pkg/PLAW-111publ203/pdf/PLAW-111publ203.pdf (archived at https://perma.cc/7BPM-JFE2)

**9** Zywicki, T. et al. (2022) The Effects of Price Controls on Payment-Card Interchange Fees: A Review and Update, *International Center for Law and Economics*, laweconcenter.org/resources/the-effects-of-price-controls-on-payment-card-interchange-fees-a-review-and-update/ (archived at https://perma.cc/2PA6-PZ7G)

**10** Board of Governors of the Federal Reserve System (2023) Additional Data Concerning the Proposed Methodology for Determining the Base Component of the Interchange Fee Cap, www.federalreserve.gov/paymentsystems/RegII_Additional_information_proposed_methodology.htm (archived at https://perma.cc/76LQ-VGKJ)

**11** Board of Governors of the Federal Reserve System (2023) Average Debit Card Interchange Fee by Payment Card Network, federalreserve.gov/paymentsystems/regii-average-interchange-fee.htm (archived at https://perma.cc/KWD3-GX9T)

**12** Prepaid Accounts Under the Electronic Fund Transfer Act (Regulation E) and the Truth in Lending Act (Regulation Z) (2016), 12 CFR 1005-1026, www.federalregister.gov/documents/2016/11/22/2016-24503/prepaid-accounts-under-the-electronic-fund-transfer-act-regulation-e-and-the-truth-in-lending-act (archived at https://perma.cc/78QV-UGTW)

**13** Rotman, F. (2015) The Hourglass Effect: A Decade of Displacement, *Confessions of a Fintech Junkie*, fintechjunkie.com/wp-content/uploads/2015/04/the-hourglass-effect.pdf (archived at https://perma.cc/E2KK-QULQ)

**14** Jayaratne, J. and Straham, P. (1997) The Benefits of Branching Deregulation, *Federal Reserve Board of New York Economic Policy Review*, www.newyorkfed.org/medialibrary/media/research/epr/97v03n4/9712jaya.pdf (archived at https://perma.cc/2H43-V34E)

**15** Federal Deposit Insurance Corporation (2024) BankFind Suite: Find Annual Historical Bank Data, banks.data.fdic.gov/explore/historical (archived at https://perma.cc/XZH8-R5GP)

**16** US Bureau of Economic Analysis (2024) Personal Saving Rate, Federal Reserve Bank of St. Louis, fred.stlouisfed.org/series/PSAVERT (archived at https://perma.cc/JRW2-CBWJ)

# 2

# Why Do Fintechs Need Banking-as-a-Service?

---

**CHAPTER OBJECTIVES**

In this chapter, you will learn about the different kinds of "fintech," which can broadly be grouped as customer-facing or infrastructure. Within the customer-facing segment, we will cover key types of fintech business models, with a primary focus on consumer and small business segments. We'll also discuss the kinds of licensing different fintech products may require, the tradeoffs of US state-level licensing versus working with a bank partner, the banking-as-a-service supply chain, and the division of labor that often exists between fintechs and their bank partners.

---

Before we dive into exploring why fintechs need banking-as-a-service, it is helpful to have a deeper understanding of the different segments and businesses within fintech. At the highest level, fintech can be divided into customer-facing applications versus infrastructure. Customer-facing businesses include those focused on consumer, small business, and enterprise users. On the other hand, a fintech that is building infrastructure is typically selling that capability to another financial services company, whether a fellow fintech, a bank, or sometimes another industry altogether.

To make matters more complicated, some fintechs may start out as customer-facing and then pivot to focus on selling infrastructure they have built or try to develop both lines of business simultaneously. For example, near-prime consumer lender Avant developed its own loan origination software in house and eventually began selling that software to other lenders.[1] It eventually spun out that infrastructure business as a standalone company, Amount. Similarly, credit card startup Petal, which uses cash flow data to underwrite applicants, began selling its underwriting algorithm to other lenders, and ultimately spun that business out as Prism Data. Fintechs that develop infrastructure often begin by selling the capabilities to other, customer-facing fintechs rather than banks, as the sales process tends to be significantly faster due to banks typically having more cumbersome due diligence and vendor management processes, as well as generally being more risk averse.[2]

KEY LEARNING POINTS

Many fintechs that build infrastructure, like open banking connectivity, novel underwriting techniques, or fraud and anti-money laundering solutions, often start out by selling to other fintechs. As their solutions are validated in the market and as they mature, fintech infrastructure providers often expand into selling to banks, which typically have significantly longer sales cycles and more constraints on the qualifications of vendors they buy from due to regulatory oversight and expectations.

Customer-facing fintechs can be segmented as focusing on consumer, small business, and enterprise. Historically, many customer-facing fintechs have focused on underserved market segments, including lower-income consumers, consumers with poor credit, consumers with "thin" or no credit file, and needs of small businesses that are not well met by incumbent banks. Selling customer-facing products to enterprises, like selling infrastructure to banks, has generally been lower down the priority list for fintech startups. Enterprise customers typically already have a solution in place, meaning that winning a sale requires convincing the company the switching costs are worth it. Further, given that most fintech startups are young, unprofitable companies, many enterprise customers are reluctant to use them as mission-critical vendors, in the event they go out of business.

KEY LEARNING POINTS

Targeting these "underserved" segments with tailored solutions, like no-fee neobanks, helped fintechs drive adoption. Likewise, small businesses, especially the quintessential "mom and pop" store and emerging segments, like gig workers or digital nomads, have often been ignored by establishment banks as too small of an opportunity.[3]

Finally, while the term "fintech" is often used in contrast to "banks," there are several examples of fintech companies that have *become* banks, especially in countries where obtaining a new bank charter, often referred to as a "de novo," is easier. In the United States, examples of companies many consider to be fintechs that went on to become banks, typically by acquiring an existing institution, include SoFi, LendingClub, Jiko, and Green Dot. Fintechs that applied for and were awarded charters include Varo and Square.[4] In the UK and Europe, fintechs that have obtained bank charters include names like Monzo, Starling, N26, bunq, and, in some jurisdictions, Revolut. The juxtaposition of companies thought of as "fintechs" becoming regulated banks illustrates the imprecision and ambiguity of fintech as a category.

## What Are Key Segments Within Consumer and SMB Fintech?

Within the consumer and small and midsize business (SMB) spaces, there are a wide variety of business models and formulations. Some clearly require state licensing in the US (becoming a bank, or working in collaboration with a bank partner), some obviously do not, and some exist in a gray area. Key segments within customer- and small business-facing fintechs include:

- Neobanks: One of the earliest and perhaps most popular incarnations of fintech, what counts as a "neobank" can also be quite confusing. The key criteria include offering checking account-like functionality, meaning the ability to hold and spend funds. In the

US, most companies that would be described as such do not hold their own bank license but rather partner with banks to operate. Some countries offer an "e-money license," with holders of such licenses commonly referred to as e-money institutions (EMIs). While specifics vary by jurisdiction, such licenses generally enable holders to issue payment cards and process transactions, but customer funds must be safeguarded in separate accounts at insured depository institutions.[5] Examples of neobanks in the US include Chime, which leverages a bank partner, and Varo, which holds its own license.

- Personal financial management (PFM): These consumer-facing services usually deal more in aggregating, analyzing, and displaying financial information in order to allow consumers to better manage their finances than they do in directly offering financial services. Classics of the category include Mint, which was acquired by Intuit and folded into its CreditKarma subsidiary, and cult-favorite You Need A Budget (YNAB).

- Digital wallets: The primary characteristic of a digital wallet is that it holds a user's payment credentials, most commonly debit and credit cards from other issuers. An end user can then use their digital wallet at online or physical points of sale to pay using the stored payment card information. Many digital wallets have expanded beyond this core capability, however. Common additional features include peer-to-peer payments and the ability to store and spend funds directly from the wallet itself. Examples of digital wallets include Apple Wallet, Google Wallet, Venmo, Cash App, and PayPal.

- Credit building: Given the paramount importance of a good credit score and fintechs' focus on underserved segments of the financial services market, it is no surprise that credit building is a popular product segment. Credit-building capabilities can be part of a broader offering, such as a neobank, or offered as a standalone product. The two most common formulations of consumer credit-building products include credit-building loans and secured credit/charge cards.

- Traditional lending: As discussed in Chapter 1, one of the original use cases of fintech was peer-to-peer lending, a model pioneered in the US by companies like LendingClub and Prosper. Although the peer-to-peer nature of these products failed to scale with borrowing demands, the lender-bank partnership model has endured.[6] The bulk of consumer products falls into two categories: Unsecured installment lending and revolving loans, most commonly as credit cards. Fintech lenders have also focused on lending to small businesses, offering products including term loans, lines of credit, invoice factoring, and merchant cash advances.

- Buy now, pay later: The onset of the Covid pandemic and spike in online shopping drove an explosion of popularity of buy now, pay later financing, popularly known as BNPL. The exact formulation of BNPL offering varies by provider. Short-term pay-in-four plans, which allow a shopper to make an initial down payment and three subsequent payments over several weeks, may not require a lending license or bank partner, whereas providers offering longer-term financing typically make use of a bank partner.[7] Many BNPL providers also make use of "virtual cards," or single-use payment cards, behind the scenes to facilitate paying merchants that the providers do not have a direct agreement with.

- Cash advance: Another immensely popular category in consumer fintech is offering cash advances, which are small loans generally repaid in short time frames of less than a month. Like BNPL, the exact product structure varies by provider. Depending on how a fintech structures the product, a license or bank partnership may or may not be necessary. Licensing requirements for such small-dollar loans vary substantially country to country.

- Earned wage access (EWA): Sometimes also referred to as "on-demand pay," EWA meets a similar need as cash advances but through a distinct product structure. Unlike cash advances, EWA enables users to obtain a portion of accrued but not yet disbursed pay from employment. Again, different models exist, with some EWA providers integrating with or being offered through an employer's payroll provider, while others are offered directly to consumers. EWA is a nascent category, and state and federal approaches in the US to regulating it are continuing to evolve.[8]

- Vertical SaaS: In Chapter 1, we introduced the idea of software-as-a-service. The concept of vertical SaaS describes platforms designed to solve problems or offer an operating system to specific industries. For example, Toast for restaurants, Squire for barbershops, or Mindbody for fitness boutiques. While the core focus of these platforms usually is not financial in nature, they often embed financial capabilities, whether accepting payments from customers, offering a wallet- or bank account-like capability to business owners, enabling payroll for employees, and so on.

- Marketplaces: Similarly to vertical SaaS, a marketplace offering's primary purpose is not necessarily financial, but can often be enabled or enhanced with financial capabilities. A classic example is auction marketplace eBay's acquisition of wallet and payment processor PayPal in 2002. A more recent example is Shopify, which partners with Stripe as a payment processor and to offer Shopify Balance, which merchants on the platform can use as a business bank account.

This is not meant to be an exhaustive list, but rather to represent some of the historically most popular consumer and small business fintech products that have emerged in recent years. Nearly all of these examples involve products and services that require some kind of financial services-related licensure or exist in a gray area. The only example above that would clearly *not* require a fintech to obtain a state license or to partner with a bank is the personal financial management category. To the extent that PFMs are aggregating, analyzing, and displaying information, rather than offering a specific financial product, they would not be subject to licensure.

---

### KEY LEARNING POINTS

Many fintech offerings involve novel product structures or distribution channels and do not always fit neatly in existing regulatory frameworks. Earned wage access, no-fee overdrafts/cash advances, and variants of buy

now, pay later exist in a gray area, with state and federal regulators still
determining if incremental legislation or regulation is necessary or how
existing rules apply.

A handful of these examples exist in a gray area, where whether or
not certain licensing requirements apply are a point of contention.
Buy now, pay later, earned wage access, and some cash advance products are examples of emerging fintech products where the
applicability of some existing regulations is unclear. All three categories are credit-like products but do not fit neatly in existing definitions
of "credit" or "lending," leading to confusion about whether or not
US regulations like the Truth in Lending Act (TILA), Fair Credit
Reporting Act (FCRA), Electronic Funds Transfer Act (EFTA), or
Equal Credit Opportunity Act (ECOA) apply. Other countries have
also struggled with how to categorize novel products, with regulators
sometimes taking diverging approaches in different jurisdictions. In
the absence of clear federal requirements, US states have taken differ-
ing approaches to these products. For instance, California has
proposed treating EWA products as "loans" under state law and
requiring providers to be licensed under applicable legislation.[9]
Numerous other states have taken the exact opposite view, explicitly
defining EWA offerings that meet certain criteria as *not* being loans
and exempting providers from licensing requirements.

A limited number of these business models are possible via state
licensing. For example, it is possible to obtain state licenses to offer
consumer credit products in most states. However, there are multiple
downsides to this approach. Acquiring and maintaining state lending
licenses in each state a company plans to operate can be time consuming and expensive. Further, the product structures and terms permitted
can vary significantly state to state. For instance, the maximum
permissible interest rate in California is 10 per cent annually, though
there are numerous exceptions, and the state prescribes the minimum
and maximum loan amounts creditors may offer for certain types of
products. By contrast, in nearby Utah, a significantly more permissive

state, there is no regulation governing the maximum interest rate that may be charged. The result for lenders operating on state licenses is often, functionally, that they are running a distinct business in every state in which they operate.

It is also possible to run a digital wallet or payments business on state licenses. For instance, popular wallets and "peer-to-peer" payments services in the US, including PayPal, Venmo (which is owned by PayPal), and Cash App hold state-level money transmission licenses (MTLs) and are registered with the federal US financial crimes regulator, FinCEN, as money services businesses (MSBs). But, as in the lending use case, businesses typically must obtain a license in each jurisdiction they plan to operate. In the US, all states, except for Montana, require licensure for money transmitters. This generates not insignificant overhead, especially for earlier-stage fintechs, of applying for and maintaining numerous MTLs. Banks, and fintechs that partner with banks, are generally exempt from this requirement.

KEY LEARNING POINTS

Even for fintech business models where state licensure is possible, many products, like lenders, digital wallets, and peer-to-peer payments, still have a critical dependency on the banking system.

It is also worth noting that holding state licenses does not eliminate the need for some level of dependence on the banking system and other key third parties. State-licensed lenders still require payment-processing partners to disburse loan proceeds and collect loan repayments. This is most commonly done via ACH payments, which a bank, acting on behalf of the lender, would handle. Non-bank lenders also require external debt capital to reach any significant scale of lending, though this most often is provided through private credit markets, rather than bank lenders.

Similarly, wallet and peer-to-peer payment providers, even when holding state MTLs, still have critical dependencies on banks in order to operate. While requirements vary by state, money transmitters are typically required to segregate and safeguard customer funds. A common method of achieving this is by holding customer funds in a segregated, insured bank or trust account. Wallet providers also need a method for users to move funds in and out of their wallet, sometimes referred to as "on" and "off ramps." There are multiple rails available to do this, but the most ubiquitous and least expensive is ACH, which, again, requires leveraging established bank infrastructure.

> **KEY LEARNING POINTS**
>
> Not all fintech businesses that leverage services provided by a bank are considered to be banking-as-a-service. The key distinction is whether a firm itself is a customer of a bank, or if it is offering a bank's regulated products to its end users.

It is worth noting that in the case of state-licensed lenders and digital wallets, although they may leverage banks in some aspects of their businesses, these relationships would not generally be considered to be "banking-as-a-service" relationships. The distinction being that, while a wallet or lender *itself* uses a bank's services, they are not offering a bank's regulated products (deposits, payment cards, etc.) to the end user. Many digital wallets *do* offer ancillary capabilities, like a debit card that enables users to spend from the underlying wallet, which would be considered a banking-as-a-service-powered capability.

## Most Fintech Capabilities Depend on Banking-as-a-Service

The large majority of fintech business models do require capabilities made possible through banking-as-a-service. Neobanks, one of the most prevalent categories of fintech, necessitate holding customer deposits and issuing debit cards, both of which, at least in the US, only a licensed bank can do. In other jurisdictions, it is possible to be a principal member of card schemes and thus to issue payment cards *without* a bank charter. Regulated e-money institutions, which exist in the UK, Europe, LatAm, Middle East, and Asia, can issue payment cards but must hold customer funds in segregated accounts at insured depository institutions, in an arrangement somewhat comparable to how US neobanks operate.

Many US fintechs offering credit products either require or substantially benefit from having an underlying bank partner. Partnering with a bank allows a lending-focused fintech to avoid having to obtain licenses in each state it plans to operate in, to offer a largely consistent product across the country, and to benefit from state interest rate preemption in most circumstances. US fintechs offering charge or credit cards must partner with an issuing bank to offer their products.

The upshot is that fintech-bank relationships, powered by banking-as-a-service, often amount to a kind of division of labor. Historically, this has meant fintechs focus on creating value in their areas of strength: Design, user experience, product management, branding, marketing/customer acquisition, data science, software engineering, and the like. Banks that partner with fintechs, meanwhile, benefit from capitalizing on their key attributes and strengths: Above all else, holding a bank license and all that goes with that, but also strong risk management and compliance capabilities, which are functions that are often less-developed at fintechs, especially for earlier-stage companies.

In this division of labor, one can consider a user-facing fintech to be the "front end," while its partner bank is the "back end." Using popular US neobank Chime as an example, Chime built, operates, and maintains a customer-facing mobile app and website, defines the brand, determines the marketing strategy and execution, handles user onboarding and customer service. Chime's bank partners, The Bancorp Bank and Stride, hold insured customer deposits and, together with processor Galileo, issue Chime's debit and secured credit cards. That is not to say there is not incredibly close collaboration between fintechs and their bank partners. Ultimately, in the eyes of bank regulators, non-bank customer-facing fintechs are third-party vendors to their bank partners.[10] It is the bank that holds the ultimate responsibility for supervising their fintech partners to ensure compliance with applicable regulations.

Why would a fintech not just get its own bank license, instead of depending on a partner? Well, a number have done just that, and the decision has not always paid off. In the US in particular, the process to obtain a de novo bank license or to acquire an existing bank tends to be lengthy and expensive.[11] But there are other factors at play as well. With most fintechs being backed by venture capital, they tend to attempt to develop business models that enable rapid growth with low marginal costs, which is more difficult to do with the constraints that go along with being a regulated entity like a bank.

True software companies and, later, web businesses are the classic example of this. For example, Microsoft spends a significant amount upfront to develop a piece of software, like Windows or Office, but the cost to scale, or to produce and sell an incremental unit, is low. Likewise, with a web-era company like Google or Facebook (now known as Meta), a substantial amount is invested upfront, but the marginal cost of revenue—another ad showing when someone searches on Google or scrolls on Facebook—is very low. Software business models, especially in their early, hyper-growth phases, tend to demand outsized valuation multiples which can earn early venture capital investors handsome returns.

Investors and operators, seeking to repeat the magic of earlier eras of Silicon Valley, have attempted to apply the same mentality to fintech. This has led to many fintechs positioning themselves as "technology" companies, rather than financial ones, and focusing on the software and data components of their businesses. For most of its history, fintechs were all too happy to leave the risky, legally complicated, capital-intensive part of offering financial products to their bank partners.

---

EXAMPLE: THE UNBUNDLING OF CONSUMER MORTGAGES

The unbundling of a single financial product is not new. In the US, a good example is consumer mortgages. A product lifecycle that used to be contained in a single bank is now spread over numerous entities, including brokers, originators, government sponsored entities, servicers, and so forth.

---

It is worth noting that this disaggregation of a single product across multiple players is not, in and of itself, new. A classic example in the US market is consumer mortgages. While generations ago, a single bank might market, underwrite, originate, and hold and service a customer's mortgage until they paid it off, that value chain looks radically different today. Without diving into the complex reasons why, the unbundling of the retail mortgage has given rise to specialized companies that focus on each step of the process: Marketing, brokering, origination, bundling and securitization, servicing, and so on.

With the rise of non-bank fintechs and banking-as-a-service, we have seen a similar segmentation of players and capabilities across other consumer financial products, including checking and savings accounts, personal loans, and credit cards. Acting Comptroller Michael Hsu, who leads the US national bank regulator, the OCC, has referred to this as a sort of bank-fintech "supply chain."[12]

That is not to say there are no risks or hiccups in this emerging banking-as-a-service supply chain. There are novel risks to building and delivering financial products this way, which fintechs and bank partners may not be prepared to adequately mitigate. Novel fintech business models are unproven over a longer time horizon and may not prove to be viable. For instance, neobanks that charge no fees, which users like, but are dependent on interchange income have yet to demonstrate the model is viable.[13] Fintechs offering credit products have even greater uncertainty to deal with, as they are exposed to the whims of debt capital markets for their lending capacity, interest rate risk, and repayment risk. Lending fintechs that began operating post-2008, which is most of them, have yet to see a full credit cycle.

Perhaps most importantly, time horizons and incentives between fintechs and their bank partners can be mismatched. Venture-backed fintechs tend to be more risk tolerant, as they seek to hit certain key metrics or milestones in order to raise their next round of funding. This tends to drive a more aggressive, growth-oriented culture, whereas most, though certainly not all banks tend to be more risk-averse. Banks that experience rapid growth but fail to make commensurate investments in compliance and controls risk raising concern from their regulators.

## Most Fintechs Require a Partner or License

The term "fintech" encompasses a wide variety of business models, products, and services. But when you drill down into customer-facing fintechs, those offering products and services used by everyday consumers and small businesses, the majority either explicitly require partnering with a bank, state-issued licenses, or exist in a gray area that is likely to become subject to additional regulation. One of the most popular categories of consumer and SMB fintech, neobanks, require the ability to hold insured customer deposits and issue payment cards, necessitating fintechs and banks working together. And while another popular category, credit, can, in some circumstances, be done without a bank partner, there are numerous benefits to working with a chartered bank than through state-issued licenses. Banking-as-a-service relationships between fintechs and banks represent a kind of disaggregation of the value chain of banking, with fintechs owning pieces they are better at, like product, technology, marketing, and banks taking responsibility for areas like balance sheet management, risk, and compliance. The banking-as-a-service model has potential to foster innovation and expand access and inclusion, but it also comes with risks that must be mitigated. And, for better or worse, in the current regulatory paradigm, the ultimate responsibility for most of those risks sits squarely with the banks that provide fintechs with the ability to distribute their regulated products.

## Endnotes

**1** Amount (2020) Avant Spins Out SaaS Business Amount, *PR Newswire*, prnewswire.com/news-releases/avant-spins-out-saas-business-amount-300999069.html (archived at https://perma.cc/HU7Q-NH6R)

**2** Board of Governors of the Federal Reserve System (2021) Conducting Due Diligence on Financial Technology Firms: A Guide for Community Banks, www.federalreserve.gov/publications/files/conducting-due-diligence-on-financial-technology-firms-202108.pdf (archived at https://perma.cc/Z8YH-D7S4)

**3**   Pangestu, M. (2023) Fintech and Financial Services: Delivering for Development, *World Bank Blogs*, blogs.worldbank.org/en/voices/fintech-and-financial-services-delivering-development (archived at https://perma.cc/2U6X-4WL4)

**4**   Office of the Comptroller of the Currency (2020) Acting Comptroller of the Currency Presents Varo Bank, N.A. Its Charter, www.occ.gov/news-issuances/news-releases/2020/nr-occ-2020-99.html (archived at https://perma.cc/796Y-JV2A)

**5**   Michelin, E. et al. (2023) Electronic Money and Payments Institutions: Supporting your Regulatory License and Authorisation Journey, *EY*, assets.ey.com/content/dam/ey-sites/ey-com/en_uk/topics/banking-and-capital-markets/ey-electronic-money-and-payment-institutions.pdf (archived at https://perma.cc/UU84-9QPR)

**6**   Renton, P. (2020) LendingClub Closing Down Their Platform for Retail Investors, *Fintech Nexus*, www.fintechnexus.com/lendingclub-closing-down-their-platform-for-retail-investors/ (archived at https://perma.cc/CE92-JYCG)

**7**   Mikula, J. (2020) Buy Now, Pay Later vs POS Lending, a Crash Course, *Fintech Business Weekly*, fintechbusinessweekly.substack.com/p/buy-now-pay-later-vs-pos-lending (archived at https://perma.cc/3EP3-28H3)

**8**   Mikula, J. (2023) Maryland Latest State to Issue EWA Guidance, *Fintech Business Weekly*, fintechbusinessweekly.substack.com/p/maryland-latest-state-to-issue-ewa (archived at https://perma.cc/3HDL-GAKP)

**9**   Mikula, J. (2023) Earned Wage Access Regulatory Update: California & Wisconsin, *Fintech Business Weekly*, fintechbusinessweekly.substack.com/i/138938192/earned-wage-access-regulatory-update-california-and-wisconsin (archived at https://perma.cc/JE99-6CB3)

**10**   Federal Deposit Insurance Corporation (2023) Interagency Guidance on Third-Party Relationships: Risk Management, www.fdic.gov/news/financial-institution-letters/2023/fil23029.html (archived at https://perma.cc/3GG3-YF4Q)

**11**   Hrushka, A. (2020) Varo Becomes First Challenger Bank to Get National Charter from OCC, *Banking Dive*, www.bankingdive.com/news/varo-first-challenger-bank-charter-occ/582686 (archived at https://perma.cc/F2FC-NA6Y)

**12**   Hsu, M. (2024) Preventing the Next Great Blurring, Office of the Comptroller of the Currency, www.occ.gov/news-issuances/speeches/2024/pub-speech-2024-17.pdf (archived at https://perma.cc/3CCZ-Z5LZ)

**13**   Mikula, J. (2022) Varo, First Chartered Neobank, Could Run Out of Money by End of Year, Regulatory Filings Show, *Fintech Business Weekly*, fintechbusinessweekly.substack.com/p/varo-first-chartered-neobank-could (archived at https://perma.cc/VN8K-AQQP)

# 3

# The House that Durbin Built: US Fintechs' Love Affair with Interchange

CHAPTER OBJECTIVES

In many ways, at least in the United States, legal and regulatory changes passed after the 2008 financial crisis are more responsible for the rise of fintech than any individual change in technology itself. We already touched on this in Chapter 1, and in this chapter, we will take a deeper dive into interchange. You will gain a deeper understanding of what interchange is, the role it plays in the card payment system, and the stated purpose of the Durbin amendment versus its actual impacts. We'll also explain how Durbin and interchange revenue helped power an explosion of fintech, driving demand for an easier way of working with partner banks, helping to give rise to banking-as-a-service. We will also touch on constraints on interchange income in regions outside of the US, and how those constraints have shaped banking and fintech in various other markets.

## What Is Interchange, a Key Revenue Driver in Banking-as-a-Service?

But first, what is interchange, and why does it matter? To understand the role interchange plays in card payment systems, it is helpful to have a basic understanding of the stakeholders and economic model behind card payment networks. For illustrative purposes, we will focus on Visa and Mastercard, which use a "four-party" model.[1] The main players in the four-party model are cardholders (someone buying something), merchants (a store selling something), acquirers (service providers that enable a merchant to accept card payments), and issuers (entities that provide payment cards to cardholders). There are often additional providers involved in facilitating card payment transactions, such as payment gateways, payment processors, payment facilitators, and, of course, the network schemes, like Visa and Mastercard.

While we will not fully unpack the role of each player, a basic understanding of the stakeholders helps to explain the intended purpose of interchange. The term "interchange" is often used interchangeably (pun not intended) with the generic terms "swipe fee," "transaction fee," or the more technical "merchant discount rate," though this is actually not correct. The merchant discount rate (MDR) is in fact the total share a merchant pays to accept a card payment, calculated as a percentage of the transaction value. The MDR is composed of interchange fees, which are typically the largest component, card scheme fees, and an acquirer markup.[2]

KEY LEARNING POINTS

The merchant discount rate, sometimes called a "swipe fee," is the total cost to a merchant to accept card payments, as a per cent of the transaction size. The MDR typically consists of interchange, card scheme fees, and an acquirer markup.

The interchange fee, ultimately borne by the merchant accepting the card payment, goes to the card issuer. The stated purpose of this payment is to help cover issuers' costs associated with building and maintaining their systems, customer support, costs of fraud and fraud mitigation, and risk of non-payment. Revenue from interchange is also commonly used to support rewards programs.[3]

Interchange rates are set by the card networks and can be subject to country-specific regulation. Additional factors that can influence interchange rate on a given transaction include:[4]

- Network: Visa, Mastercard, Discover, American Express, JCB, etc.
- Card type: Prepaid, debit, credit, charge
- Card type: Consumer, commercial (business, corporate, purchasing, fleet)
- Card tier: For example, Visa Signature, Visa Signature Preferred, Visa Infinite; card tiers often denote levels of rewards
- Transaction type: Card present (swipe, EMV, wallet/token) or card not present
- Merchant category: For example, grocery, restaurant, taxi, travel
- Region: Interchange can vary based on where a card is issued and used, including due to regulatory limits on interchange fees
- Risk level: Certain categories of transaction, based in part on above attributes, may be considered higher risk and thus charge higher interchange

Of the above factors, the most significant is regulatory caps on interchange rates. For example, consumer transactions made at merchants and on debit cards issued within the European Economic Area are capped at 0.2 per cent of the transaction value. Consumer credit card transactions within the EEA are capped at 0.3 per cent, helping to explain the relative rarity of rewards credit cards that are so popular in the United States.

KEY LEARNING POINTS

Region-specific regulatory caps on interchange help explain wide variations country to country. For instance, most consumer credit and debit transactions within Europe are capped at 0.3 per cent and 0.2 per cent, respectively, whereas credit and Durbin-exempt debit interchange rates in the US can be five to ten times higher.

Like so many other parts of the US financial system, practices around interchange are incredibly complex and an ongoing source of tension, particularly among card networks, merchants, and issuing banks. Despite occasional efforts to implement reforms governing credit card fee practices, as of early 2024, none of these initiatives have gained substantial traction. This is relevant for fintechs and BaaS partner banks, as it provides added incentive to build credit card-like offerings, as they generate higher interchange income than debit.

---

KEY LEARNING POINTS

US fintech programs and BaaS partner banks have built-in incentives to favor credit and charge cards, as they earn higher rates of interchange. This helps explain the rise of product structures that take advantage of this difference, like "credit-building" cards, which typically use a secured charge card structure.

---

## Durbin Amendment Explains the Appeal of BaaS for Smaller Banks

On the debit side, as we touched on in Chapter 1, Dodd-Frank, passed in 2010, included what is commonly referred to as the Durbin amendment, which required the Federal Reserve to formulate regulations that set a cap on interchange for debit cards issued by banks with more than $10 billion in assets. The intention was to determine a cap that was "reasonable and proportional" to card issuers' actual costs.[5] In 2011, the Fed issued its final rule, which capped debit interchange fees for cards issued by large banks at $0.21 plus 0.05 per cent of the transaction value plus an additional $0.01, if issuers implemented certain fraud-prevention measures. After leaving this cap in place for over a decade, in 2023, based on data indicating issuers' costs had declined, the Fed proposed updating this cap. The Fed's proposal, which had not been finalized as of early 2024, would lower the cap on covered debit transactions to $0.144 plus 0.04 per cent of transaction value plus $0.013 for issuers implementing certain fraud-prevention measures.[6]

KEY LEARNING POINTS

The Durbin amendment and its implementing regulation capped debit interchange for cards issued by banks with over $10 billion in assets at $0.21 plus 0.05 per cent of transaction size, plus $0.01 if issuers implement certain fraud prevention measures. Banks with less than $10 billion in assets are exempt from this cap, making them the preferred choice for fintechs that offer debit cards.

Stated goals of the Durbin amendment at the time it was proposed and adopted included addressing concerns from merchants, particularly small businesses, about high payment processing fees; saving consumers money, by reducing interchange fees borne by merchants; and enhancing competition, including by carving out smaller, sub-$10 billion asset banks from the cap. However, empirical data from other countries that have passed fee caps and in the US since the passage of Durbin suggests this is not exactly what has happened.[7]

The precise impact to a given merchant was dependent on numerous factors, including their type of business (more precisely, their merchant category code), their average transaction size, and their mix of card and transaction types: Present versus non-present, credit versus debit, covered debit versus exempt debit, and so on. For merchants that did see payment processing costs decline, there is little evidence that those savings were passed along to end consumers, though it is possible payment processing savings results in slower increases in consumer prices.

## The Unintended Consequences of Durbin

But Durbin also came with a host of unintended consequences. For instance, merchants with small average transaction sizes actually tended to see their payment processing costs go up.

Why did that happen? Prior to Durbin, card networks often offered preferential interchange pricing to merchants with small ticket sizes—think your local coffee shop or neighborhood convenience store. The networks' motivation was simple: To increase card acceptance, making payment cards more useful for consumers and encouraging them to use them more frequently. With the passage of Durbin, networks generally eliminated these incentives. Given the structure of the cap, specifically the $0.21 fixed-fee component, the result was many merchants with small average transaction sizes actually ended up paying more.[8] This helps (though does not entirely) explain the proliferation of minimum spend requirements and the more recent rise in card surcharge fees, both of which network rules have historically prohibited.

The architects of the Durbin amendment almost certainly did not envision how it would end up enabling the explosion of fintech and driving the growth of partner banking and banking-as-a-service. The idea of "free checking," typically meaning no set monthly "service" or "maintenance" fee, really began to take root in the late 1980s and early 1990s. Its emergence was concurrent with the wave of banking deregulation, the beginning of consolidation that continues to this day, and rise of technologies, like the ATM and, later, online banking.

Who can say no to "free"? But marketing checking accounts this way belied a simple fact: Acquiring customers and serving and maintaining their accounts is decidedly *not* free. Prior to the passage of Dodd-Frank and its Durbin amendment, banks relied on a number of strategies and revenue streams, including interchange income, to support offering free checking accounts.

Strategically, many banks relied on a cross-sell strategy. In retail parlance, checking accounts were a loss leader, to get a customer into the bank. Once a bank had acquired that customer, it would then market other, revenue-generating products to them: Credit cards, auto loans, mortgages, investment products, and so forth. This approach intuitively made sense in the era pre-dating widespread internet and online banking use. Customers were, in a sense, a captive audience. For many transactions, they had to physically walk into a bank branch and interact with a human teller or a personal banker—someone who they might develop a relationship with, who could suggest products and services to them. Combined with the benefits of low-cost deposits from checking customers and, with the rise of debit cards starting in the 1990s, interchange income, banks could generally make the math work, on average, across their customer base. While deposit accounts could carry fees, including overdraft and non-sufficient funds fees, these were generally in the range of $10 to $20 through the 2000s.

But as banks increasingly consolidated, service became less personal and more automated. The rise of ATMs and later internet banking dramatically reduced the need for consumers to visit a physical bank branch. The growth of the internet as a distribution channel also meant that consumers could more easily shop for and compare financial products from institutions beyond their primary bank. Over time, these forces have steadily eroded loyalty and banks' ability to cross-sell products to their customers.

Following the rise of internet banking in the 2000s, the sharp reduction in interchange revenue for the largest banks following the passage of Dodd-Frank in 2010 encouraged them to take a hard look at their customer base. Analyzing the costs versus revenue of customer segments would yield an unsurprising outcome: Lower-income checking account holders were often unprofitable for banks to serve. They historically brought few deposits to banks, they were poor targets to cross-sell other products and services, like loans or investments, and they tended to have disproportionately high customer service utilization. The response from most banks was to, over time, increase fees to compensate: Overdraft fees, non-sufficient fund fees, minimum balance fees, and so on. Almost by definition, the costs of these fees, for "free" checking accounts, disproportionately fell on lower-income account holders. While pre-Durbin, many banks had something approaching an even distribution of earnings by customer income group, over time, that changed to something of a barbell. The highest- and lowest-income customers would drive the bulk of profits.[9]

KEY LEARNING POINTS

After debit caps called for by the Durbin amendment came into effect, account service fees for "free" checking accounts steadily increased. These fees are disproportionately borne by lower-income consumers, which provided a logical segment for fintechs to cater to by offering no-fee checking accounts.

This steady growth in fees made for an increasingly bad experience for lower-income consumers at major banks. Faced with expensive and difficult to predict fees, which, by definition, were assessed when consumers were least able to afford to pay them, customers that were impacted increasingly chose to give up their bank accounts to avoid the fees or had their accounts forcibly closed by their banks. Customers with a history of overdrafting, especially if it resulted in forcible closure of their account, are often reported to specialty consumer reporting agencies, like ChexSystems, which can make it difficult for them to open bank accounts elsewhere.[10] The gap in the market this created became the perfect target segment for fintechs to serve. And, with the significant difference in debit interchange rates between covered and exempt banks, there was only one segment of banks that made sense for fintechs to partner with: Those with less than $10 billion in assets.

## Why Exempt Smaller Banks from Durbin?

The intention in exempting smaller banks from the debit interchange caps Durbin called for was not to foster an explosion of non-bank fintech companies. While exempting smaller banks was a matter of debate at the time, legislators ultimately justified the carve-out by leaning on several arguments. While the number of institutions above the threshold captured a relatively low share of the total number of US banks, it would cover approximately 70 per cent of consumer checking accounts, thereby substantially achieving the amendment's stated goal of effectively lowering interchange rates and payment processing costs for many merchants. At the same time, the carve-out preserved interchange as an important revenue source for smaller banks, which supporters argued was necessary and justified to enable them to compete effectively in a marketplace that was rapidly consolidating around the country's largest banks. Supporters also argued that because of their relatively smaller size, sub-$10 billion banks were justified in collecting higher interchange, because their operating costs on a per transaction basis are likely to be higher.

## A Slow Start for Early Neobanks

The marriage of customer-facing fintechs with sub-$10 billion banks did not immediately explode in the wake of Dodd-Frank and the Durbin amendment. In fact, BankSimple (later rebranded as Simple) was founded in 2009, before these laws were passed. BankMoven (later rebranded as Moven) was founded in 2011, just as the Durbin amendment's debit interchange cap for larger banks went into effect. Chime, probably the most well-known US neobank that partners with a chartered institution, was founded in 2013 and launched publicly the following year.

But by the end of the decade, there were dozens of neobanks, and seemingly every consumer fintech was offering users a branded debit card. What accounted for this slow start and eventual shift? In the early 2010s, there were not many bank partners interested in or capable of partnering with young, tech-focused, and venture-backed startups. At the time, banks with experience in the prepaid space were arguably the most well suited to work with these new tech companies that were interested in offering regulated financial products. The emerging crop of fintechs, however, had different goals and expectations than the prepaid card issuers that preceded them. Steeped in the ethos of Silicon Valley, these companies tended to be engineering and product led and had the goal of building "disruptive" products. This even came across in the positioning and marketing of early fintech consumer products, much of which positioned fintech companies as modern, innovative, and consumer-focused, going so far as to be explicitly anti-bank (despite partnering with banks in most cases).

Fintechs looking to work with bank partners often found the experience to be highly manual, time consuming, and expensive. Many banks, especially the smaller ones that benefited from being exempt from Durbin and were looking for new sources of revenue, relied on legacy core banking technology from behemoths like FIS and Fiserv. Banks' commercial agreements with these core providers often made it economically unattractive to have accounts with small amounts of deposits "on core," or where an end-user's account was individually titled in their name in the bank's system of record. This gave rise to the growing use of "FBO" accounts, or "For the benefit of," which became key for facilitating non-bank fintechs partnering with chartered banks. In the chartered bank's core system of record, one or a small number of accounts would hold all of a fintech's end-customers' funds.[11] The fintech, in turn, would have its own sub-ledger and virtual accounts that would track individual users' deposits and transactions. While this approach provides both banks and fintechs with greater flexibility, it also introduces challenges, including reconciling records between a bank and its fintech partners, and banks' oversight of their fintech partners' compliance practices.

Located away from the coastal metropolitan centers of banking and technology in New York and San Francisco, and instead based in states like Tennessee, Utah, and South Dakota, likely partner banks often lacked the caliber of tech and engineering talent fintechs were accustomed to from their other counterparties. Bank culture, especially smaller banks, tends to include a strong focus on risk and controls—resulting in slow, manual, expensive negotiations and integrations between fintechs and early bank partners.

The pain points of fintechs working with bank partners would give rise to a new segment aiming to streamline these collaborations: "Middleware" providers, also sometimes referred to as "connectors" or "banking-as-a-service platforms." There are a variety of middleware operating models, which we will explore in more depth in Chapter 8, but the commonality among them is simplifying the technical integration between fintechs looking to build customer-facing products and underlying bank partners.[12]

Early middleware providers recognized that fintechs were reinventing the wheel, so to speak: Many were looking for the same capabilities from bank partners and were spending substantial resources to build largely similar integrations with banks' legacy cores to do so. Instead, middleware platforms could do the hard part of integrating with one or multiple bank partners, and provide fintechs with a modern set of developer-ready APIs, simplifying their integration process. Some middleware providers were also able to take on some of the work that would typically have been done by a bank partner, including preparing due diligence information and some level of compliance responsibility, for instance. Synapse, widely credited as the first banking-as-a-service platform company, was founded in 2014 and went on to support the underlying technical infrastructure of numerous fintechs.

As the middleware model gained traction with both fintechs and partner banks, more companies entered the space with their own variants on the approach. Treasury Prime was founded in 2017. Solid, Bond, and Unit were founded in 2019 (Bond was acquired by FIS in 2023). And Synctera was founded in 2020. The pitch to fintechs was simple: Replace the lengthy, expensive process of onboarding and integrating with a bank by working with a middleware intermediary who has already done the heavy lifting. The promise was a quicker, cheaper path to market. The exact pitches from middleware platforms to bank partners varied, but all promised to bring fintech clients and a new source of revenue to bank partners often desperate for diversification and growth. Concurrently, venture funding to fintech startups exploded. These ingredients combined to drive dramatic growth in the number of fintechs that sought to monetize users through interchange income. It felt like, all of a sudden, every company wanted to put a debit card in your wallet.

## The Interchange Business Model

At its most simple, for each player, the interchange business model boils down to providing a piece of the puzzle in return for a share of the interchange generated when end customers swipe their card, though, of course, some of the particulars can be more complex. The responsibilities and value chain also will vary depending on the exact partners and operating model.

To illustrate, let's first look at the responsibilities and revenue share for a hypothetical fintech neobank that works directly with a bank— for simplicity, let's call our neobank FinCo and our bank State Bank & Trust. In this configuration, FinCo holds all of its end customers' funds in a single account for the benefit of its users at State Bank & Trust. FinCo, in turn, has built its own technology stack, including to handle customer onboarding, customer service, ledgering, security, reporting, and so forth. FinCo likely works with multiple external vendors to provide mission-critical capabilities, including an issuer-processor, which facilitates end users' card transactions by connecting payment networks, like Visa or Mastercard, to FinCo and its bank partner. In this example, when an end customer uses their card to make a hypothetical $100 purchase, the merchant receives $97.80— the amount the customer spent, less a 2.20 per cent merchant discount rate. From the $2.20 the merchant pays, a share, let's say $0.50, goes to the merchant acquirer and acquiring bank, which enables the merchant to accept card payments. The remaining $1.70 interchange fee gets split between the network (Visa/Mastercard), the issuer-processor (Galileo, i2c, Lithic, etc.), the underlying bank partner, State Bank & Trust, and the customer-facing fintech, FinCo. While the customer-facing fintech is likely to take the lion's share of the interchange, the split between bank, issuer-processor, and fintech will depend on the particulars of their negotiated agreements.

KEY LEARNING POINTS

The cost to merchants of accepting payments has long been a point of contention, driving lawsuits, legislation, and regulation in an attempt to rein in the fees merchants pay. For example, Reg II, which requires debit card issuers to enable two unaffiliated networks, was extended to include e-commerce transactions in July 2023, potentially lowering the interchange rates card issuers earn.[13] The proposed Credit Card Competition Act of 2023 would extend a similar requirement to credit cards issued by banks with more than $100 billion in assets.[14] A long-running dispute between merchant trade organizations and Visa and Mastercard also holds the potential to lower interchange rates.[15] And account-to-account payments, popular in some European countries, would bypass card networks and the interchange they generate altogether. This is all to say that business models focused primarily on revenue from interchange face a number of threats, which, should they come to pass, would reduce income for fintechs, middleware providers, and banks that depend on them.

Typically, larger fintechs (more customers, more transaction volume) are able to negotiate preferential rates compared to earlier-stage and smaller fintechs. Given the relatively high costs to onboard and work with a fintech partner and the relatively small proportion of interchange that flows to the bank partner, historically, banks preferred to work with larger programs or programs that could demonstrate the opportunity to become meaningful contributors to a bank's bottom line. In addition to the share of interchange, bank partners like our hypothetical State Bank & Trust can also benefit from the low-cost deposits fintech partners like FinCo can bring to their banks, particularly in times of elevated or rising interest rates. We will explore this further in the next chapter.

Working more closely with a bank partner may allow a fintech to claim a larger share of interchange revenue, but, on the flip side, the fintech must build substantially more infrastructure, including technical, legal and compliance, to get to market. The promise of middleware platforms was to remove much of this friction for both fintechs and banks by building reusable and scalable technology and compliance infrastructure in return for a share of the interchange. Reducing barriers to entry enticed more banks to enter the partner banking business. It also meant that niche programs that previously may have been too small to make sense as a potential partner to banks and as a standalone fintech business appeared to be viable.

Yet, by the early 2020s, there were signs of stress in the middle-ware model, as numerous banks that partnered with middleware intermediaries like Unit, Synapse, and Treasury Prime were cited by bank regulators for compliance violations.[16] The viability of the financial model for middleware providers has also been called into question, with multiple players in the space exiting to larger incumbents, and, in early 2024, Synapse collapsing into a chaotic bankruptcy.[17]

## Banking-as-a-Service's Promise vs. Reality

If the lofty promise of banking-as-a-service was a quick, low-cost route to market for customer-facing fintechs and an easy, diversified source of revenue for small banks, the reality has proven to be somewhat different. Partner banks with less than $10 billion in assets, those exempt from the constraints of the Durbin amendment, are the only logical choice for debit interchange-driven business models. But, by definition, these banking organizations tended to be smaller and less sophisticated. Asset size, number and types of customer accounts, and transaction volumes can be used as very rough heuristics to assess a bank's level of risk. However, as fintech and banking-as-a-service really began to take off in the mid-2010s, only a very small number of banks had experience running and monitoring these kinds of programs. Some estimates show the number of partner banks grew by five times from 2010 to 2020. And as banks flocked to what appeared to some to be an easy new revenue stream, compliance investments did not always scale with the number and type of risks some banks, wittingly or unwittingly, began to take on. Eventually, this kind of risk-taking would bear consequences, with a number of banks facing public enforcement actions related to their banking-as-a-service partnerships.

The economic model of banking-as-a-service, for banks, fintechs, and middleware providers, remains unproven. During the boom times, customer-facing fintechs often focused on growth at all costs, prioritizing being able to show their investors an ever-increasing number of users, and not worrying about unit economics or profitability. Downstream providers, both middleware and bank partners, were happy enough to work with these fintechs, as long as they were being bankrolled by venture capital. Looking to grow sources of revenue beyond interchange, customer-facing fintechs have tried, but largely failed to add and cross-sell into additional products, particularly credit offerings. Because of the customer segment fintechs were most able to appeal to, those disfavored by large establishment banks as undesirable in the wake of Dodd-Frank, users of neobank services tend to skew lower-income and lower credit score. This limited the upside from interchange income while also limiting viable product offerings. In the saturated market of the late 2010s, consumer fintechs struggled with high costs of customer acquisition, low average revenue per user, and low customer retention rates. Prioritizing "frictionless" experiences and offering signup or referral bonuses also often made fintechs a favorite target for fraudsters.

We will explore the challenges to customer-facing fintechs, middleware platforms, and bank partners more thoroughly in Chapter 8.

## What About Interchange-Driven Models *Outside* of the US?

It is worth noting that the dynamic portrayed above is mostly specific to the United States. Other regions have significantly lower debit interchange rates, which are capped by regulation in many cases. At first blush, this would seem to favor neobank business models in the US, that benefit from higher interchange rates, and disadvantage the model in other countries. But the interchange question exists in a wider regulatory context. Obtaining a full banking license has proven substantially easier in other jurisdictions. Many of the major "neobanks" in the UK and Europe, for instance, are fully licensed banks, including Monzo, Starling, N26, and bunq (confusingly, despite being fully chartered banks, these companies are often still referred to as "fintechs"). And while it is true that the interchange rates they earn tend to be substantially lower, they have built their businesses with this in mind. Actually being banks, rather than dependent on an underlying bank partner, has enabled many licensed fintech players in the UK and EU to benefit from core elements of the business of banking: Holding deposits and making loans. For instance, during the Covid-19 pandemic, the UK's Starling, which focuses on banking small businesses, benefited enormously from facilitating the country's Bounce Back Loan Scheme (roughly comparable to the Paycheck Protection Program in the US). And as central bank interest rates rose sharply to combat inflation following the pandemic, fully licensed neobanks stood to benefit. We will dig into these important differences in the detailed case studies later in the book.

## Is Interchange Sufficient to Sustain US Fintech?

The importance of interchange, particularly in the US market, in powering the dramatic growth in fintech, banking-as-a-service, and partner banking cannot be understated. The Durbin amendment, even though it was not its intention, is largely responsible for the disaggregation of the value chain of deposit accounts and consumer debit payments in the United States. Combined with the rise of mobile phones and apps beginning in the late 2000s, the negative experience for lower-income consumers at large banks after Durbin, and plentiful venture capital funding, made for a golden age of consumer fintech in the mid- to late 2010s. But interchange was never intended to support a standalone business. Rather, the payment, from merchants and acquirers to card issuers, is intended to cover the issuing bank's costs of operating, serving customers, and bearing the cost of fraud losses. It remains to be seen whether the disaggregation of both the economics but also the responsibilities of building, marketing, and maintaining a customer deposit and payments program between fintechs, middleware platforms, and bank partners is sustainable on a long-term basis.

# Endnotes

**1**  CGAP (2019) Acquiring Models, www.cgap.org/research/publication/acquiring-models (archived at https://perma.cc/R58B-7QL8)

**2**  Scott, A. (2021) Merchant Discount, Interchange, and Other Transaction Fees in the Retail Electronic Payment System, *Congressional Research Service*, crsreports.congress.gov/product/pdf/IF/IF11893/1 (archived at https://perma.cc/4Y89-W5QW)

**3**  Durham, K. and Reed R. (2024) Redefining Rewards: The Future of Loyalty Programs in the FedNow Era, *Capco*, www.capco.com/intelligence/capco-intelligence/the-future-of-loyalty-programs-in-the-fednow-era (archived at https://perma.cc/6WND-M9G5)

**4**  Visa (2024) Visa USA Interchange Reimbursement Fees: Visa Supplemental Requirements, usa.visa.com/content/dam/VCOM/download/merchants/visa-usa-interchange-reimbursement-fees.pdf (archived at https://perma.cc/9WU4-R3X8)

**5**  Durbin, D. (2024) Durbin Urges the Federal Reserve to Hold Banks and Card Networks Accountable & Charge Reasonable Interchange Fees, www.durbin.senate.gov/newsroom/press-releases/durbin-urges-the-federal-reserve-to-hold-banks-and-card-networks-accountable-and-charge-reasonable-interchange-fees (archived at https://perma.cc/K4SW-44TM)

**6**  Marek, L. (2024) Fed Bombarded by Debit Card Fee Commentary, *Payments Dive*, www.paymentsdive.com/news/federal-reserve-debit-card-interchange-fee-cap-rule-proposal/716059/ (archived at https://perma.cc/JUP2-2PNW)

**7**  Lunde, A. et al. (2020) Study on the Application of the Interchange Fee Regulation, *Copenhagen Economics*, copenhageneconomics.com/publication/study-on-the-application-of-the-interchange-fee-regulation/ (archived at https://perma.cc/6G2A-MTKL)

**8**  Haltom, R. and Zhu Wang (2015) Did the Durbin Amendment Reduce Merchant Costs? Evidence from Survey Results, *Federal Reserve Bank of Richmond*, www.richmondfed.org/-/media/richmondfedorg/publications/research/economic_brief/2015/pdf/eb_15-12.pdf (archived at https://perma.cc/A964-PRGS)

**9**  Miroshnichenko, O. and E. Iakovleva (2022) Banking Sector Profitability: Does Household Income Matter?, *Sustainability*, www.mdpi.com/2071-1050/14/6/3345 (archived at https://perma.cc/GK92-3J24)

**10**  Consumer Financial Protection Bureau (2020) When Can I Be Denied a Checking Account Based on my Past Banking History?, www.consumerfinance.gov/ask-cfpb/when-can-i-be-denied-a-checking-account-based-on-my-past-banking-history-en-1113/ (archived at https://perma.cc/ZA9Z-VSZM)

**11**  Berge, E. et al. (2023) FBO Accounts: What Banks and Fintechs Need to Know, *Venable LLP*, www.venable.com/insights/publications/2023/01/fbo-accounts-what-banks-and-fintechs-need (archived at https://perma.cc/E24J-QGTU)

**12**  Cross, M. (2024) Banking-as-a-Service Middleware is Going "Direct." What Does that Mean?, *American Banker*, americanbanker.com/news/banking-as-a-service-middleware-is-going-direct-what-does-that-mean (archived at https://perma.cc/5T6L-FTJV)

**13**  Barnett, K. (2022) Federal Reserve Finalizes Rule Eliminating Exclusive Debit Card Networks for E-Commerce, *Troutman Pepper*, www.troutman.com/insights/federal-reserve-finalizes-rule-eliminating-exclusive-debit-card-networks-for-e-commerce.html (archived at https://perma.cc/J95Q-DQWK)

**14**  McBeain, J. (2023) Key Elements of the Proposed Credit Card Competition Act, *Troutman Pepper*, www.troutman.com/insights/key-elements-of-the-proposed-credit-card-competition-act.html (archived at https://perma.cc/7YLJ-3FBW)

**15**  Stempel, J. (2024) Visa, Mastercard can Likely Handle Settlement Much Bigger than $30 Billion, judge Says, *Reuters*, www.reuters.com/legal/visa-mastercard-can-likely-handle-settlement-much-bigger-than-30-billion-judge-2024-06-28/ (archived at https://perma.cc/A83F-775K)

**16**  Mikula, J. (2024) Consent Order Double Header Suggests Tough 2024 for Fintech, Banking-as-a-Service, *Fintech Business Weekly*, fintechbusinessweekly.substack.com/p/consent-order-double-header-suggests (archived at https://perma.cc/5Y8X-7M5R)

**17**  Mikula, J. (2024) Leaked Treasury Prime Docs Show Risks of BaaS Business: Churn, Concentration, Slowing Growth, *Fintech Business Weekly*, fintechbusinessweekly.substack.com/p/leaked-treasury-prime-docs-show-risks (archived at https://perma.cc/G5QK-CYNB)

# 4

# What's in It for Banks? Primarily, a Low-Cost Source of Deposits

CHAPTER OBJECTIVES

If interchange is a key ingredient for many fintechs, then deposits are the lifeblood of pretty much *all* banks. In this chapter, we will explore different ways banks fund their balance sheets and the unique role customer deposits, protected by deposit insurance schemes, play in banking business models. We will also explore factors that have reshaped the deposit-gathering landscape over the past several decades and how and why banking-as-a-service can be an important channel for smaller banks to gather deposits outside of their geographic area. We will unpack the most common examples of fintech business models that bring deposits to their bank partners, including consumer and business neobanks, peer-to-peer payments, neobrokerages, treasury management startups, and vertical SaaS applications.

While the interchange revenue detailed in Chapter 3 has obvious appeal, for many banks, the deposits fintech programs can bring with them may actually be more important. We briefly touched on the idea of net interest margin, or NIM, in Chapter 1. NIM is the difference between the interest a bank earns from its lending less the bank's interest expense, including rates paid on customer deposits. Historically, retail and corporate deposits have been some of the most desirable for banks to hold, as they tend to be "sticky," meaning customers are less likely to move funds elsewhere, and they are often less expensive (lower rate) than other forms of funding.

While we will not do a deep-dive on how banks fund the liability side of their balance sheets or how fractional reserve banking works, it is helpful to have some context on the pros and cons of various funding sources, which will provide a backdrop on why sourcing deposits through fintech and banking-as-a-service relationships holds such appeal to many banks. Sources of funding are their lifeblood. It is with the core ingredient of funding that banks work their magic to generate revenue, by deploying that funding into loans to consumers and businesses, using it to buy third-party loans or securities (thereby redeploying liquidity to other lenders), or even just parking funds at the central bank.[1]

Historically, deposits have been the bedrock source of funding for most banks, though there are exceptions to this, for banks that have atypical business models. Going back to that quintessential *It's A Wonderful Life* example, banks took in deposits from customers in a defined geographic area they served and deployed those deposits to fund loans in that same community. As long as banks charge more on their loans than they pay on deposits (and manage credit risk prudently), they earn a positive spread. There are two key levers to determining what that spread, the net interest margin, is: How much a bank has to pay depositors for entrusting the bank to hold their money, and how much the bank can charge customers who seek to borrow funds.[2]

Banks typically offer depositors interest rates that are below the central bank rate (the Fed Funds rate in the US). During rate-cutting cycles, when central banks are lowering rates, banks tend to immediately pass along these rate cuts to depositors. But, on the flip side, when central banks are raising rates, there tends to be a delay, and typically only a portion of the rate hike is passed along in the form of higher rates on deposits. This concept is known as the "deposit beta," which measures what percentage of a policy rate hike is passed along to depositors.[3] The reason why banks could get away with not passing along the full value of rate hikes goes back to the idea of "sticky deposits." Most consumers are not actively monitoring the rates checking and savings accounts are paying. Opening a new account or switching one's primary banking relationship was, historically, a laborious, high-friction process. Likewise, small businesses that have an established banking relationship have historically been unlikely to bear the cost of disruption of switching for a higher rate. On the corporate side, while yield and treasury management are certainly considerations, for day-to-day operational funds, finance executives often have considerations beyond yield. This idea that banks benefit from depositors' inertia, and thus don't have to pass along the entirety of interest rate increases, is often referred to as a bank's deposit "franchise value."[4]

KEY LEARNING POINTS

The "deposit beta" measures the share of increase in baseline interest rates that is passed along to depositors. A bank's deposit "franchise value" reflects the economic benefit of deposits tending to be "sticky," thus enabling banks to pay lower rates than if every depositor sought to maximize the interest rate they received.

In addition to retail and corporate deposits mentioned above, banks have various other ways to raise funding to support their balance sheet through "wholesale" funding markets. One of the most common forms of such wholesale funding is brokered deposits. Banks can make use of "brokered" deposits, so named because, historically, an actual person would act as a matchmaker to place deposits in bulk from one institution, whether another bank, broker-dealer, or other kind of institution, with a bank that was seeking deposits.[5] Brokered deposits tend to be more expensive and less "sticky." The end customer does not have a direct relationship with the bank accepting the brokered deposits and typically prioritizes rate over other characteristics. Because the end customer has no loyalty to the bank accepting their deposit via broker, they are more likely to shift those funds if a higher rate is on offer elsewhere or if a bank is exhibiting any sign of distress. However, these risks to the bank can be mitigated through product structure, such as by offering brokered certificates of deposit (CDs) rather than demand deposits, or by accepting deposits only up to a maximum of each individual depositors' deposit insurance coverage limit. Brokered deposits are sometimes referred to as "hot money" because of a perceived propensity to be less "sticky" or reliable than other types of funding.[6]

Other examples of wholesale funding include interbank lending, the "repo" market (repurchase agreements), and the commercial paper market. There are also a number of other government or government-backed facilities in the United States for banks to access liquidity, including the Federal Home Loan Bank system and the Federal Reserve's discount window. These facilities allow banks to pledge assets they hold in return for access to liquidity.[7] They are typically used as forms of emergency or "last resort" funding, as they can be as or more expensive than other market sources and may be viewed negatively by market participants. Banks also can raise funding by issuing debt (bonds) or equity (stock), though these methods can be expensive, and, in the case of equity, dilutive to existing shareholders, and are not typically primary funding channels for most banks.

The various funding mechanisms come with tradeoffs. Two key considerations include cost and how deposits are likely to behave in a stress scenario. These considerations, in turn, are influenced by law and regulatory policy. For instance, the FDIC charges banks a deposit insurance assessment, which is determined, in part, by both the amount of insured deposits, and also the composition of these deposits. Brokered deposits carry a higher assessment rate, as they are viewed as riskier. Likewise, regulatory requirements for banks to maintain a given liquidity coverage ratio (LCR), implemented after a wave of bank failures in the 2008 crisis, also take into consideration the composition of a bank's liabilities, including the composition of its deposits.[8]

## From Branch-Led Growth to Direct Banking

In the not-so-distant past, if a bank were looking to grow retail and corporate deposits, it would do so by expanding its branch footprint.

After all, before the rise of internet banking and digital account open-ing, how else would you grow your customer base? This could be done organically, by a bank building and opening incremental branches, or through merger and acquisition activity. Organically growing a bank's branch footprint is time consuming and resource intensive. Not only does it require physical infrastructure, but it also requires incremental personnel, to staff the new branches, and increased marketing outlays, to acquire new customers. Marketing spend and new account-opening incentives can be significant, as banks expanding their branch footprint into a new geographic area are almost certainly competing to win customers who already have a banking relationship. Growth in a bank's branch network is also likely to generate incremental compliance and regulatory overhead. For all this investment and incremental expense, a bank's upside, in terms of deposit growth, is constrained by the density and proximity of potential new customers to the branch. While in the pre-online banking age, a branch strategy was pretty much the only game in town, growing internet adoption starting in the mid-1990s heralded new, potentially radically more-efficient methods of gathering customer deposits.

KEY LEARNING POINTS

Traditional branch strategies relied on physical proximity, marketing, account-opening incentives, and foot traffic to source new customers, but often paid low rates on customers' deposits. By contrast, direct banks often had no branches, and used near-top-of-market rates and online deposit listing services as customer acquisition tools.

Beginning in the late 1990s and early 2000s, an alternative model began to emerge that was not dependent on physical bank branches. Some would refer to this as "branchless" banking or "direct to consumer." Security First Network Bank, often considered the first internet-only bank, launched in 1995. Telebank launched in 1996 and was acquired by E*Trade in 2002. First Internet Bank was founded in 1997 and began operating in 1999. Dutch bank ING launched a branchless concept in the US, dubbed ING Direct, in 2000 (it sold to Capital One in 2011). Some of the most successful banks deploying a direct-to-consumer deposit-gathering strategy did so as a funding tactic to support an existing lending franchise. For instance, GMAC, the one-time captive finance arm of automaker General Motors, became a bank in the course of the 2008 crisis and launched direct savings, CDs, and money market accounts as a cheaper source of capital to make loans to vehicle buyers. GMAC was ultimately renamed as Ally Bank, which is now a full-service online-only bank. Historically, monoline credit card-issuing banks, like MBNA, Providian, and Capital One, have also made use of the direct bank model for gathering deposits as a less expensive source to fund credit card-lending portfolios. The basic premise of direct banking for deposit gathering was, and remains to this day, quite straightforward. Instead of investing huge sums in building, maintaining, and staffing a physical branch network and on advertising to drive customers to it, go direct to depositors via the internet and let market-leading interest rates do the work of acquiring customers.

By contrast, the major money center banks, owing to their sheer size and ubiquity, have long benefited from their scale and perceived safety, even more so as "too big to fail" institutions in the wake of the 2008 crisis. While direct banks compete on rate, and smaller and community banks leverage their legacy geographically defined customer base and compete on service, banks like JPMorgan Chase, Wells Fargo, and Bank of America compete on size and the economies of scale that come with it. On a typical consumer checking and even savings accounts, money center banks often pay next to nothing (or literally nothing) in interest. Although establishment mega-banks may have been slower to adapt to internet and mobile distribution, once they made the investment in digital infrastructure, they have been able to benefit from their economies of scale. Major banks have even experimented with their own versions of digital-first direct banking models in markets where they did not already have a branch footprint. For instance, JPMorgan Chase memorably launched its neobank-like app Finn, though the effort was ultimately folded into Chase proper.[9] Chase's effort with Finn was widely viewed in the industry as a failure, though that may be an oversimplification. With

Chase's existing brand recognition and mammoth marketing budget, there was little reason to launch a new consumer brand instead of capitalizing on existing consumer awareness of Chase, even in markets where the bank lacked a branch presence.

Where did this evolving banking landscape leave community banks? On one side, they had direct banks offering the highest rates in the market, which tended to attract savvy, larger depositors looking to maximize yield. On the other hand, they faced the ever-encroaching presence of the mega-banks, which offered ubiquity and convenience, especially as digital capabilities began increasing as an important competitive feature set in the mid-2000s. Community banks generally could not (or did not want to) compete on rates with direct banks, at least in their home markets. Some did pursue a segmentation strategy, creating a distinct, online-only brand that offered higher rates, in an effort not to alienate loyal customers and their sticky deposits in a bank's local market.

But many community banks also lacked the infrastructure, budgets, and expertise to compete with mega-banks or to launch their own direct-to-consumer online-only bank brand. The ability to walk into a branch and the level of personalized customer service is where community banks historically have shone, but, for many consumers and businesses, these attributes were of declining importance. Even in the 2010s, community banks looking for growth were still heavily reliant on the same two tactics: Build branches or merger and acquisition (M&A) activity. But with customers increasingly comfortable with opening and managing their financial accounts online, the returns, in terms of deposit growth, of opening incremental branches has tended to decline over time, though the ratio of deposits to branches has increased as overall volume of deposits has gone up while the total number of branches has declined.[10] Bank mergers and acquisitions, while a tried-and-true method of bulking up to gain scale, have their own issues and complexities. Shareholders and regulators need to bless such deals, and regulators' view of bank mergers, and the implicit negative impact on competition, tends to oscillate with which party is in charge in Washington, DC. Deal economics and bank accounting rules can also influence the appeal of M&A as a growth strategy. As interest rates began rising in 2022, the value of many banks' securities portfolios declined. Banks could avoid recognizing these losses if they planned to hold underwater securities to maturity. However, in an acquisition scenario, the acquiring bank would have to mark such securities to market, making such an acquisition potentially significantly more expensive from a capital perspective.

## Fintech and BaaS: The Answer to Community Banks' Prayers?

When consumer fintech and especially banking-as-a-service came along, in many ways, they appeared to be the answer to community banks' prayers. Customer-facing fintechs promised to function as nationwide deposit-gathering front ends for small, local banks. The financial risk to banks appeared to be low. After all, venture-backed fintechs would foot the bill for building out their own tech infrastructure. Fintechs' agreements with partner banks often included a fixed-fee component or minimum monthly revenue commitment, meaning, in addition to bringing deposits, fintech relationships also often generated a direct revenue stream for these small, local banks. And perhaps best of all, at least until the VC funding winter arrived in 2022, fintechs had war chests of venture funding to deploy in marketing campaigns to acquire users—users who would bring their deposits to partner banks.

Despite the promise of customer-facing fintechs, banks still faced barriers in tapping into this potentially huge deposit-gathering channel. Banks would need to identify, negotiate with, and onboard these fintechs, which tended to be small, early-stage companies, often located thousands of miles from where banks interested in pursuing these models were. Onboarding fintech partners would require, at least in theory, a bank to conduct thorough diligence reviews and have appropriate risk and compliance controls in place to oversee their partners. But these capabilities—business development, sales, solutions engineering, account management, compliance oversight of third parties—are ones most community banks looking to partner with fintechs lacked. And, as we have touched on previously, the culture and priorities and VC-backed fintech startups tend to look radically different than at sometimes centuries-old community banks. These gaps meant that even small banks that understood the opportunity of partnering with fintechs as a deposit-gathering strategy often lacked the skills and culture to do so effectively.

KEY LEARNING POINTS

Middleware intermediaries, like Synapse, Unit, Treasury Prime, and others in the US, found product-market fit by solving key pain points for their two key constituencies: Banks, on the one hand, that often lack the resources and skills to build BaaS businesses on their own, and fintechs, on the other, whose focus tends to be getting products live in market quickly and efficiently.

Solving this pain point for banks, or at least promising to, is what made banking-as-a-service middleware platforms so appealing. Middleware platforms, also a beneficiary of the generous venture funding environment of the 2010s, by definition were dependent on cutting deals with chartered banks to make their offering work. While some of the specifics vary, middleware platforms are like any two-sided marketplace: They facilitate matching supply (banks) with demand (fintechs) by building and operating a technology platform. In this way, middleware platforms solved at least two key barriers to community banks partnering with fintechs. They would functionally do (and pay for) the business development/sales to attract fintech clients and, once integrated with a bank, would handle technology integrations with customer-facing fintechs. Some middleware platforms even attempted to take on various levels of due diligence and compliance functions on behalf of their bank partners, with mixed success. This could range from facilitating these processes on behalf of their partners, for instance, by collecting and doing an initial review of materials for a standardized diligence onboarding packet, to taking on execution of compliance obligations on behalf of bank partners. Indeed, the sales pitch of some middleware platforms, to both fintech clients and bank partners, was that they need not worry about compliance, because the middleware platform would handle much of it on their behalf. A part of the theory of this model was that middleware platforms could scale compliance capabilities in a way that neither banks nor fintechs could. Middleware players have often pitched their "proprietary" technology as enabling them to achieve compliance, at scale, with lower costs and less staff than would otherwise be possible.

## How Do Deposit-Gathering Business Models Work?

While the specifics can vary substantially by bank partner, middleware provider if applicable, and customer-facing fintech, the basic principle of the economic model in play here is simple. Customer-facing fintechs, whether making use of demand deposit accounts, cash management accounts, or offering a sweep network, function as a front-end customer acquisition channel that funnels deposits to underlying bank partners. Banks use those deposits as a source of funding for their various lines of business, which could include directly funding loans, like consumer credit cards or commercial real estate, buying securities, like agency-issued mortgage-backed securities, investing in government-issued debt, or even parking funds at the central bank. In return, banks pass along a share of the revenue generated to middleware platforms, if applicable, and to customer-facing fintechs. For legal reasons, this type of revenue sharing may be described as something other than "interest," for instance as "deposit rebates," but, regardless of what it is called, functionally that is what is happening. Customer-facing fintechs may or may not pay end-users any interest on their deposits. Transactional accounts, especially neobanks aimed at lower-income consumers, often do not offer any interest. The upshot for banks can be a lower-cost source of funds, which drive a larger net interest margin.

For customer-facing fintechs, revenue derived from generating deposits for bank partners helps to supplement interchange income revenue streams detailed in the last chapter. But while a non-bank fintechs' cost structure is simpler than the bank partners that hold its customers' deposits, fintechs still face substantial capital and operating expenses, including the cost of acquiring and servicing customers, which can be quite high. Likewise, middleware platforms, where fintechs and banks have chosen to work with them, generally derive most of their revenue from fintech partners, in the form of platform fees and revenue sharing from interchange and deposits. But, like fintechs, middleware platforms also have substantial capital and operating expenses. The relatively novel business models of customer-facing fintechs remain largely unproven through the economic cycle. Questions remain about the sustainability of fintech and middleware business models, which we will explore in greater depth in Chapter 9. There also can be incentive mismatches between fintechs and middleware platforms versus their underlying bank partners. Most fintechs and middlewares are early-stage, venture-backed companies that are often unprofitable and place an emphasis on rapid growth. This can introduce risks and place them at odds with their bank partners, where rapid growth can pose myriad challenges, including compliance and balance sheet management.

## Deposit-Gathering Fintech Business Models

Banking-as-a-service middleware layers have enabled community banks to develop partnerships with fintechs with a variety of business models that drive deposits to the banks. There are countless examples of fintechs that can act as deposit-gathering networks for their bank partners. Chances are, any customer-facing fintech that holds users' funds is partnering with a chartered bank to do so, though legal structures and business models can vary. Examples of categories and fintechs that exemplify them include:

- Consumer neobanks: Nearly all consumer neobanks in the US operate with a bank partner. Notable examples in the category include Chime, Current, Dave, and MoneyLion. Neobanks generally enable end users to open a demand deposit account (DDA) at an underlying bank partner (though some might use a cash management structure). These accounts typically pay little or no interest, though neobanks may also offer savings accounts that have more competitive interest rates. As previously discussed, these products are often designed for and appeal to lower-income and lower-credit score users, who may have negative experiences of incurring hefty fees at moneycenter banks. Average account balances per user are often quite low.

- Savings-focused: In contrast to many consumer neobanks, savings-focused services are often designed to appeal to higher-income users looking to earn a competitive return on their savings. HMBradley typified this category, with tiered interest rates that incentivized users to set aside larger portions of their paycheck, though the company shut down its consumer-focused product and pivoted to selling software to banks in 2023. Apple's partnership with Goldman Sachs to offer a savings feature is another, high-profile example of features targeted at mid- and upper-income users as a deposit-gathering vehicle for bank partners.[11]

- Peer-to-peer (P2P) and remittance: Though the primary use case of peer-to-peer payments and remittance services, like Cash App, Venmo, Apple Cash, and Wise is to send and receive money, increasingly, they have the capabilities to function as bank accounts. Many of these services provide users with bank account credentials, like routing and account numbers, and an associated debit card. While many users may actually store only minimal or no funds in these services, the number of users can be significantly higher than neobanks, given P2P and remittance services are often used in conjunction with an existing bank account, rather than intended as a replacement. The legal structures of these products vary but often can involve a bank partner holding insured customer funds.

- Neobrokerages: Neobrokers, as the name suggests, are focused on offering investment capabilities. Companies in this space include names like Robinhood, Public.com, and eToro. And while the focus is on investing, like any brokerage, these companies typically offer users options about how to handle uninvested cash, which may include parking it in a money market fund, certificates of deposit, or in a bank-powered sweep network. Neobrokers, like Robinhood, may also offer cash management accounts, which rely on a bank partner and operate similarly to traditional checking accounts.

- Small business neobanks: Like most consumer neobanks, those focused on small and medium businesses (SMBs) partner with chartered banks to hold customer deposits and issue payment cards. The SMB segment tends to focus more on the classic "mom and pop" type of business, like retail stores, coffee shops, bakeries, and so on. SMBs can be a bigger lift than consumer accounts from an onboarding perspective, as more documentation is often required. On the flip side, the average balance is usually significantly higher than a consumer neobank.

- Spend/treasury management: Fintechs in this segment often focus on building products for and marketing to high-growth, venture-backed startups. They do this by providing features tailored to this segment, like managing burn and runway projections, or by offering products, like corporate charge cards, that startups often have a difficult time obtaining from traditional issuers. Fintechs in this segment leverage demand deposit and cash management account structures. Examples include Brex, Mercury, Meow, and Arc. Startup clients of these platforms can often bring millions each in deposits to underlying bank partners, making them an attractive target, though they may be more sensitive to interest rates, resulting in a higher cost of funds.

- Vertical SaaS: As previously mentioned, vertical software-as-a-service platforms do not typically have as their primary use case-solving a banking or financial problem. Rather, a bank-enabled capability enhances what is often a subscription software product. For instance, a platform for managing a homeowners' association could offer embedded banking capabilities to hold and manage the association's financials. Or a rental management platform for landlords could offer the ability to collect and hold renters' security deposits. Both of these examples could represent sticky, low-cost sources of funds to underlying bank partners.

## Additional Considerations for Bank Partners

Banks leveraging banking-as-a-service business models as a tactic to source deposits have numerous and evolving considerations to take into account. Is it better to work directly with customer-facing fintechs, partner with a middleware platform, or both? What kind of fintech programs fit a bank's risk tolerance? Is a bank readily positioned to take advantage of deposits sourced through such relationships?

Being able to answer such questions is key for banks considering BaaS strategies, particularly as they are likely to influence a bank's cost of supporting such programs. Taking on fintech partners can substantially change a bank's risk profile, necessitating additional investments in compliance resources. For instance, regulatory expectations for complying with know your customer (KYC) or know your business (KYB) and anti-money laundering requirements can vary if a customer is physically walking into a bank branch versus opening an account remotely. The risk level of a consumer account that might hold hundreds of dollars and transact primarily via debit card is quite different from a business account that could hold millions and frequently send large value international wire transfers, for instance. The sheer number of accounts and transactions from fintech partners can quickly grow to dwarf a community bank's existing business, necessitating new or different kinds of transaction monitoring and regulatory reporting.

### KEY LEARNING POINTS

From a regulatory perspective, banks are generally responsible for compliance with applicable regulations, even when they are working with third parties, like banking-as-a-service middleware platforms and customer-facing fintechs. These third parties are treated as vendors or service providers to the bank, and it is the bank's responsibility to design and implement a compliance management system that enables it to effectively monitor and mitigate risk from its partners.

Banks, whether intermediated by a middleware platform or not, are ultimately responsible for ensuring their vendors, including fintechs, are compliant with applicable regulations. This generally means banks having second- and third-line compliance programs in place to oversee numerous aspects of their fintech partners' businesses, including areas like KYC/KYB, consumer protection, EFTA Reg E, TILA Reg Z, and ECOA Reg B for lending consumer credit, and so on. Even managing and classifying deposits sourced through fintechs requires special care. Rules defining "brokered deposits," which are treated differently in assessing deposit insurance premiums and in certain regulatory calculations, were updated in the US in 2020, though ambiguity remains. Smaller banks may not wish to exceed $10 billion in assets, requiring careful management of how quickly deposits through fintech partners grow, and strategies to shift deposits off balance sheet if needed. We will further explore these and other risks in Chapter 8.

## BaaS Deposits Offer Small Banks a Lifeline, with Risks

Deposits are the lifeblood of nearly every bank. But the last three decades have seen a sea change in how consumers and businesses use banks. The rise of online and then app-based banking has gradually eroded the importance of the local bank branch. "Direct" banking models enable institutions to source deposits without geographic restriction. Direct banks reduced their cost base by eschewing bricks and mortar locations and, instead, attracted depositors by paying market-leading rates. At the same time, market and regulatory forces have led to a steady consolidation in the number of chartered banks, which has been declining since 1984. Even the number of bank *branches*, which continued to grow for decades after the peak number of banks, began declining in 2012. Money center banks like JPMorgan Chase and Bank of America benefit from ubiquity, massive scale, and the implicit guarantee of government backing as they are deemed "too big to fail," and offer nearly zero interest on many standard checking and savings accounts. On the flip side, smaller community banks have faced unrelenting pressure on their business models, especially on the deposit side. Their key differentiators, geographic location and customer service, have been steadily undermined by the rise of mega-banks and digital distribution. Yet they often lack the budgets and capabilities to build and operate competitive digital offerings. Fintechs and middleware have, in many ways, stepped in and enable small banks to gather lower-cost deposits in ways they otherwise would not be able to. But these novel operating models come with novel risks, which regulators and banks themselves are still trying to understand. And, perhaps most importantly, whether or not the economic model is workable for all parties—fintechs, middleware platforms, *and* banks—remains to be seen.

## Endnotes

**1** Chen, J. and Vera, G. (2017) Bank Balance Sheets and the Value of Lending, *IMF Working Paper*, www.imf.org/-/media/Files/Publications/WP/2017/wp17111.ashx (archived at https://perma.cc/X2CY-SSYU)

**2** Corporate Finance Institute (n.d.) Net Interest Margin, corporatefinanceinstitute.com/resources/accounting/net-interest-margin/ (archived at https://perma.cc/5Q9Y-9MET)

**3** Kang-Landsberg, A. et al. (2023) Deposit Betas: Up, Up, and Away?, *Liberty Street Economics*, https://libertystreeteconomics.newyorkfed.org/2023/04/deposit-betas-up-up-and-away/ (archived at https://perma.cc/P6EU-ACJK)

**4** Kulkarni, N. and Singh, H. (2022) Bank Deposit Franchise, Interest Rate Risk, and Default Risk: Evidence from India, *NYU Stern*, www.stern.nyu.edu/sites/default/files/2023-01/Kulkarni%20Singh%20-%20Bank%20Deposit%20Franchise%2C%20Interest%20Rate%20Risk%2C%20and%20Default%20Risk--Evidence%20from%20India.pdf (archived at https://perma.cc/875W-R5FQ)

**5** Sidley Austin (2020) FDIC Final Rule on Brokered Deposits, www.sidley.com/en/insights/newsupdates/2020/12/fdic-final-rule-on-brokered-deposits (archived at https://perma.cc/L9HK-AQA3)

**6** Heeb, G. and Eisen, B. (2023) Banks Lean On "Hot" Deposits to Shore Up Balance Sheets, *Wall Street Journal*, www.wsj.com/amp/articles/banks-lean-on-hot-deposits-to-shore-up-balance-sheets-2677a931 (archived at https://perma.cc/TSH6-FP3X)

**7**  Anderson, H. et al. (2024) Overdependence on Short-term Wholesale Funding: A Historical Perspective, *Bank Policy Institute*, bpi.com/overdependence-on-short-term-wholesale-funding-a-historical-perspective/ (archived at https://perma.cc/9GK9-MESH)

**8**  Bank for International Settlements (2018) Liquidity Coverage Ratio (LCR)—Executive Summary, www.bis.org/fsi/fsisummaries/lcr.htm (archived at https://perma.cc/3DCK-BTPP)

**9**  Benoit, D. and Rudegeair, P. (2019) JPMorgan Scraps New App Service for Young People, *Wall Street Journal*, www.wsj.com/articles/jpmorgan-closing-down-finn-digital-bank-a-year-after-nationwide-launch-11559819232 (archived at https://perma.cc/E43P-W2S2)

**10**  Benmelech, E. et al. (2023) Bank Branch Density and Bank Runs, *NBER Working Paper Series*, www.nber.org/system/files/working_papers/w31462/w31462.pdf (archived at https://perma.cc/4FKD-EM6J)

**11**  Apple (2023) Apple Card's Savings Account by Goldman Sachs Reaches over $10 Billion in Deposits, www.apple.com/newsroom/2023/08/apple-cards-savings-account-by-goldman-sachs-sees-over-10-billion-usd-in-deposits/ (archived at https://perma.cc/KD3S-A64F)

# 5

# BaaS Business Models: Loan Origination-to-Distribute

CHAPTER OBJECTIVES

In this chapter, we will cover variations of bank-fintech lending partnerships and their key components. Consumer lending can be substantially more complicated than deposit and debit programs and comes with significantly more risk and regulation. For banks, powering banking-as-a-service lending models can be a key strategy to source lending assets and generate income as part of a "capital light" strategy. For fintechs, banks can enable a simpler licensing and product strategy, especially in the US market, but require close coordination with their partner banks. Regulatory risks, particularly around "true lender" issues, cast a shadow of uncertainty over this model, especially for consumer credit at rates above state usury limits.

Lending, a key component of the business of banking, is another common product segment in fintech. As we touched on in Chapter 1, non-bank lending is not itself new. For US fintechs offering lending products, there are three primary approaches: Obtain their own state lending licenses, partner with a chartered bank, or develop products that may not require licensing. Fintechs may also take a hybrid approach and employ more than one of these strategies, especially if they offer multiple kinds of lending products.

We discussed some of the benefits and drawbacks to the state-license model in the case study examining storefront payday lenders' use of the so-called "rent-a-bank" or "rent-a-charter" model in Chapter 1. A non-bank lender typically must secure and maintain a license in every US state it plans to operate. The products and terms permitted can vary considerably state to state, with differences in core product specifications, like minimum and maximum permitted loan amounts, interest rate caps, minimum term lengths, and so forth. Accommodating these differences, while absolutely possible, can generate significant administrative overhead. Pursuing a state-license strategy does not obviate a non-bank lender's need to comply with applicable US federal lending regulations, which can be quite complex and onerous, especially for consumer credit products. The Equal Credit Opportunity Act (ECOA), Truth in Lending Act (TILA), Fair Credit Reporting Act (FCRA), Electronic Funds Transfer Act (EFTA), anti-money laundering requirements, consumer protection, and so forth all generally still apply, regardless of whether a fintech lender is working with a bank partner or not. And some products simply are not possible without a bank partner: Namely, credit cards. Operating a credit card program as a non-bank will, at a minimum, require having a "BIN sponsor," or a bank partner, that is a principal member of a card scheme like Visa or Mastercard (at least in the US).[1]

> **KEY LEARNING POINTS**
>
> A bank license is not a requirement to offer consumer credit products. However, non-bank lenders, including fintechs, generally must obtain a license in each state they plan to operate. And federal consumer credit protections, like FCRA, ECOA, and TILA generally still apply.

So, while you do not have to be a bank to lend, being one certainly comes with plenty of advantages. By virtue of holding a charter, banks do not have to obtain licenses in each state they plan to lend in. Instead, banks can typically lend nationally, with the same product structure and terms, based on what is permitted in a bank's home state. The right of preemption dates to the National Bank Act, passed in 1863, though interpretations and limitations of this right continue to evolve.[2] Perhaps most importantly, banks, unlike non-bank fintech lenders, generally enjoy a stable, low-cost source of funding: Their deposits! By contrast, non-bank lenders are dependent on capital markets to enable their lending. This can lead to a variety of different business models. For example, non-bank lenders, including fintechs, can market, acquire, and service loans, but they then can sell the bulk or all of the loans (and its accompanying credit risk) to investors, realizing a gain on the sale of the loan and charging a fee to service the loan. This can be an attractive model, but also comes with risks that we will explore more later in this chapter.

## How Do Bank-Fintech Lending Partnerships Work?

There are various operating and financial models for how fintechs can partner with banks to offer lending products. Typically, a non-bank fintech will own many of the customer-facing functions, including marketing, customer acquisition, onboarding, and servicing. A bank partner will be the legal lender of record and thus typically appears on a borrower's loan agreement. Once the loan is consummated, the partner bank may retain the loan on its own balance sheet, or sell part of or the whole loan. Technically, the bank may be selling a "participation stake" or receivables tied to the underlying loan, but the effective outcome is the same: To transfer some or all of the credit risk from the bank that originated the loan to another party, often the customer-facing fintech.

Fintech partners, in turn, often tap capital markets to fund their own lending. This could take the form of revolving credit lines, warehouse facilities, forward-flow agreements, asset-backed securitizations, and the like. The capital markets strategy a fintech pursues will depend on its products, origination volume, maturity, and business model. In cases where bank partners do not retain the entire loan on their own balance sheet, they will typically hold a participation stake of at least 5 per cent, which helps defend against regulatory charges that the bank is not the "true lender," an idea we will discuss in greater depth later in this chapter.

---

KEY LEARNING POINTS

Banks that partner with fintechs in lending programs typically have two potential business models: Retain the loan on their own balance sheet and earn interest income or sell much or all of the loan to their fintech partner, collecting a fee for originating the loan and limiting their credit risk and capital commitment.

---

In these partnership structures, the bank is typically legally the lender of record. A customer-facing fintech functions, essentially, as a service provider to its partner banks. Responsibility for compliance with many of the applicable lending regulations ultimately lies with the chartered bank whose name appears on the loan agreement. While a fintech engaging in lending will generally do its own marketing, propose its own credit box and underwriting strategy, and need to pull data from and furnish data to the credit bureaus, its policies and procedures for ensuring compliance ultimately must align with and be approved by its bank partner. The bank, in turn, must have adequate oversight and controls over fintech lending partners that are acting on its behalf. This can become quite complicated if, as is often the case, a single bank is working with numerous fintech lending partners. Given the greater complexity and risk, there are relatively fewer banks that specialize in partnering with fintechs on lending programs vs. deposit and debit card issuing programs. Well-known examples in the US market include Cross River Bank, WebBank, Celtic Bank, Transportation Alliance Bank, and FinWise Bank.

There are relatively few types of lending products offered through these kinds of fintech-bank partnerships, and many banks develop a specialization in a certain lending niche. Examples of popular credit products include:

- Unsecured personal loans: In many ways, this product, popularized by fintech lenders like LendingClub and Prosper to consolidate credit card debt, is the earliest example of bank-fintech lending in the modern fintech era.

- Small-dollar loans: Capitalizing on banks' preemption rights and ability to export interest caps of their home state, fintech lenders focused on small-dollar, shorter-term products have partnered with banks to offer such products nationally.

- Credit builder loans: Legally, these are just unsecured personal loans. But rather than the loan proceeds going to the borrower, they are placed in an escrow account. A borrower makes payments as normal, and receives the funds from the escrow account at the end of the loan term.

- Charge cards: Charge cards function like a credit card, but the balance must be paid in full at the end of each billing period. Charge cards, especially *secured* charge cards, have become a popular product structure, as they claim to help users build credit and also allow fintechs to benefit from higher interchange rates compared to debit cards. Charge cards are not subject to the interchange caps called for by the Durbin amendment as discussed in Chapter 3.

- Credit cards: Non-bank fintechs and brands looking to offer their own credit card need a bank partner to do so. The technical integration and economic and operating models can vary substantially.

- Commercial/business variants of some of the above, including charge cards and term loans. Lending to businesses is substantially less regulated than consumer credit, though issuing credit/charge cards does still require working with a bank partner.

## Direct vs. Middleware Models

Lending is substantially more complex than deposit accounts and debit programs. And, within lending, revolving credit—charge and credit cards—are significantly more complicated to build and operate than close-ended products, like installment loans. Fintechs offering installment loans, both for larger amounts at rates below 36 per cent APR and smaller high-APR loans, tend to work directly with a bank partner to build and operate their products. Because their structure and compliance requirements are simpler, less infrastructure is required to launch these close-ended credit products. By using a simpler structure with fewer intermediaries, lending fintechs and their bank partners can capture a greater share of the economics for themselves.

There are examples of fintechs leveraging middleware platforms to offer close-ended credit products. Examples include credit-building loans and small cash advances, which tend to be ancillary products that might make sense as part of a larger neobank offering. Examples of middleware platforms that have attempted to facilitate such models include Synapse and Onbo, both of which used their own state-level licenses to originate loans for third-party fintechs. Onbo shut down in late 2022, and Synapse declared bankruptcy in early 2024, casting doubt on the viability of this approach.

### KEY LEARNING POINTS

"Close-ended" credit products have a defined term. Consumer products in this category are commonly known as personal loans or installment loans. Because the term and interest rate are typically fixed, close-ended products are structurally simpler to offer.

"Revolving" or "open-ended" credit products do not have a defined term. Popular consumer products in this category include credit and charge cards, where the revolving credit is tied to a card payment instrument, and lines of credit. Interest rates on open-ended products are typically variable and the term is, by definition, not fixed, making these products structurally more complex.

Revolving credit products are substantially more complex for a number of reasons. Managing credit risk for revolving products is a more difficult proposition, as borrowers are assigned a credit limit when approved and are able to repeatedly borrow and repay, up to that limit, as long as they remain current on their account. Because cardholders only need to make a minimum payment, which can be as little as a few per cent of the outstanding balance, "bad credits," or delinquencies and charge-offs, can take some time to appear.[3] This process of portfolio "seasoning" can be particularly painful for new issuers and creditors using novel approaches to underwriting, both of which tend to be true of fintech lenders.

Perhaps a more significant piece of complexity comes from the fact that charge and credit cards actually function as two distinct products in one: a loan and a payment mechanism. This can create a lot more utility for users, but also requires a lot more work behind the scenes to operationalize. Unlike with fintech lenders offering installment loans, which tend to work directly with a bank partner, fintechs offering card products exist on a continuum. There are examples of programs where a fintech (or brand) works and integrates closely with a bank partner, like Apple and Goldman Sachs' collaboration on the Apple Card, which we will explore in a case study in Chapter 9. At the opposite end of the spectrum, there are operating models where fintech credit card issuers rely heavily on intermediaries to act as program managers, including to connect them with BIN sponsors, issuer-processors, and card networks and to take on certain operational and compliance responsibilities. How responsibilities are disaggregated between a customer-facing fintech, supporting intermediaries, and a bank partner will heavily influence the economics for each participant in the value chain.

## Bank-Fintech Lending Business Models

The wider variety of product structures and operating models in lending drive a more diverse set of potential business models. Who holds the credit risk is the primary driver influencing each party's business and economic model. A bank partner, a customer-facing fintech, or a third-party investor can ultimately hold most or all of the credit risk from loans originated through banking-as-a-service lending models. The product structure also plays a role. Charge and credit cards, like their debit counterparts, drive interchange income as well as potentially driving interest income.

Bank partners that specialize in fintech-bank lending partnerships tend not to retain more than a small participation stake in the loans they originate, typically 5–10 per cent. Lending partner banks' models tend to focus on supplying the infrastructure to originate loans, including their charter but also regulatory risk and compliance expertise. In this model, the bank partner may receive a per-loan fee, fees based on the size and performance of a fintech partner's portfolio, and/or monthly account fees based on the number of fintech customers. Banks that retain a slice of loan receivables would also earn interest income. For charge and credit card programs, partner banks also typically receive a share of interchange income generated. Normally, banks need to contribute capital toward loans they fund and set aside funds to cover potential loan losses, known as provisions. But, by selling much or all of the loans a partner bank originates to their fintech partners, the bank reduces its credit risk and, as a result, the structure can be substantially less capital intensive. This can allow banks pursuing this model to post impressive financial results when measured by return on assets (ROA) or return on equity (ROE), two common approaches to measuring bank profitability.[4]

There are, however, banks that are more concerned with finding diversified, high-quality assets into which they can deploy their deposits. Rather than focusing on earning fee-based revenue in the short term, these banks may have excess deposits they are looking to deploy profitably. In this model, a partner bank can serve both as the lender of record and hold much or all of the originated receivable themselves, rather than selling them to a customer-facing fintech. The quintessential example of this in the US market is fintech lender Upstart, which works with a network of banks, including popular partner bank Cross River but also a host of smaller banks and credit unions, like Ridgewood Savings Bank, First Federal Bank of Kansas

City, Kemba Financial Credit Union, and Patelco Credit Union.[5] In this approach, Upstart operates largely as a front-end for its partner banks, by generating demand, underwriting applicants, and matching them to bank partners who actually originate and hold those loans. Upstart typically collects an origination fee and servicing fee, while the bank partner collects interest income.

For lending fintechs, the same primary question applies: Do they actually hold the credit risk themselves, or do they shift it to another party? Because non-bank fintechs, by definition, cannot hold customer deposits to leverage as a source of funding, to grow to any meaningful scale, they need to tap external sources of funding. In the case of Upstart, the company taps a network of banks that functionally pay Upstart to find, help underwrite, and service loans that the banks originate and hold. An alternate funding model for fintechs is to tap private credit markets to scale their ability to extend credit. A fintech's capital market strategy will heavily influence its economic model. There are a variety of structures a non-bank lender can use to tap liquidity: Revolving lines of credit, warehouse facilities, whole loan sales, securitizations, and so forth.

Exploring the pros, cons, and economic implications of each of these is beyond the scope of this book. But to boil it down, fintech lenders basically have two choices. One, to hold on to the credit they originate, collect interest and any fee income, and access liquidity by pledging those assets for access to debt capital. Alternatively, as is the case with Upstart, fintech lenders can seek to offload some or all of the credit they originate to third parties. In this second model, fintechs benefit from a "gain on sale," where the party buying a loan pays more than the par value (face value) of a loan, reflecting the present value of the future stream of principal and interest payments. Fintechs may also charge borrowers an upfront origination fee, and, in cases where they sell some or all of the loan receivable, earn a percentage fee for servicing the loan. It is also possible to blend these methods, where a fintech lender taps multiple sources of debt capital, and will hold some loans and sell others. While fintech lenders' non-bank structure can mean less regulatory overhead, it does create risks, in that fintech lenders are highly dependent on capital markets to fund their lending.

The card side functions similarly, though the ability to sell on receivables from charge card programs can be more limited, owing to their short duration. Non-bank fintechs offering credit cards, on which cardholders can revolve a balance, tend to have similar funding strategies available to them as those offering close-ended loans. A bank partner may hold much or all of the credit risk, as is the case in the Apple Card-Goldman Sachs partnership. A fintech may tap debt capital but hold much of the loan book on its own balance sheet, earning interest income. Or a fintech may sell on receivables to third-party investors. Charge and credit card programs also have the benefit of generating other fee streams, including interchange income and fee revenue, though some of this may be passed back to cardholders in the form of perks, points, and rewards.

Middleware platforms' involvement in facilitating fintech-bank lending partnerships is generally more limited. As mentioned previously, there are examples of non-bank middleware platforms holding their own state lending licenses—Onbo and Synapse, both of which have shut down. The reliance on state-issued licenses constrains the flexibility of this approach, and the uptake of these capabilities by customer-facing fintechs so far has been limited. In Synapse's model, customer-facing fintechs originate loans on Synapse's behalf, meaning interest and fee revenue accrue to Synapse, which likely pays a per-loan fee or similar revenue share to fintechs for customer acquisition. Given Synapse's collapse into bankruptcy in early 2024, it is not clear that this model is economically viable. Middleware platforms play a more significant role in card-based lending, in that they generally help facilitate transaction authorization, settlement, and reconciliation. Middleware platforms that offer capabilities in the space include platforms like Synapse and Unit but also issuer-processors, which may include some aspects of program management, like Marqeta, Galileo, Lithic, i2c, Deserve, and so forth. These platforms' revenue typically derives from a share of transaction volume, based on the number of customer accounts, and may involve other service or professional services fees.

## Risks in Bank-Fintech Lending Partnerships

Bank-fintech lending partnerships are not without risk. Consumer credit, as a category, has substantially more regulatory oversight than deposit and debit products discussed in the previous chapters. In addition to broad-based consumer protection requirements, such as prohibitions on unfair, deceptive, and abusive acts and practice (UDAAPs), there are a host of complex laws and regulations that apply specifically to consumer credit in the US, including the Equal Credit Opportunity Act (ECOA), the Fair Credit Reporting Act (FCRA), and the Truth in Lending Act (TILA). Much of consumer credit regulation in the United States dates to the 1960s and 1970s and was not designed with modern, internet distribution of products in mind—let alone the disaggregation of a product across a bank, middleware, and fintech. At a high level, ECOA prohibits lenders from illegally discriminating against applicants on the basis of a "protected class," which includes race, color, religion, national origin, sex, marital status, age, receipt of public assistance, or the good faith exercise of any right under the Consumer Credit Protection Act.[6] FCRA governs creditors' obligations when accessing data from or furnishing data to credit reporting agencies.[7] And TILA mandates lenders to make certain disclosures, including of finance charges and the corresponding annual percentage rate (APR), as well as imposing certain requirements on how lenders market credit products.[8] Even when a bank partner sells some or all of loan receivable post-origination, because it is the lender of record, it is ultimately responsible for ensuring its third-party partners—middleware platforms, if applicable, and customer-facing fintechs—are in compliance. In practice, this requires a bank partner to work closely with their fintech partners in developing and overseeing their compliance programs, which can be a labor- and cost-intensive task for partner banks.

### KEY LEARNING POINTS

Even in cases where a bank partner sells much or all of a loan it originated on behalf of a fintech partner, because the bank is the "lender of record," it is responsible for ensuring its partners' compliance with applicable regulations.

Compliance risks in bank-fintech lending are not the only threat. The legal structure itself, in which banks act as the lender of record but typically go on to sell most of the resulting loan receivable, has been and remains a point of ongoing conflict between banks/fintechs that leverage the model, consumer advocates, and various state and federal regulators. At issue is who is legally the "true lender" of loans originated using bank-fintech partnerships.[9] The question is paramount, as chartered banks historically enjoy the ability to preempt many state laws, but the same is not true for non-bank fintechs. The area where this has garnered the most attention is when fintechs partner with banks to originate loans at interest rates above a state's usury cap. As discussed previously, a non-bank fintech lender that relied on a state license would clearly be bound by a state's interest rate cap. Partnering with a bank potentially offers a way around these restrictions, but some states and consumer advocates view these arrangements as a kind of replay of the "rent-a-bank" structures used by payday lenders in the early 2000s.[10]

The "true lender" debate is ongoing and multifaceted. A full discussion is outside of what is relevant to this book, but it is helpful to understand the recent history around the issue. Much of the current angst around "true lender" dates to the 2015 case *Madden v. Midland Funding, LLC.* The decision in that case called into question the long-standing doctrine of "valid when made," by finding that the originating bank's preemption of a state's rate cap did not apply if the loan purchaser was not a bank. In other words, the decision called into question banks' ability to sell the loans they originated with interest rates above a given state's usury cap to their fintech partners. In the wake of the decision, there was substantial fear and uncertainty about the future of fintech-bank partnerships for lending, which relied in many cases on banks' ability to preempt state law. Subsequent actions in different branches of government and different court jurisdictions had the effect of narrowing the scope of Madden, but, in 2017, the Colorado attorney general filed suit against two fintech lenders, accusing them of violating the state's 21 per cent usury limit. The matter was ultimately settled, but limited fintech-bank partnerships to charging a maximum of 36 per cent in Colorado.[11] The settlement also required lenders that offered loans above Colorado's 21 per cent rate to obtain a license from the state regulator and agree to certain requirements, thereby eroding some of the benefits of partnering with a bank.

In 2019 and 2020, the Office of the Comptroller of the Currency (OCC), which regulates national banks in the US, proposed two rules in response to Madden in an attempt to clarify the situation. The "valid when made" rule sought to clarify and codify that whether or not the interest rate of a loan is permissible is determined at the time the loan is originated, and that subsequent sale or assignment of a loan does not impact the enforceability or validity of the rate.[12] The "true lender" rule sought to create a simple, bright line test for determining which party in a partnership is the actual lender. The rule specified that a bank is considered to be the lender if, on the date of origination, it is named as the lender in a borrower's loan agreement, or if the bank funds the loan.[13] The FDIC, which regulates state banks, adopted a "valid when made" rule consistent with the OCC's guidance, but it did not adopt a corresponding "true lender" rule. And indeed, the OCC's "true lender" rule was later nullified by Congress through its use of the Congressional Review Act, leaving a cloud of uncertainty over bank-fintech lending partnerships, particularly those used to originate loans in excess of states' usury caps.[14]

In the time since the reversal of the OCC's "true lender" rule, there have been a handful of state actions that demonstrate the risk to the bank-fintech partnership model. OppFi, which partners with three Utah-based banks, has been sued in both Washington, DC, and California for offering loans at rates as high as 160 per cent APR, in alleged violation of those jurisdictions' interest rate caps. Both cases make the argument that OppFi, not its bank partners, is the "true lender," and thus does not enjoy the right to preempt the rate caps. Conversely, OppFi argues it offers a platform that enables its bank partners to market, underwrite, and service borrowers, and that the banks are the true lenders. As the banks are based in Utah, which has no usury cap, and enjoy the right of preemption, the loans are permissible, even in states with lower rate caps, OppFi argues.

The "true lender" issue is the most salient, but there are also emerging challenges to banks' right of preemption itself. In other words, the right of a bank, regardless of working through a fintech partner, to originate loans into another state that exceed that state's own rate cap. For example, state-chartered Transportation Alliance Bank, known as TAB, also based in Utah, faced a challenge from Iowa's attorney general, who argued TAB should not enjoy rate preemption rights in Iowa, as Iowa had opted out of a voluntary provision of a 1980 law known as DIDMCA, which allows state-chartered banks to charge interest rates and fees permitted by their home state on a nationwide basis.[15] Iowa's argument hinged, in part, on determining where the loans in question were "made," which, in an era of cross-state digital distribution, is open to debate. Since that case, Colorado has enacted a measure that would also have the state opt out of the provisions of DIDMCA, and Washington, DC has considered such a measure. Some jurisdictions are also considering "anti-evasion" bills, which seek to codify elements of "true lender" theory in state law and regulation in such a way as to challenge the ability of out-of-state lenders, including those operating through bank-fintech partnerships, from exceeding state rate caps.

Finally, while most of the above is aimed at out-of-state state-chartered banks, which are the most common partners for fintech lenders, there is an ongoing case that threatens to undermine nationally chartered banks' right of preemption. The US Supreme Court has agreed to hear a case to determine whether state laws requiring banks to pay 2 per cent interest on residential mortgage escrow accounts are preempted by the National Bank Act. While the topic is unrelated to lending or fintech-bank partnerships directly, the decision could curtail national banks' right of preemption. Separately, Democratic US Senators have pushed back on the OCC's expansive definition of preemption rights for national banks, arguing that the regulator is not operating consistently with requirements set forth in Dodd-Frank and is undermining states' abilities to protect consumers from harmful practices.

## Banks and Fintechs Face Credit, Business Cycle Risks

Beyond the compliance risks and challenges of any lending business and potentially existential "true lender" risks, fintechs pursuing bank partner lending models also face garden variety business and credit cycle risks. Although many fintech lenders have marketed themselves to investors by claiming novel approaches to identifying and underwriting applicants that traditional lenders miss, academic analysis suggests that many fintech lenders have actually captured market share by taking on riskier borrowers and charging correspondingly higher rates.[16] That is not to say no fintech lenders have deployed new approaches to underwriting, including using "alternative data," like applicants' rental payment history, or cash flow-based underwriting, where lenders use bank account data in addition to or instead of a traditional credit report. But many fintech lenders using these approaches are relatively new ventures, and have not been tested through the cycle. How their underwriting models stand up to a recession largely remains to be seen.

Likewise, as non-bank lenders, fintechs are reliant on capital markets to supply necessary funds to lend. Their ability to access lending capital is dependent both on the performance of lenders' own portfolios—if they are able to accurately forecast losses and returns—as well as market-wide conditions. If lenders' ability to access capital is constrained, it is likely to have an abrupt and serious impact on their origination volume, revenue, and overall health of their business. This is not purely theoretical. Around 2016, when the Federal Reserve began raising rates after nearly a decade of them being at functionally 0 per cent, capital market funders grew skittish, conditions tightened, and non-bank lenders' access to funding dropped considerably. The predictable result was significantly curtailed origination volumes, drops in revenue, and employee layoffs.

Partly as a hedge to this kind of capital markets volatility, and also as a mechanism to access a lower cost of capital, several fintech lenders have made the decision to *become* banks. SoFi and LendingClub, both of which primarily originate unsecured consumer loans, acquired banks. This provided them with a stable, lower-cost source of funding in the form of deposits. Becoming banks also gave SoFi and LendingClub greater flexibility, in that they could choose to hold loans they originated on their balance sheet and earn interest or to sell the loans they originated, depending on market conditions and their own balance sheet needs. Still, numerous fintech lenders have chosen not to pursue a charter, demonstrating the range of business and operating models possible in consumer lending.

## Evolving Models to Match Savers with Borrowers

One of the core roles of banking is matching savers with borrowers by holding deposits and making loans. The spread between what a bank pays savers and what it charges depositors, the net interest margin, is traditionally a primary source of revenue in banking. But, as we have examined, running a lending business is rife with risks and challenges, and thus comes with significant regulation. The lending business model, done via banking-as-a-service, takes what is a single product to an end customer and disaggregates the capabilities necessary over multiple partners. Fintech lenders typically focus on "customer-facing" capabilities, like marketing, customer acquisition, underwriting, and servicing and collections. Their bank partners bring the most important ingredient, a bank license, but also compliance and risk management expertise, and sometimes supply capital as well. The upside for both fintechs and banks is quite clear: Fintechs are generally able to offer a consistent product, nationwide, without the hassle of securing state licenses. Banks leverage their license and compliance expertise and can generate outsized returns thanks to the capital-light structure. That is not to say there is no risk or uncertainty in the model. Particularly for bank-fintech partnerships that offer loans at rates above states' usury cap, uncertainty over who the "true lender" is and the permissibility of such loans in certain jurisdictions is likely to remain.

# Endnotes

**1** Horowitz, C. (2022) Fintech Guide to Bank Identification Numbers (BINs), *Lithic*, www.lithic.com/blog/bank-identification-numbers (archived at https://perma.cc/Q32G-A4W3)

**2** Federal Reserve History (2022) National Banking Acts of 1863 and 1864, www.federalreservehistory.org/essays/national-banking-acts (archived at https://perma.cc/P8FV-X86E)

**3** Federal Deposit Insurance Corporation (n.d.) Credit Card Activities Manual, www.fdic.gov/regulations/examinations/credit_card/ch12.html (archived at https://perma.cc/MQ7T-V3BK)

**4** Mikula, J. (2023) BaaS Is No Silver Bullet for Community Banks, De Novos, Analysis Shows, *Fintech Business Weekly*, fintechbusinessweekly.substack.com/p/baas-is-no-silver-bullet-for-community (archived at https://perma.cc/2Q6G-FJH4)

**5** Upstart (2024) Upstart Powered Lenders, www.upstart.com/lenders/partners/ (archived at https://perma.cc/N5BU-TKMQ)

**6** Federal Deposit Insurance Corporation (2022) Consumer Compliance Examination Manual, www.fdic.gov/resources/supervision-and-examinations/consumer-compliance-examination-manual/documents/5/v-7-1.pdf (archived at https://perma.cc/ER8L-Z6TZ)

**7** Jones Day (2016) Understanding the Fair Credit Reporting Act, www.jonesday.com/-/media/files/publications/2016/04/understanding-the-fair-credit-reporting-act-ipract/files/understanding-the-fcra/fileattachment/understanding-the-fcra.pdf (archived at https://perma.cc/78BX-ERKZ)

**8** Federal Deposit Insurance Corporation (2024) Consumer Compliance Examination Manual, www.fdic.gov/resources/supervision-and-examinations/consumer-compliance-examination-manual/documents/5/v-1-1.pdf (archived at https://perma.cc/D9HE-5Y9D)

**9** Perkins, D. (2018) Marketplace Lending: Fintech in Consumer and Small-Business Lending, Congressional Research Service, crsreports.congress.gov/product/pdf/R/R44614 (archived at https://perma.cc/G95J-N2KN)

**10** National Consumer Law Center (2022) High-Cost Rent-a-Bank Loan Watch List, www.nclc.org/resources/high-cost-rent-a-bank-loan-watch-list/ (archived at https://perma.cc/57PL-LZNN)

**11** Reczka, B. (2021) Continuing Uncertainty after Colorado Compromise: The Limited Impact of the Avant-Marlette Settlement on True Lender Risk for Nonbank-Bank Partnerships, *The FinReg Blog*, sites.duke.edu/thefinregblog/2021/02/02/continuing-uncertainty-after-colorado-compromise-the-limited-impact-of-the-avant-marlette-settlement-on-true-lender-risk-for-nonbank-bank-partnerships/ (archived at https://perma.cc/38M5-8E2D)

**12**  Office of the Comptroller of the Currency (2019) OCC Proposes Rule to Clarify "Valid When Made" Doctrine, www.occ.treas.gov/news-issuances/news-releases/2019/nr-occ-2019-132.html (archived at https://perma.cc/RA5N-R4UP)

**13**  Office of the Comptroller of the Currency (2020) Office of the Comptroller of the Currency Issues True Lender Rule, www.occ.gov/news-issuances/news-releases/2020/nr-occ-2020-139.html (archived at https://perma.cc/BAU4-NRVW)

**14**  Office of the Comptroller of the Currency (2021) Acting Comptroller Statement on the Vote to Overturn OCC True Lender Rule, www.occ.gov/news-issuances/news-releases/2021/nr-occ-2021-69.html (archived at https://perma.cc/MNR4-QXZD)

**15**  Mikula, J. (2023) Affairs of State: Chime's License Push, Iowa Usury Case, Afterpay Quits New Mexico, EWA in Arizona, *Fintech Business Weekly*, fintechbusinessweekly.substack.com/p/affairs-of-state-chimes-license-push (archived at https://perma.cc/2C2M-EB8T)

**16**  Johnson, M. et al. (2023) FinTech Lending with LowTech Pricing, *Fisher College of Business Working Paper*, papers.ssrn.com/sol3/papers.cfm?abstract_id=4396502 (archived at https://perma.cc/5JKS-HDEW)

# 6

# What Are the Different BaaS Operating Models?

---

CHAPTER OBJECTIVES

At this point, we have covered the basics of how fintechs and banks partner in banking-as-a-service relationships to offer end users regulated products and services. In this chapter, we will explore those models in greater depth. At a high level, operating models can be divided into direct bank-fintech partnerships versus those that utilize a middleware platform. But within each of these high-level categories, each player exists along a continuum of taking on more or less responsibility for delivering the regulated components of a product. At one extreme, this could look like a customer-facing company white-labeling a bank's existing offerings and focusing primarily on marketing and distribution (though some would object to describing this as banking-as-a-service). At the other extreme, a customer-facing service could be composed of products from multiple underlying bank partners, facilitated through a middleware platform, with the service owning much or all of the responsibility for program management. The operating model will heavily influence the economics, how compliance responsibilities are allocated, and the flexibility and customization of the product and user experience.

---

## Direct Operating Models

The most simplistic operating model is arguably a non-bank company "white labeling" an existing bank's products or entire application. In fact, it is a stretch to even call this banking-as-a-service, as control over almost all of the key parts of the business still rests with the bank partner. It is probably more accurate to think of this as a precursor to more contemporary BaaS relationships. In a white label operating model, the partner's brand is used for customer-facing marketing, acquisition, and servicing, but, behind the scenes, pretty much everything is run by the partner bank. Technical integration between the two is minimal and possibly even zero. The main assets a white label partner brings are typically its brand and distribution. Basically, white label partnerships are often mere distribution and customer acquisition strategies for the underlying bank partners. The economic model is such that non-bank partners may earn a per-customer referral fee or revenue share on the program. Touchpoints requiring bank review and approval are much more limited and typically focus on marketing strategies and material in order to mitigate potential UDAAP risk.

The quintessential example of this light-touch partnership strategy is Green Dot's relationship with Walmart to power its Walmart MoneyCard. While customers may think of Walmart as providing this service, the arrangement functions much more akin to a branding and licensing deal, in which Green Dot pays Walmart for the right to use its intellectual property and to distribute its cards in Walmart's stores.[1] Private label credit cards, or "store cards," are functionally analogous on the credit side. While a customer might hold a Bass Pro Shop or Victoria's Secret store card, almost all of the responsibility for operating the program sits with the bank partner. Retail stores serve as a distribution and customer acquisition channel in return for some kind of commission or revenue-sharing arrangement.

---

EXAMPLE: GREEN DOT

Green Dot has evolved through various operating models, including leveraging white label distribution through retail partner Walmart. In its earliest incarnation, Green Dot was a non-bank prepaid card issuer. Eventually, Green Dot acquired Bonneville Bank and transitioned its product

portfolio from prepaid cards to traditional demand deposit accounts.[2]
Throughout that evolution, Green Dot has pursued multiple distribution
strategies, including under its own Green Dot and GO2Bank brands and a
partnership with retail behemoth Walmart. The arrangement with Walmart
is a classic example of a white label product. The product is branded as
Walmart's MoneyCard and distributed through Walmart stores and on a
Walmart-branded microsite, but the program is run primarily by Green Dot.

If white-labeling is a sort of proto-banking-as-a-service operating
model, early bank-fintech partnerships that enabled fintech partners
to take on much of the responsibility for program management can
be thought of as its mirror image. Program management encompasses
designing and running key aspects of banking and card businesses,
including customer onboarding, card fulfillment, bank partner selection and management, payment network operations, risk and fraud,
reconciliation and settlement, customer identification, data management, customer service, marketing, and more. Taking on the
responsibility of program management gives fintechs much more
ability to build their own solutions and customize aspects of their
products. Providing these capabilities, either through building or
buying, enables a fintech to capture a larger share of revenue versus
a white label arrangement but also comes with significant incremental expenses and risk.

What started with a handful of banks like The Bancorp and
Pathward (formerly known as MetaBank) that operated such direct
fintech-bank partnerships has grown substantially since the early
2010s. While the specifics vary by bank and by program, most legacy
banks have been constrained by their software architecture, specifically, their "core banking" solution.[3] Banks working with legacy
cores historically have been unwilling or unable to provide direct API
integrations to their fintech partners. As a result, the most common
work around has been for fintech partners to use a shared account
structure, often referred to as an "FBO" or an "omnibus" account,
with their bank partner, and, for all intents and purposes, build (or
buy) their own entire banking technology stack outside of the bank.

EXAMPLE: PATHWARD

Pathward, previously known as MetaBank, is an exemplar of early versions of direct bank-fintech partnerships. Pathward has a long history of powering prepaid debit and stored value card programs, which are functionally precursors to the many fintechs that followed them. Pathward enables spending account programs through direct relationships and integrations with brands and fintechs like H&R Block, Ace Cash Express, MoneyLion, Coinbase, and Clair.

On the one hand, this approach provides fintechs with a significant amount of flexibility. End customer funds are *held* at a partner bank, protected by that bank's deposit insurance, but nearly everything else is happening at the fintech or other third parties the fintech engages, like fraud screening vendors or an issuer-processor. The flip side of this increased flexibility can be significantly higher costs and complexity. A fintech operating in this legacy partnership model is, functionally, building its own complete banking technology stack to act as its own program manager, which can be time consuming and expensive. And, at the end of the day, end customer funds are held at the partner bank, necessitating penny-perfect reconciliation between a fintech's systems and the system of record at the bank.

This approach also leads to a dramatically more complicated regulatory compliance model. If in a white label model, a bank is limited to needing to oversee the marketing and customer acquisition efforts of its third-party partner, in the classic bank-fintech partnership, a bank has significantly more activities to supervise. This typically necessitates a bank building out its own compliance management system that is designed with third-party partners in mind, as well as operationalizing and staffing it appropriately. The reliance on an FBO (for the benefit of) or omnibus account structure can limit a bank's direct visibility into the day-to-day operations of their fintech partners, making it more complicated to effectively fulfill their compliance obligations. For instance, if a fintech is handling its own customer onboarding and KYC processes, its bank partner should not only have policies and procedures in place that define how the processes them-selves work, but the bank should also be monitoring its fintech partner to ensure it is adhering to the agreed-upon process. To the extent a fintech's system of record for its customers is not integrated with the bank—remember, the bank partner often has one big account that is titled to the fintech "for the benefit of" its customers—how the bank goes about ensuring its fintech partners' compliance can be time consuming, manual, and expensive.

For fintechs, this operating model can be a limiting factor on how quickly the company can move. Getting a first product live in market requires a lengthy selection and negotiation process with a bank part-ner, undergoing a due diligence process, building out compliance policies and procedures, and having more or less every aspect of their program blessed by their partner bank. While the direct model does give fintech partners substantially more flexibility, it also dramati-cally increases the capabilities a fintech has to buy or build to launch. For banks, those that engage with multiple fintech partners under this operating model do not necessarily achieve returns to scale, as each fintech program they work with may be bespoke with their own products, processes, and mix of homegrown and vendor-supplied technology.

## Middleware-Enabled Operating Models

The middleware or connector banking-as-a-service model arose in an effort to solve some of the pain points of the direct fintech-bank model outlined previously, especially the high time- and cost-to-market that functioned as barriers to earlier stage companies launching regulated products. As more providers have entered this middleware space, there have been diverging approaches to bridging the gap between fintechs and banks, each with varying pros and cons. The middleware space is rapidly evolving in response to expectations from their supply side (banks) and demand side (fintechs), as well as the ongoing impact of numerous regulatory actions.[4] While there is room for debate, middleware platforms can be grouped as those providing "tech only," meaning they focus on streamlining the technology integration between fintechs and bank partners, and those that take on components of program management. Middleware companies that also provide elements of program management may seek to provide certain "off-the-shelf" capabilities, like customer onboarding/KYC, and provide some level of compliance oversight and support on behalf of their underlying bank partners. Middleware providers that provide program management capabilities can be further divided into those that hold some type of license, like state lending licenses or a broker-dealer license, versus those that rely entirely on the licenses of their underlying bank partners.

The "tech only" approach is the least complicated middleware model. In this framework, the primary problem to be solved is streamlining how a fintech integrates with one or multiple partner banks. A middleware platform operating under this model builds its own integrations with a network of bank partners. Rather than needing to integrate with those underlying banks, fintechs simply integrate with the middleware provider. But customer-facing fintechs contract directly with their bank partner(s) and compliance processes are generally overseen directly between the bank and fintech, though a middleware platform may help guide and facilitate these discussions. In this model, the middleware platform operates primarily as a technology service provider to the bank, streamlining the process of how fintechs integrate with a given bank. Middleware platforms in this segment may also offer some level of "matchmaking" services, helping to guide fintechs and connect them with the most appropriate prospective partner banks on their platform.

---

EXAMPLE: TREASURY PRIME

Banking-as-a-service middleware platform Treasury Prime typifies the approach of providing primarily a technology platform that enables banks and fintechs to work together. It focuses on creating software to enable this, rather than offering program management capabilities. Treasury Prime offers compliance support, in the form of best practices and pre-built integrations with relevant vendors, but it generally does not take on compliance functions on behalf of the banks or fintechs it works with. The company historically has facilitated "matchmaking" between prospective fintechs and partner banks Treasury Prime works with, but, amid escalating regulatory scrutiny, pivoted in early 2024 to focus on selling software to banks. In this approach, fintechs have a direct relationship and communication with their bank partner(s), and Treasury Prime focuses on supplying APIs that enable those relationships.

Rather than seek to build and offer its own solutions for aspects of program management, like KYC/KYB, fraud risk, anti-money laundering and sanctions compliance, open banking connectivity, payment processing, card issuing, and so forth, technology-focused middleware platforms can be thought of as an "orchestration" layer, or a sort of one-stop shop for the APIs necessary to build a financial product or service. Customer-facing fintechs can integrate with a tech-focused middleware and, through that platform, access many of the capabilities they need to operate their own program.

While tech-focused middleware platforms aim to solve the challenge of technology integrations, they leave the bulk of the commercial and compliance questions for fintechs and their bank partners to work through directly, making for a process that is far from turnkey. An alternative middleware approach is for the intermediary platforms to include aspects of program management. The idea is that by taking on responsibilities normally handled by bank partners, middleware platforms and their fintech partners are able to move more quickly. For example, a middleware provider may act as the primary touchpoint for a fintech partner. In some circumstances, a fintech may not have any direct contractual relationship with its underlying bank partner, though there are questions about the suitability of such an approach. It is worth noting that, even in situations where a middleware platform is taking on due diligence or compliance functions, it is typically doing so on behalf of its bank partners. The legal and regulatory requirements on the bank side remain the same, even if it is working with a third party to carry out those responsibilities.

Working with an intermediary platform that handles some aspects of third-party risk management and compliance on behalf of the bank does not necessarily mean a bank is fulfilling their regulatory responsibilities, as the bank in such a model still needs to have appropriate policies and procedures in place to oversee the middleware provider (and the middleware provider's fintech customers, and the fintech customers' end users). As became clear from the numerous regulatory enforcement actions over the course of 2023 and early 2024, the middleware approach introduces additional operational complexity and thus risk to banks.

The theory of the case is that purpose-built middleware providers can handle program management, at scale, in a way that their underlying bank partners cannot. Middlewares that incorporate elements of program management attempt to achieve this efficiency with reusable "Lego block"-style elements, like software development kits (SDKs), white-label user interface elements, out-of-the-box integrations and APIs, and templated compliance policies and procedures. So-called "low-code" and "no-code" tooling aim to make it easy for any startup—fintech or otherwise—to launch financial products, including by embedding them in existing applications or websites. Middleware platforms with program management aim to reduce the lift from both sides of the market, bank partners and fintechs, by taking what would normally be their responsibilities onto their own shoulders. The original vision was that such an approach would allow a bank partner to enter the banking-as-a-service space with little incremental effort, staffing, and cost and that companies could get a new fintech product or feature to market without needing to onboard numerous vendors and hire an in-house compliance team.

---

### EXAMPLE: SYNAPSE

Synapse, which collapsed into bankruptcy in early 2024, has also iterated through various operating models over time, but has generally emphasized the relationship between Synapse and its fintech clients and de-emphasized direct relationships between fintechs and partner banks. This became even more the case when the company obtained its own broker-dealer license and transitioned to a cash management account model. In this model, fintechs and their end customers are clients of Synapse's brokerage and have no direct relationship or communication with bank partners Synapse uses to hold insured customer funds, do payment processing, and so forth.

However, this approach to middleware is not without drawbacks and risks. Creating reusable elements does help reduce complexity and thus the time and cost necessary to develop a financial offering, but it can also mean a lack of flexibility. Barriers to customization can result in a crop of look-alike products with little differentiation that end up struggling in market. For example, neobanks that leveraged middleware solutions have been able to launch quickly, but are constrained in their ability to innovate or tailor their offerings to their market segment. Likewise, the attempt to apply templated approaches to compliance may streamline the process of developing a compliance program, but the resulting infrastructure may not be adequately tailored to the risks of a given fintech's products and customers. We will explore some of the compliance and regulatory challenges in middleware providers taking on certain compliance functions in greater detail in Chapter 8.

An additional variation to the middleware with program management model involves the middleware platform obtaining its own licenses, though not generally a bank license. This approach most often coincides with taking on some or much of the program management lift as well. The logic here is similar: By obtaining some level of licensure, even if not a full bank license, a middleware platform has greater vertical integration and thus more control over its processes. Examples in the US include obtaining a broker-dealer license and state lending licenses. In countries where e-money or payments institution licenses exist, that can also be a viable route to a middleware platform reducing its dependency on external bank partners. Specifics vary by license type and country, but, generally speaking, obtaining some level of licensure does not necessarily reduce the overall compliance burden, but rather shifts some elements to being more in the license holder's control. If the benefit to this approach is greater control, the primary drawback is increased complexity, particularly for the middleware platform itself. This approach generally still requires some level of partnership with banks, plus the platform is taking on the regulatory overhead of applying for and maintaining their own licenses.

For fintechs that select middleware providers using this model, the appeal is theoretically less complexity (for the fintech) and a faster and cheaper route to market. The major drawback, even if a fintech does not think of it this way, is that a fintech may not have any direct relationship or ability to communicate with underlying bank partners, exposing them to uncertainty and risk if the banking relationship with the middleware platform is disrupted.

## Tech-Native Partner Banks

The initial promise of middleware platforms was a simplified technical integration with underlying banks that were largely dependent on legacy core infrastructure. The evolution of offering program management capabilities as part of a middleware platform arose as a product-led growth strategy. By offering to do much of the heavy lifting of compliance for banks and for fintechs, middleware platforms could, in theory, substantially lower the barrier to entry for both sides, thus growing the market substantially.

But what if that root problem, banks' old tech, was no longer an issue? That is exactly the approach a number of institutions and entrepreneurs have taken in the US and other countries. These new financial institutions, not bound by legacy systems and technical debt, could approach the problem space from first principles and start building from scratch. That approach has not been without complication, particularly in the US. Given the difficulty of obtaining a new ("de novo") license since the 2008 financial crisis, nearly all efforts to build an API-native bank have relied on acquiring an existing institution or launching a new business unit at an existing bank. The notable exceptions in the US market being Cross River Bank, which applied for a de novo license prior to the 2008 financial crisis and began operating in 2008, and Piermont, which obtained a de novo charter in 2019. Other examples of existing banks that either were acquired, added, or pivoted to a business model focused on API-driven distribution include Column, Lead, and Grasshopper. Goldman Sachs' efforts in its consumer initiatives, including its Apple partnership, and its partnerships with Stripe and Modern Treasury through its Transaction Banking unit, represent similar efforts to build net-new, API-native platforms for third parties to consume and build upon.

---

EXAMPLE: COLUMN

Column is a key example of a "BaaS-native" or "API-first" bank. Column, started by a cofounder of open banking infrastructure company Plaid, acquired a small community bank in California, which continues to operate, and used its charter as the foundation to build a beginning-to-end modern technology stack that attempts to solve the pain points of fintechs working with legacy community banks.[5] The company refers to itself as a "developer infrastructure bank," in the sense that it provides core capabilities, like account creation, payment processing, ledgering, card programs, and so forth without having to rely on intermediaries, like middleware providers, or workarounds, like FBO and omnibus accounts.

---

The biggest differentiator with these BaaS-native banks, which eliminate the need to use a middleware provider, is avoiding the original sin of being locked in to one of the major core banking providers, like FIS or Fiserv. The early community banks to recognize the marketing opportunity in banking-as-a-service generally lacked sophisticated technical talent and relied on workarounds like FBO accounts and having fintech clients functionally build their own bank tech stack. The emerging crop of BaaS-native banks have learnt from the challenges and limitations faced by the community banks that have been vanguards in the space and by the challenges faced by middleware platforms. Instead, BaaS-native banks tend to focus on and have deep understanding of their target market: Fintechs. They offer modern, developer-friendly APIs with thorough documentation, flexible products, development sandboxes, and sales and support staff that speak fintechs' language. Solving the technical integration problem without relying on a third-party middleware reduces complexity and should improve the share of economics that flows to the bank and its fintech partners.

Some BaaS-native banks do have legacy community-banking operations, but those are generally run and evaluated separately from the nascent BaaS business lines. This is distinct from how many community banks think about BaaS, which is often used as a source of cheap deposits to fund business lines typical of small banks, including things like commercial real estate.

## BaaS Operating Models Around the World

While the specifics of banking-as-a-service operating models vary country to country, the general approaches are largely similar: Either a direct partnership between a customer-facing fintech and a bank or one intermediated by a middleware platform. Some of the major differences in the US versus other markets are driven by the comparative ease of obtaining a de novo bank license and the existence of other categories of licenses that have no analog in the United States, like e-money and payments institution licenses. For example, while most neobanks in the US work through a bank partner, many popular neobanks in the UK and the EU are fully licensed in their own right, including well-known names like Monzo, Starling, N26, and bunq. Even neobanks that are not licensed as banks in the UK or Europe have the more clearly defined regulatory model of applying for an e-money license. The e-money license functions somewhat akin to the US fintech/bank partner model, insofar as end-customer deposits are typically segregated and safeguarded in an insured depository institution. E-money institutions are generally able to be principal members of network schemes and issue their own cards, without relying on a partner bank. Codification in a license regime provides greater clarity and stability to fintechs choosing to operate under this model.

However, it is worth noting most would not describe the relationship between an e-money institution and an underlying bank partner that holds customer deposits as "banking-as-a-service," even if it is roughly analogous to some direct bank/fintech partnerships in the US that would be considered as such. The emerging model of API-native banks also exists in other markets. Startup entities like Griffin, in the UK, and Solarisbank, in Germany, are fully licensed institutions that are attempting to build API-driven banking models by offering "programmatic" access to offering end customers savings accounts, current accounts, payments infrastructure, credit products, and more. As in the US, the different models are not without tradeoffs and have business and regulatory models that remain to be proven. We will explore some examples of these in greater detail in the case studies later in the book.

## More Intermediaries Means More Complexity

It is worth remembering that the modern banking-as-a-service era is roughly a decade old. And, in that time, banking and fintech business models and regulatory issues have continued to evolve. A helpful frame is to think about customer-facing companies as acting as distributors for banking products. Those customer-facing entities may work directly with a bank partner, or have one or potentially even multiple intermediaries between them and a partner bank. As a general rule of thumb, the more intermediaries, the more complex the operating model is, particularly from a regulatory compliance standpoint. More intermediaries also means splitting a defined revenue pool across more parties. In theory, this can work, if intermediary platforms like BaaS middleware unlock increased efficiency and thus bring economies of scale. But the ability of middleware platforms to achieve those promises will be determined, at least in part, by whether or not their efforts pass muster with regulators. We will further unpack these regulatory compliance and economic model challenges in subsequent chapters.

# Endnotes

**1** *Business Wire* (2020) Walmart MoneyCard Adds 2% High Yield Savings Account, Free Cash Deposits and Family Accounts, www.businesswire.com/news/home/20200526005264/en/Walmart-MoneyCard-Adds-2-High-Yield-Savings-Account-Free-Cash-Deposits-and-Family-Accounts (archived at https://perma.cc/QE8Z-RZQZ)

**2** Green Dot (2011) Green Dot Completes its Acquisition of Bonneville Bank, ir.greendot.com/news-releases/news-release-details/green-dot-completes-its-acquisition-bonneville-bank (archived at https://perma.cc/HU7Y-43EL)

**3** Alcazar, J. et al. (2024) Market Structure of Core Banking Services Providers, Federal Reserve Bank of Kansas City: Payments System Research Briefing, www.kansascityfed.org/research/payments-system-research-briefings/market-structure-of-core-banking-services-providers/ (archived at https://perma.cc/R8A7-WX83)

**4** Mikula, J. (2022) With Blue Ridge's OCC Agreement, BaaS "Rumors" Spill into Public View, *Fintech Business Weekly*, fintechbusinessweekly.substack.com/p/with-blue-ridges-occ-agreement-rumors (archived at https://perma.cc/D3BF-557L)

**5** Kauflin, J. (2022) Plaid's Billionaire Cofounder is Back with a New Startup–A Fintech-Friendly Bank He's Running with his Wife, *Forbes*, www.forbes.com/sites/jeffkauflin/2022/04/21/plaids-billionaire-cofounder-is-back-with-a-new-startupa-fintech-friendly-bank-hes-running-with-his-wife/ (archived at https://perma.cc/LL9N-BR23)

# 7

# What Is the Difference Between Banking-as-a-Service and Embedded Finance?

CHAPTER OBJECTIVES

Banking-as-a-service is often mentioned alongside another recent trend: Embedded finance. In this chapter we will cover the difference between the two and how banking-as-a-service enables embedded finance. We will examine popular embedded capabilities, including payments, lending, and full-stack banking services. Specific examples will illustrate how and why non-financial firms choose to add embedded financial capabilities to their products and services.

Like the term "banking-as-a-service," the idea of "embedded finance" has exploded in recent years. And although the two concepts are intertwined, they represent distinct concepts and operating models. Also, like banking-as-a-service, embedded finance, or the practice of making a financial product or service available within another context, is not an inherently new idea.

Embedded finance is, at its core, a delivery and distribution channel. Making financial products and services available on-demand and in a context where they are likely to be needed benefits both the financial services provider and the firm embedding their capabilities. For the financial services company, distribution through embedded channels may offer access to desirable customers, a lower cost of customer acquisition, or opportunities to create uniquely advantageous product integrations. For the companies embedding financial capabilities in their products, the addition of financial capabilities can increase customer engagement, reduce churn, offer additional insight into customers' needs, and generate incremental revenue streams.

Examples of categories of embedded finance products and services include banking services, payments, lending, insurance, and taxes. Historically, examples of these embedded offerings often took place in person at the point of sale, even if these were not referred to as being "embedded" at the time. For instance, using a furniture retailer's offer of promotional financing is an example of embedded lending at the point of sale—something that now might be referred to as "buy now, pay later." Private label credit cards, which we discussed in Chapter 5, are another example of lending embedded in a traditional retail sales context. Similarly, a loan to purchase an automobile arranged through the dealer selling the vehicle is a classic example of lending embedded in context. Or an insurance product sold as an add-on to a car rental as an example of an embedded insurance product. In some cases, revenue from these ancillary embedded products has eclipsed a company's primary business—like the car dealership that makes more from arranging financing than it does on the actual sale of vehicles. The context of distribution in person at point of sale and occasionally high-pressure sales tactics may have given this model a less-than-savory reputation historically.

KEY LEARNING POINTS

Think of banking-as-a-service and embedded finance as two sides of the same coin: Banking-as-a-service is often the "how" while an embedded capability is the "what." More complex embedded features, like a digital wallet or full-stack banking services, generally require BaaS behind the scenes, whereas simpler capabilities like payments acceptance or disbursement may not.

As more and more commerce has moved from offline to online and with the growth in banking-as-a-service, the capabilities, use cases, and adoption of embedded finance has evolved. Think of banking-as-a-service and embedded finance as opposite sides of the same coin: Increasingly, banking-as-a-service *enables* both financial and non-financial firms to seamlessly integrate financial capabilities. In addition to a changing user experience, from analog and bricks and mortar to digital and online, net new capabilities also enable altogether new use cases.

## How and Why Firms Embed Their Financial Capabilities

Banking-as-a-service enables companies to seamlessly add banking capabilities to their existing products and services: Holding funds, making or facilitating payments, and credit and lending, for example. These capabilities manifest through app features like digital wallets, buy now, pay later, streamlined payment options, contextual commerce, and more. There are a variety of motivations for companies to add such features. Motivations tend to fall into a few categories, including reducing friction, making customers stickier, and as an incremental revenue stream or way to reduce costs. A single embedded capability may check more than one of these boxes.

KEY LEARNING POINTS

Firms adding embedded financial capabilities may do so with the goal of reducing friction, increasing customer retention, and creating new revenue streams.

"Reducing friction," or making it easier and faster to complete a transaction, is a quintessential motivation for embedding supporting financial capabilities. In-app payments, through stored payment credentials or a digital wallet, are one classic example of simplifying transactions in order to boost merchants' conversion rates. Making credit available alongside a transaction can both boost conversion rates and increase revenue, as embedded credit often boosts shoppers' average order size. In consumer apps, these kinds of built-in capabilities often tick and tie to loyalty and rewards programs, reducing customer churn and boosting lifetime value. In small and midsize business (SMB) or enterprise and SaaS contexts, offering additional features can increase customer engagement and revenue opportunities, driving better customer and revenue retention. Embedded capabilities may also represent cost savings for merchants that add them. For instance, encouraging customers to use a digital wallet to hold funds and make payments may reduce a merchant's payment processing costs.

## Embedded Payments

Payments represent the most common and lowest hanging fruit for embedded capabilities. Some might push back and argue that merchants have *always* needed to be able to accept payments. What is different about "embedded" payments versus everything that has come before?

Companies in the so-called "sharing economy," like Uber, Instacart, and Postmates illustrate numerous facets of embedded payments that are relevant for all stakeholders in these transactions: The end user, the gig worker providing the services, but also the platform connecting the two and, in some cases, third-party merchants, like the grocery stores or restaurants a gig worker visits. Banking-as-a-service capabilities enable non-financial firms to go beyond mere payment acceptance to offering products and services typically reserved for banks, like holding funds, offering credit, and issuing payment credentials. In some cases, embedded capabilities are "nice to haves" that improve the user experience, but aren't, strictly speaking, necessary. In other cases, these capabilities are critical pieces of functionality, like how Instacart relies on debit cards and "just-in-time" funding to power its shopper experience.

*How Uber Reduces the Friction and Pain of Paying*

The simplest and most familiar piece of this will be the end user-facing component. It may be difficult to remember now, but there was a time when making a payment within a mobile app for a "real life" service was a novelty. No longer did a taxi driver run a meter, punch the fare amount into a payment terminal, and swipe or tap your card (if you were lucky enough that the driver actually accepted card payments). Instead, your payment card is stored within a ride-sharing app, like Uber, the app calculates the fare and total charge, and automatically charges your card. How quickly consumers have grown accustomed to this shift is a testament to how powerful a change it has been. While apparently relatively minor on the surface, embedding payments solved multiple pain points thus reducing friction. Riders no longer had to worry about whether or not their driver would accept card payments. Indeed, they no longer had to pull out their wallet or think about the fare total at all—just get into the car, travel, and get out at your destination. This seemingly small but important difference, combined of course with the ability to request a ride from anywhere, has dramatically transformed the experience of transportation. And separating the utility of the experience from the pain of paying increases the likelihood that consumers use the service.

But the opportunities of embedded payments in this scenario go beyond the rider. Remember, services like Uber are a marketplace that connects consumers with drivers—technically, independent contractors that use Uber's platform. The use case of embedded finance for this side of Uber's platform is perhaps even more important. The company developed Uber Money, a digital wallet-like offering, in certain markets to enable drivers on the platform to instantly access their earnings, though this was eventually replaced with the ability to instantly cash out earnings to an external bank account.[1] This is not just a nice-to-have for the drivers, but a key ingredient to keeping them on the road and using the platform. First and foremost, drivers are incurring expenses as they work, primarily fuel costs. With many drivers living paycheck to paycheck, they cannot afford to wait for a typical "pay cycle" to access their earnings. They *need* those funds to fill up their car if they want to keep earning. So beyond a simple perk or increasing loyalty of its drivers, embedding a wallet that unlocks instant access to earnings is actually a key ingredient in supporting the supply side of Uber's two-sided marketplace.

### How Starbucks Builds Loyalty with Embedded Payments

Another tangible example many readers will be familiar with: Starbucks. While many have erroneously argued that Starbucks is "actually a bank," it is a shining example of the success of leveraging embedded payments to foster customer loyalty. Starbucks' mobile app has two core functionalities, both of which are designed to appeal to frequent customers: Ordering ahead of time for pickup and paying, both for app-based orders and in person.

Starbucks' app functions like a stored value payment card. Users can add funds to their wallet via debit, credit, or bank transfer. But recognizing that paying with their Starbucks app versus paying with a typical card offered little incremental benefit, Starbucks coupled the payment mechanism with a loyalty program. For each $1 spent through the app, users earn one "star." But the company has gone beyond a simple points mechanism and gamified the experience, with opportunities to earn bonuses by completing challenges, playing games, and making purchases on designated days.[2] Stars can then be redeemed for food, beverages, or Starbucks merchandise. And the effort has been wildly successful, with 34.3 million users as of early 2024.[3] Loyal customers had more than $1 billion in aggregate stored in the app as of 2022, leading some analysts to incorrectly describe Starbucks as a "bank that happens to sell coffee."[4] The app is estimated to be used for more than 30 per cent of transactions at US company-operated stores as of the end of 2023.[5] Beyond fostering customer loyalty, Starbucks can benefit from cost savings on payment processing. Even if users load their wallet via credit or debit rather than a bank transfer, in aggregate, that means fewer, larger card payments for Starbucks, likely driving savings in their payment processing costs.

And while perhaps less favorable for its customers, Starbucks also benefits from breakage and float. Starbucks benefits from "float" in the sense that the funds users load to their apps function akin to a zero-interest loan to the company. "Breakage," a common term in the stored value/gift card industry, refers to funds that are loaded but never spent, which, after a period of time, can often be claimed as revenue by the company that holds the funds. In 2021, Starbucks made some $155 million in profit from such unused funds.[6] Key factors that have helped Starbucks' wallet reach scale include that its most loyal customers are high frequency, making purchases multiple times a week or even a day, and that the amounts are relatively low, making it feel less risky to keep $20 or $50 at a time in the app in exchange for earning loyalty rewards they otherwise would not get.

### How Cash App Can Reduce Cost for Parent Company Block

If Uber's use of embedded payments originated with reducing friction, and Starbucks' focus has been on cementing customer loyalty, one area of emphasis of payment infrastructure company Block has been on reducing costs. Block, previously known as Square, got its start by offering a small device that turned any mobile phone into a payment terminal that could accept card payments.

The company has expanded its merchant offerings from there to include point-of-sale equipment that functions as a cash register with card processing built in. On the consumer side, Block offers popular peer-to-peer payment app Cash App. By integrating these offerings and embedding the ability to pay via Cash App in its merchant points-of-sale, Block has the potential to realize meaningful cost savings. Block is able to reduce its payment processing expenses because, if a customer pays via Cash App at a Square payment terminal, the transaction is effectively "closed loop," meaning it happens entirely within Block's ecosystem and without needing to touch card schemes or a customer's issuing bank. But Block/Square still assesses the same flat fee to the merchant to accept such payments, capturing those cost savings as improved margins for itself.

*Embedded Virtual Cards Act as Key Infrastructure*

Embedded payment capabilities also play a key role in powering another fintech segment that has recently exploded in popularity: Buy now, pay later, often abbreviated as BNPL. We will discuss how BNPL is an example of embedded lending later in this chapter, but, in some circumstances, BNPL is dependent on embedded payments, specifically programmatically issued virtual cards, to enable consumers to use BNPL as payment method at a wider selection of merchants.

In its original incarnation, BNPL relied on merchants having a direct, contractual relationship with a BNPL provider. When a user chose to use BNPL at checkout, the user would apply and check out through an embedded flow from the BNPL provider. Behind the scenes, the BNPL provider would remit the full purchase price, less applicable fees, to the merchant, typically in batches via a bank-to-bank transfer, like ACH in the US, and the user would make their payments to the BNPL provider itself. This integration proved popular with merchants and consumers but faced a major limitation: Users could only use a specific BNPL provider if it had a relationship with the merchant they were shopping at. Recognizing this limitation, and seeking to own the customer relationship rather than be relegated to an afterthought at checkout, BNPL providers have leveraged embedded payments to make it possible for shoppers to use their services at nearly *any* merchant that accepts card payments.

BNPL providers achieve this through the use of embedded virtual cards and, more recently, physical payment cards. If a user wants to split their payments at a merchant that does not contract with a given BNPL provider, in the background, the BNPL provider can create a one-time use debit card authorized for the precise amount of a given transaction. That one-off debit card is used to process payment to the merchant via card rails, and then the user re-pays the BNPL provider. While this increases the utility of a given BNPL provider to a user by expanding the universe of where they can use the service to nearly any merchant, there is one notable downside. Because BNPL providers generally lack a bilateral agreement with these merchants, the revenue earned is limited to typical debit interchange income, rather than the higher merchant discount rates typically negotiated in direct BNPL agreements.

EXAMPLE: APPLE

Some BNPL providers *exclusively* use this merchant-agnostic approach. For instance, Apple's Apple Pay Later feature does not rely on bilateral contracts with merchants. Rather, users who have enrolled in the feature can use Apple Pay Later to split qualifying transactions into four payments at almost any merchant that accepts Apple Pay, both online and in person. To achieve this, Apple, together with underlying infrastructure partners, in a process that is invisible to the end user, creates a one-time use virtual Mastercard for the exact purchase amount. When a user checks out, a merchant is effectively running a typical debit transaction (and paying the corresponding merchant discount rate), pulling the money from Apple over card rails. Simultaneously, the user pays Apple their first of four payments. Apple, however, announced in June 2024 it would end its own-operated BNPL capability in favor of partnering with third-party providers.[7]

Delivery services, like Instacart, Doordash, and Uber Eats, are additional examples of embedded payments in action. Couriers for these types of services often need to make purchases on behalf of end customers. To enable couriers to make payments without relying on their personal funds, such services typically provision a digital or physical debit card that can be used to make payments. To reduce fraud risk and ensure that couriers are using payment cards for their intended purposes, cards are often provisioned with a zero-dollar balance. When a courier attempts payment at a merchant and in an amount that matches the end user's order, funds are made available in a "just-in-time" manner to facilitate the transaction.

### Extending Vertical SaaS Platforms with Embedded Finance

Vertical software-as-a-service platforms, commonly referred to as "vertical SaaS," which often aim to act as a kind of operating system for specific types of businesses, also make heavy use of embedded payment functionality. Examples of vertical SaaS offerings include platforms like Squire, a "business management system" for barbershops, MindBody, for fitness and wellness businesses, and Toast, a restaurant point-of-sale and management system. While the specifics vary by industry and by platform, embedded payment acceptance and fund disbursement to employees or contractors are common features. These capabilities typically require partnering with a BaaS middleware or directly with a bank.

For example, in addition to acting as an appointment booking and management system, Squire enables shops that use it to accept payments, both online and in person, collect chair rental payments from barbers, and pay out barbers for their earnings in real time.[8] Embedded payments capabilities both add core functionality to vertical SaaS platforms and can serve as a supplemental revenue stream to commonly charged subscription fees. In addition to payments acceptance and disbursement, some vertical SaaS platforms may offer credit products or even a full-stack bank account as ancillary offerings.

## Embedded Lending

If payments are an incredibly powerful enabling capability to embed, credit is a close second. Like payments, embedding lending options can be enabled by banking-as-a-service infrastructure. Embedded credit is relevant to both consumer and business segments.

For consumers, the most prevalent example of embedded lending is one we have already touched on: Buy now, pay later. While thought of as a single category, BNPL actually comprises a range of products, from shorter-term, 0 per cent interest financing to longer-term interest-bearing loans. The idea of making credit available to facilitate a consumer purchase is not new. Indeed, merchant-provided credit has arguably existed for centuries, only more recently being displaced by bank-issued general purpose credit instruments, namely, the dawn of the credit card age beginning in the 1960s.[9] Even so, bricks and mortar merchants have remained a key acquisition channel for lenders, providing credit products, often for larger purchases, including auto loans, promotional financing, and private label credit cards. The growth of e-commerce has made embedded digital distribution a growing channel and powered the resurgence of point-of-sale financing, including novel product formulations, like pay-in-four BNPL. For merchants, providing embedded financing (or lending) can help boost conversion rates, increase average order value, and improve customer retention. For shoppers, it can facilitate making purchases they otherwise might not, though this has opened BNPL providers to critiques that the ease of applying and underwriting approach of the product risks causing users to become overly indebted.

Digital wallets, like PayPal and Cash App, offer additional examples of embedded lending with different distribution mechanisms and product structures. Long before BNPL became a phenomenon, PayPal offered six-month no-cost financing directly to consumers as a line of credit for qualifying purchases. Consumers can use the offering, dubbed PayPal Credit, at any merchant that accepts PayPal as a payment method. Like the Apple Pay Later example, PayPal Credit's distribution is via a consumer's relationship with *PayPal*, rather than with any specific merchant. Cash App, the consumer digital wallet operated by Block, offers a different example of embedded credit. Cash App offers consumers direct loans, rather than financing a purchase at a merchant. Cash App offers qualifying users the ability to borrow up to $200 for a flat fee of 5 per cent of the principal amount.

## Embedded SMB Lending Can Benefit from Improved Data and Repayment

There has arguably been even more innovation in providing embedded credit to business than to consumers. The forms of commercial lending products are largely similar: Structures like merchant cash advances, invoice factoring, term loans, and lines of credit. But embedding these products in platforms businesses already use dramatically improves what has long been a pain point for specialty lenders serving small and medium-sized businesses: Cost of customer acquisition.

Previous generations of standalone SMB lenders often relied on expensive marketing campaigns or ethically dubious brokers to generate leads. Since businesses nearly universally already have banking relationships, non-bank SMB lenders are de facto competing with a business's existing bank, often limiting the potential market and driving a negative selection bias in those open to using non-bank lending, in which riskier borrowers gravitate to non-bank lenders due to their easier application process. Embedded distribution provides not only a new avenue of customer acquisition, but also provides novel, proprietary data that can strengthen underwriting and can offer repayment mechanisms that de-risk such transactions.

Examples of SMB-focused platforms that have expanded into offering credit products include payment processor Stripe, point-of-sale platform Square (owned by Block), e-commerce platform Shopify, and even household names like Amazon and Walmart. These platforms may originate their own loans or serve as intermediaries to offer credit on behalf of third parties. SMB platforms benefit from access to merchants' data, which can be leveraged for underwriting. The platforms have access to sellers' performance across a number of metrics, including transaction data, revenue and sales performance, history on the platform, industry and business type, and more. Further, because many of the platforms sit in the flow of funds, they may be able to condition extension of credit on SMBs agreeing to repay any loan directly from revenue processed by the platform, helping to lower repayment risk.

In the vertical SaaS space, an example would be embedding invoice factoring within a bookkeeping or accounting platform. In this scenario, the primary offering might be an invoicing and payments solution for businesses. But because the invoicing platform has visibility into a business's receivables, including the payee, the platform can intelligently assess and underwrite offering an advance against, or discounted purchase of, the invoice receivable. The embedded lending capability both boosts utility to businesses on such an invoicing platform while offering an incremental revenue stream to the platform operator.

## BaaS and Embedded Finance Continue to Evolve

Some services go beyond merely payments or lending and embed a full suite of banking services, including the ability to hold insured customer funds and use them to make payments. Embedding full-stack banking is most common within e-commerce and vertical SaaS platforms, like those discussed above. Examples include Shopify, which offers Shopify Balance built on top of Stripe's BaaS offering, Invoice2Go, an invoicing platform that offers banking capabilities through BaaS platform Unit, and AngelList, a fundraising platform for startups that also leverages Unit. These examples further illustrate the synergy between embedded finance and banking-as-a-service, where platforms whose primary offering is *not* financial services extend their functionality by adding those capabilities through partnerships with underlying providers. While these additional capabilities are optional to businesses on these platforms, the idea is that offering ancillary features enhances the core product offering, deepening the customer relationship and offering additional monetization opportunities.

There is understandably confusion between what is "banking-as-a-service" and what constitutes "embedded finance." A simple paradigm to delineate between the two is that embedded finance is the *what*, while banking-as-a-service is the *how*. Hopefully, the examples in this chapter help to illustrate that relationship. Not every instance of an embedded financial capability requires BaaS, and, conversely, not every BaaS use case is an example of embedded finance. Embedded finance often takes the shape of a non-financial company leveraging a third-party to offer a financial capability—payments processing, credit, banking—seamlessly within their application, frequently by making use of banking-as-a-service capabilities behind the scenes.

## Endnotes

1   Semple, C. (2019) Uber Hails BBVA as it Launches Uber Money, *BBVA*, www.bbva.com/en/innovation/uber-hails-bbva-as-it-launches-uber-money/ (archived at https://perma.cc/Y3GW-TWJQ)

2   Starbucks (2024) Starbucks Rewards, www.starbucks.com/rewards (archived at https://perma.cc/HR24-6GHR)

3   Wassel, B. (2024) Starbucks to Capitalize on Record Loyalty Membership with App Improvements, *Marketing Dive*, www.marketingdive.com/news/starbucks-rewards-loyalty-q3-personalization/706322/ (archived at https://perma.cc/J9W6-PKNR)

**4** Meisenzahl, M. (2022) Starbucks Customers Have More Than $1 Billion Sitting on Gift Cards, *Business Insider*, www.businessinsider.com/starbucks-says-over-1-billion-is-sitting-on-cards-2022-5 (archived at https://perma.cc/H6UH-9D82)

**5** Soper, T. (2024) Starbucks Mobile Orders Surpass 30% of Total Transactions at U.S. Stores, *GeekWire*, www.geekwire.com/2024/starbucks-mobile-orders-surpass-30-of-total-transactions-at-u-s-stores-for-the-first-time/ (archived at https://perma.cc/5X6T-CGHP)

**6** MJV (2023) Starbucks Breakage: Discover How Unused Gift Cards Are Pushing Profits Forward, www.mjvinnovation.com/blog/starbucks-breakage-discover-how-unused-gift-cards-are-pushing-profits-forward/ (archived at https://perma.cc/762S-4ZQS)

**7** Peters, J. (2024) Apple Is Shutting Down Apple Pay Later Just Months After Launch, *The Verge*, www.theverge.com/2024/6/17/24180340/apple-pay-later-shutting-down-months-after-launch (archived at https://perma.cc/D7WJ-JVJY)

**8** Contrary Research (2023) Squire, research.contrary.com/company/squire (archived at https://perma.cc/R8P2-W4B4)

**9** Mikula, J. (2020) Buy Now, Pay Later vs. POS Lending, a Crash Course, *Fintech Business Weekly*, fintechbusinessweekly.substack.com/p/buy-now-pay-later-vs-pos-lending (archived at https://perma.cc/K9V6-TMNV)

# 8

# Banking-as-a-Service Challenges Pose Questions about the Model's Sustainability

CHAPTER OBJECTIVES

In the previous chapters, we have covered the benefits and opportunities banking-as-a-service can bring to its different stakeholders: Banks, middleware platforms, and fintechs, as well as end users of the fintech services. But with these benefits come new kinds of risks and challenges, which include aspects of the operating model itself, regulatory compliance implications, and even questions of whether or not the economic model is sustainable for the various participants. In this chapter, we will touch on the challenges in banking-as-a-service, including from operational, legal and regulatory compliance, and economic perspectives. We will also take a look at the sustainability of standalone banking-as-a-service companies, a number of which have been acquired or failed outright.

## Operational Challenges in Banking-as-a-Service

Many of the challenges in banking-as-a-service operating models are not necessarily *new*. Banks themselves face all sorts of challenges and risks. In Chapter 1, we talked about broad categories of risk: Credit, market, liquidity, interest rate, compliance and legal, reputational, strategic, model, operational, and so forth. While BaaS may introduce some novel risks, the bigger challenge is arguably from increased complexity—in some cases, exponentially more complexity. This increase in complexity is driven by layers, numbers, and the diversity of products, customers, and geographies served. This is even more so the case for banks that work with middleware providers.

While there is significant diversity in banks powering BaaS operating models, a typical BaaS bank might have between $1 billion and $3 billion in assets, tens or hundreds of thousands of customer deposit accounts, which are typically geographically proximate to the bank's branch locations, and offer a fairly vanilla set of products, such as checking and savings accounts, the deposits of which it uses to fund things like commercial and industrial loans. Asset size is commonly used as a rough heuristic in assessing risk, and, historically, many community banks would receive lighter scrutiny, given their small asset sizes, low number of customers and transaction volumes, and relatively straightforward products. But entering BaaS has introduced challenges that have changed the risk profiles of many community banks in ways not necessarily reflected by a simple measure like asset size.

In the following section, we will examine how the additional layers and scale that BaaS introduces and the new kinds of customers, products, and geographies introduce risks that smaller community banks are not always well equipped to deal with.

**Layers:** In a classic banking delivery model, banks have a one-to-one direct relationship with their customers. Historically, that looked like a customer physically walking into a bank branch, where they could open an account by filling out a paper application, signing a "signature card," and showing a government-issued ID. With the transition to digital, this process moved from pen and paper to online, but still generally took place directly with a bank, through its website or app. The move to banking-as-a-service has changed this dynamic, introducing potentially multiple layers between a bank, which has legal and regulatory obligations to verify its customers' identities, and those end customers. In a structure where a bank works directly with its fintech partners, the customer-facing fintechs would typically have first-line responsibility for acquiring and verifying customers, for instance.

For a bank that works with a BaaS middleware provider, there can be at least *two* layers between the bank and its end customer. So, instead of a bank designing policies, procedures, and systems to verify that customer itself, the bank needs to develop policies, procedures, and systems to oversee that its third parties are effectively verifying end customers' identities. But identity verification, known as Know-Your-Customer (KYC) for consumer accounts and Know-Your-Business (KYB) for commercial accounts, is but one of many capabilities BaaS banks need to transition from operating themselves to overseeing how others operate. Moving from acting as a first party that directly interfaces with end customers to overseeing potentially *multiple* intermediaries that are acting on the banks' behalf is a substantial challenge that requires banks to design and adopt a quite different set of systems and controls, including staff with appropriate experience.

KEY LEARNING POINTS

Banks operating BaaS business models need to oversee how their third-party partners conduct regulated activities, like KYC and KYB checks. The policies and procedures, systems and tools, staff, and training to oversee that an external third party is carrying out these responsibilities in a compliant manner can be quite different than the resources necessary were the bank doing these checks itself.

Perhaps the most critical piece of a financial services business, keeping track of who is owed what, is often significantly more complicated in the layered structure of banking-as-a-service relationships. Historically, a bank would run its own core system, which keeps track of account balances, processes transactions, and so forth. In the BaaS model, a bank's core is still the ultimate source of truth, but middleware providers and fintechs may functionally run their own technology stack, introducing virtual accounts and sub-ledgers as layers on top of what the bank often sees as a single account. This gives middleware providers and fintechs more flexibility to create their own technology, but also introduces a massive challenge: Reconciliation. The bank's books need to match, hopefully down to the penny, its third parties' books. Ensuring accurate reconciliation—and running down any discrepancies that occur—can be a laborious and manual task.

In addition to the challenges posed by designing and operating a compliance framework that is functionally dispersed across multiple layers of entities, whose goals, interests, and incentives may not always be aligned, there are also more mundane challenges that result from this layered structure. Given the need for strong information security controls, banks understandably tightly control who has access to their systems and the information that passes in and out of their IT environment. While these controls help mitigate risk of hacking incidents or data breaches, they can also make it significantly more challenging to integrate with or even effectively communicate with external third parties. But for a bank to effectively oversee external third parties, bank staffers and their counterparts at middleware firms and customer-facing fintechs need to collaborate closely on everything from proposed changes to credit or fraud models to the latest marketing campaign. Often, the approach to collaboration has been highly manual and reliant on inefficient channels, such as emailing documents back and forth. While new compliance-focused tech providers like Themis, Cable, and Performline have sprung up to help streamline and automate collaboration between a bank and its middleware and fintech partners, coordination across these layers remains a challenge.

**Numbers:** In addition to the different capabilities needed to effectively operate and manage risk when there are layers between a bank and its end customers, BaaS partner banks can also see the sheer volume of customers and transactions from fintech partners grow rapidly and even dwarf their "regular" business. BaaS banks typically do not have just one or two fintech partners, but rather could be supporting dozens of programs, either directly, through middleware partners, or both directly *and* through middleware partners. The increase in scale requires resources for initial due diligence and ongoing supervision of the fintech partners themselves, as well as for the fintechs' end customers. New technology solutions have improved banks' and their partners' abilities to automate some aspects of compliance, enabling staff to be more efficient. But areas like customer due diligence, enhanced due diligence, and transaction monitoring—the volume of which all increase as customer numbers go up—often can still require manual intervention and review from analysts. Furthermore, while regulators seem to have warmed to the potential of technology to allow banks to achieve effective outcomes with fewer personnel, a recurring theme in regulator actions against BaaS banks, which we will discuss in greater detail later in this chapter, is a perception of inadequate compliance staffing in relation to the scale of programs BaaS banks are sponsoring. While middleware platforms and customer-facing fintechs can take on some of the compliance burden of overseeing growing numbers of customers and transaction volume, regulatory responsibility ultimately lies with the bank partner for overseeing their efforts.

**Products, Customer Types, and Geographies:** Fintech partners of BaaS banks often offer products, serve categories of customers, or wish to operate in geographies that can be starkly different from a bank's own business. For example, popular fintech product and service offerings, including small-dollar cash advances, credit building/secured charge cards, credit building loans, buy now pay later, and peer-to-peer payments are rarely offered by BaaS banks themselves. Unfamiliar products like these come with a host of legal, regulatory, and compliance risks that partner banks may be ill-prepared to manage, including financial crime risk, credit risk, and consumer compliance risk. Fintechs may also seek to cater to types of customers that their partner banks have not historically served. For instance, beyond the simple consumer versus business split, there is a wide spectrum of riskiness based on the type of business a company is in. Certain categories of business, including crypto, money services businesses, cannabis, firearms, online gaming, and adult entertainment, for instance, are considered higher risk. If a bank does not typically work with such businesses directly, it likely would lack the proper policies, procedures, and controls to meet regulators' expectations. Fintech partners wishing to serve such businesses would need to have compliance programs that meet heightened expectations and would necessitate their bank partners being equipped to oversee those programs.

KEY LEARNING POINTS

Many fintechs seek to serve customer segments who have historically not
had their financial services needs well met by incumbent institutions. But
there are typically reasons why this has been the case, both from an
economics or business model perspective as well as a risk perspective.
While fintechs seeking to serve segments like consumers who lack US
identity credentials or businesses in higher-risk categories arguably
expands access and inclusion in the financial system, community banks
may lack experience serving these users and not have adequate compliance
controls in place to mitigate often unfamiliar risks.

On the question of geography, given all fintechs, by definition, are
digital businesses, they generally seek to operate on a national, if not
an international scale. Although almost all banks have transitioned
into the digital age, and offer online account opening and servicing,
community banking still tends to be a heavily local affair. As a result,
even though they may have "digital" offerings, many banks with
banking-as-a-service models may still have a risk-and-control mind-
set geared toward operating in a narrowly defined geographic area.
Fintechs operating on a nationwide scale can pose new or increased
risks. Fintechs seeking to operate on an international scale, offering
US-based bank accounts to consumers or businesses outside of the
US, would typically require a substantially more sophisticated framework, capable of onboarding and serving these customers. For
instance, a risk-based approach to KYC/KYB, anti-money laundering
policies and procedures, and transaction monitoring for offering US
accounts to consumers and businesses outside of the country would
necessitate significantly heightened requirements versus a local bank
serving customers in its proximate geographic area.

## Regulatory Challenges in Banking-as-a-Service

In today's regulatory paradigm, middleware providers and fintechs
function as third-party service providers to their bank partners. But,

at the end of the day, it is the charter holder—the bank—that is ultimately responsible to regulatory authorities, including for the actions
or inactions of its partners. The bank is responsible for effectively
supervising that its partners are complying with applicable regulations for the activities they are undertaking just the same as if those
activities were being undertaken by the bank itself.[1]

While, at face value, this sounds simple, it can quickly become
orders of magnitude more complicated to supervise external third
parties than if the bank were undertaking such activities by itself. The
number and variety of partners a bank has will increase the complexity of monitoring and ensuring their compliance, particularly if the
risk profile of a bank's partners' activities differs substantially from
the bank's own activities. This is often the case, as many banks that
engage in banking-as-a-service activities are relatively small and may
have comparatively simpler businesses. For example, the physical
location, type of customer, and type of product of a bank's third party
can have a substantially different risk profile than the bank's own
customers and products. For instance, offering a standard or basic
checking account to a retail consumer who lives down the block has
different risks and thus necessitates different controls than offering a
business bank account to companies based outside of the US.

US bank regulators have made it increasingly clear that they are
paying attention to the unique risks posed by banking-as-a-service.
The three primary federal regulators, the Federal Reserve Board, the
FDIC, and the OCC, have collaborated in issuing various guidelines
in an attempt to provide a consistent framework for the banks they
oversee. Examples of guidance documents include 2021's interagency
guide for community banks on conducting due diligence on financial
technology companies and 2023's interagency guidance on third-
party risk management.[2,3]

Between general guidance documents and regulatory enforcement
actions against specific entities (more on that later), a number of
themes have become clear.

- Initial due diligence: Before embarking on a partnership with a
  third party, banks are expected to undertake due diligence of the
  prospective partner that is appropriate for the types of activities

and level of risk. Areas of due diligence can include a counterparty's business experience and qualifications; financial condition; legal and regulatory compliance; risk management and controls; information security program and systems; and operational resilience, including business continuity and incident response planning. Banks are expected to have a clear and documented system for evaluating potential partners, including a rationale for how a third party aligns with a bank's strategic and financial goals.

- Ongoing monitoring and third-party risk management: Banks' obligations do not end when their third-party partners pass an initial due diligence screen. Banks are also expected to monitor their partners and, if applicable, their partners' clients, on an ongoing basis. Regulators expect banks to have adequate policies, procedures, processes, systems, and staffing in place to oversee third parties commensurate with the types and levels of risk they present. A comprehensive approach to third-party risk management should encompass the entire lifecycle, from initial planning and identifying prospective partners, negotiation and contracting, ongoing monitoring during the life of the engagement, as well as termination.

- Bank Secrecy Act/Anti-Money Laundering (BSA/AML): Compliance with anti-money laundering requirements has been a key focus area, both of US regulators and those in other countries. Regardless of service delivery through one or multiple intermediaries, these regulations still apply. Implementing the principles and design of effective anti-money laundering programs, including taking a risk-based approach, dual controls, and the three lines of defense can become more complicated with third parties in the mix. If a middleware or customer-facing fintech is handling customer onboarding, it is the bank partner's responsibility to oversee that they are doing so in compliance with relevant regulations. Know-Your-Customer (KYC)/Know-Your-Business (KYB), customer due diligence (CDD), enhanced due diligence (EDD), transaction monitoring, suspicious activity monitoring and reporting (SAR) are all examples of key AML functions that, historically, would be managed directly by a bank, even if it made use of vendor capabilities to do so. In a banking-as-a-service model, the policies, procedures, tech, and staff carrying out these functions are often at a third party. It is the bank partner's responsibility to oversee its third parties' compliance with regulatory requirements, including that they are appropriate given the products, customers, and geographies served.

- Information technology governance: While perhaps not typically thought of as a "banking" risk, the development and deployment of information technology systems pose unique risks in financial services. When banks are working with third parties who are developing and deploying their own software, like middleware platforms or customer-facing fintechs, a bank must have adequate oversight of those processes. This would typically include ensuring that a bank's third-party partners have their own, appropriate policies and procedures as well as the bank having adequate systems and staffing in place to effectively monitor its third-party partners. An IT control program would typically address key areas like risk governance, business continuity, information security, and change management.

- Consumer compliance: To date, surprisingly little regulatory attention has been focused on issues of consumer compliance. Examples of key consumer protection-focused regulations in the US include the Electronic Fund Transfer Act, which affords consumers certain rights related to unauthorized transfers and requires timely resolution of errors, including on bank transfers and card payments. Other examples of consumer protection regulations include the Truth in Savings Act, which requires certain account disclosures and the Gramm-Leach-Bliley Act, which requires covered institutions to formulate privacy policies to protect users' nonpublic information. The prohibition on unfair, deceptive, and abusive acts and practices (UDAAP) is arguably the most far-reaching consumer protection doctrine, encompassing business functions from product design to advertising copy. While there has been little regulatory action on these issues to date, banks are still responsible for overseeing that their third parties have appropriate policies, procedures, systems, and staffing in place to comply with their requirements, if applicable.

- Lending-related: The broad-based guidance on due diligence and third-party risk management is certainly relevant to banks supporting lending BaaS use cases. In addition to those higher-level principles governing bank-lender partnerships, banks are also responsible for ensuring their lending partners comply with applicable consumer lending regulations. The Truth in Lending Act (TILA) requires certain disclosures, including in advertising materials. The Equal Credit Opportunity Act (ECOA) prohibits illegal discrimination in making credit decisions, including in the use of automated credit underwriting models. Protections like the Fair Debt Collections Practices Act (FDCPA) and Servicemembers Civil Relief Act (SCRA) are also relevant considerations. And more general consumer protections, like UDAAP, still apply. In a banking-as-a-service model, a third party is still generally functioning as a third-party service provider to the bank, making it the bank's obligation to ensure compliance with relevant regulations. However, depending on how these arrangements are structured, some regulatory obligations, like FDCPA or SCRA, may fall only on the third party that owns and is servicing or collecting on the debt, rather than the bank that originated it.

- Concentration risk and balance sheet management: To date, this also has not been as strongly emphasized by regulators in guidance or public enforcement actions, but it is still worth flagging. As discussed previously, a key component of the appeal of BaaS for banks is the ability to source deposits. But this also becomes a source of balance sheet risk to banks, particularly if a single partner brings a large proportion of their deposits or if they work with a middleware platform that, in aggregate, brings a meaningful proportion of their deposits. This kind of concentration exposes banks to the risk of a large volume of deposits leaving all at once. Proximate causes could include a partner or BaaS platform deciding to switch to another bank partner or winding down altogether. On the flip side, should a bank decide it wants to exit a specific program, for either business strategy, regulatory, or other reasons, a dependence on the deposits of said program would complicate parting ways with it.

## Where Banks Have Run into Trouble: Evidence from Regulatory Enforcement Actions and Court Cases

The operational challenges posed by banking-as-a-service operating models and their resulting legal and regulatory risks are not merely hypothetical. The timing, nature, and severity of regulatory and policy actions have varied by jurisdiction, with US banking regulators taking a more sharply critical posture beginning around 2022. The US is hardly the only country struggling to regulate risks in BaaS models. There has been a handful of cases in Europe stemming from similarly styled partnerships and focused on consistent risk areas, like anti-money laundering controls, as in the US.

In the US, cases that illustrate challenges inherent in the banking-as-a-service model and resulting regulatory risks include Evolve Bank & Trust, Metropolitan Commercial Bank, Cross River Bank, and Lineage Bank.

**Evolve Bank & Trust:** Founded in 1925 to serve a farming town in eastern Arkansas, Evolve was an early innovator in the banking-as-a-service space, thanks to its partnership with BaaS platform Synapse (profiled in the next chapter). In addition to partnering with Synapse, Evolve has partnered with another intermediary platform, Solid, and, as of mid-2024, has direct relationships with high-profile fintechs that include Stripe, Affirm, Dave, Airwallex, and numerous others. Deposits sourced through its BaaS partnerships, what the bank refers to as its "Open Banking Division," helped Evolve rapidly grow its on-balance sheet deposits, reaching over $1.5 billion of deposits at the end of 2022.

But that rapid growth and its sprawling fintech partnerships caught up with Evolve when, in June 2024, its primary federal regulator, the St. Louis Federal Reserve, issued a wide-reaching enforcement action against the bank.[4] The cease and desist focused squarely on the activities of Evolve's Open Banking Division—its BaaS programs—and flags serious deficiencies in the bank's risk management practices and BSA/AML and Office of Foreign Asset Control (OFAC) requirements. Specifically, the order highlights shortcomings in how Evolve and its fintech programs handle consumer compliance and complaints, the bank's capital planning framework, liquidity risk management, lending and credit risk management, interest rate risk management, information technology security deficiencies, insufficient internal audit processes, inadequate customer due diligence processes, among numerous other issues.

The enforcement action carries serious consequences for Evolve. It requires Evolve's bank holding company to serve as a "source of strength" by making financial and managerial resources available to the bank. The order further requires Evolve to obtain supervisory nonobjection before onboarding any new fintech programs or offering new products through existing programs. And, in an unusual twist, it also requires Evolve to provide its regulators with a liquidity impact analysis before exiting existing fintech partnerships. The enforcement action prohibits Evolve from paying out dividends or conducting share buybacks with its regulators' approval. And Evolve also must seek regulators' approval before taking on or guaranteeing new debt.

The far-reaching enforcement action is likely not only to have a serious effect on Evolve's business, but also, potentially, on the businesses of fintech programs that partner with it. While Evolve is certainly far from the only BaaS-focused bank to receive an enforcement action, the scope of the order seems likely to constrain its ability to serve its current fintech programs, suggesting those companies may look to shift business to other banks, if and when they're able to do so. Some other banks that have been hit with similar actions have made the difficult decision to wind down their BaaS lines of business altogether. It remains an open question if Evolve may opt to follow that path as well.

The risks in Evolve's information security practices became abundantly clear when, in late June 2024, reports surfaced that the bank had suffered a ransomware attack.[5] The bank subsequently acknowledged it had detected the hack in late May 2024 and engaged cybersecurity specialists to investigate.[6] According to the bank's statement, a Russia-affiliated hacking group, LockBit, compromised the bank's systems when an employee "inadvertently clicked on a malicious internet link."[7] As of the end of June 2024, the exact scope of the data compromised in the attack was unknown, but appeared to be substantial and was confirmed to include sensitive, personally identifiable information, records of account numbers and balances, transaction and settlement files, and more.[8] Customer-facing firms that appear to have had data compromised in the breach include Affirm, Airwallex, Bilt, Dave, Mercury, Stripe Treasury, Wise, and numerous others.[9]

The Evolve hacking incident illustrates an often-overlooked risk in banking-as-a-service, specifically, and fintech, in general: Information security practices. Banking-as-a-service operating models typically rely on numerous, interconnected service providers and often, as described earlier in this chapter, multiple layers between a bank partner and an end user. This architecture brings with it increased information security risk in the form of additional access points bad actors may be able to exploit to gain unauthorized access to IT systems and sensitive data. The greater number of parties involved in delivering services to end users also can mean a greater number of employees across a number of firms who need to communicate and share data in the general course of business, which also can increase information security risk if appropriate mitigation measures are not taken. While data breaches are, unfortunately, exceedingly common, the sensitive data held by financial services providers poses greater risks than an e-commerce or social media site, for instance. Though the full repercussions of the Evolve data breach are not clear as of the end of June 2024, the consequences for Evolve, specifically, and the banking-as-a-service model, in general, may be significant.

**Metropolitan Commercial Bank (MCB):** Metropolitan Commercial Bank entered into agreements with its federal regulator, the Federal Reserve, and state regulator, the New York Department of Financial Services, stemming from a broadly similar set of issues as that which resulted in Blue Ridge's challenges. MCB was found to be operating in an unsafe and unsound manner because of failures in its third-party risk management program and BSA/AML compliance. A customer-facing fintech client of MCB, prepaid account issuer MovoCash, enabled fraudsters to channel as much as $300 million in illegally obtained Covid-era benefits through MCB and MovoCash. At one point, as many as 80,000 fraudulent MovoCash accounts were being opened per week and more than $2 million was being transferred out of the system a day.[10]

The orders MCB reached with its regulators require greater oversight by the bank's board of directors, a requirement to submit any new products or programs for regulatory review, a requirement that the bank strengthen its customer identification program, a requirement that the bank improve its customer due diligence program, and a requirement that the bank enhance its third-party risk management program. MCB was also ordered to pay a combined $30 million penalty.

**Lineage Bank:** Much like Blue Ridge and Metropolitan's orders, the consent order Lineage received stemmed largely from inadequate due diligence and third-party risk management practices, including related to BSA and anti-money laundering compliance and especially in light of how quickly the bank grew its deposits and number of customers through its banking-as-a-service programs. Certain services Lineage provided also entailed higher risk that the bank did not have proper policies and procedures in place to mitigate. For instance, as part of its BaaS program, Lineage operated a "third-party sender ACH business line," in which the bank would act as payment processor for entities that were not direct customers of the bank. While this is permissible, it entails greater risk and thus warrants corresponding policies and procedures.

The wide-ranging consent order also touched on a number of areas that shed additional light on the challenges and risks in BaaS operating models. The order requires Lineage to identify and address liquidity and funding concentration risks from its fintech and BaaS programs. A "funding concentration" is when a single source or multiple linked or highly correlated sources are responsible for bringing a materially significant volume of deposits to a bank. This can pose a type of "run risk" and thus potential liquidity challenge for a bank, if those funds were to leave the bank quickly and en masse. Lineage's consent order further mandated that it have a contingency funding plan in place that addresses the impact and risks associated with a high degree of fintech deposit concentration.

The order is also notable for the restrictions it places on Lineage. In addition to the extensive requirements around improving due diligence, third-party risk management, and BSA/AML compliance, the order also prohibits Lineage from entering into a new business or expanding an existing one that would result in an annual 10 per cent growth in assets or liabilities without prior regulatory approval. The bank also faces tougher capital restrictions, with a heightened requirement of a tier 1 leverage ratio of 12.5 per cent or higher and a total risk-based capital ratio of 16 per cent or higher.[11] The more stringent ratios help reduce the risk of a bank failing by becoming insolvent, but they also reduce a bank's profitability. The order also prohibits Lineage from declaring or paying a dividend without regulatory approval, which can result in a bank building its capital in profitable quarters by retaining earnings.

**Cross River Bank:** Cross River entered into a consent order with its primary regulator, the FDIC, in 2023. As we have touched on elsewhere in this book, Cross River is one of a relatively smaller number of BaaS banks facilitating lending products, including personal loans, credit cards, and charge cards. This is notable as, in addition to the kinds of due diligence and third-party risk management challenges faced by BaaS banks that enable fintech partners to hold deposits or issue debit cards, lending programs have additional, complex regulatory requirements we briefly touched on earlier in this chapter, including fair lending requirements. Cross River's consent order stems, in part, from its failure to adequately ensure that its third-party lending partners were adhering to these requirements. The FDIC found, and Cross River neither admitted nor denied, that the bank failed to establish and maintain information systems, internal controls, and appropriate credit underwriting practices consistent with safe and sound operation.[12]

Cross River's FDIC order requires the bank's board to strengthen its oversight, monitoring, and management of the bank, including its "marketplace lending" activities, in which Cross River acts as originator for third-party fintech partners. Cross River was also ordered to prepare documentation on all of the credit products and third parties offering them for the FDIC's review and comment. For all new third parties or new credit products, Cross River is required to submit a request with supporting analysis and documentation for the FDIC's review and non-objection.

This summary of these enforcement actions is by no means comprehensive but is intended to offer an illustration of how challenges in BaaS operating models can turn into regulatory actions. There have been a handful of other recent related US regulatory actions not touched on above, including those faced by First Fed, B2, Vast Bank, Evolve Bank & Trust, and others. In all likelihood, more banks involved in BaaS will receive public actions before the current round of heightened scrutiny eases.

### BaaS Regulatory Actions Not Limited to US

It is also worth noting that these types of lapses and resulting regulatory actions are not unique to the United States. In Europe, several firms providing BaaS or BaaS-like services, including German bank Solaris and two e-money institutions licensed in Lithuania, Transactive Systems and PayrNet, a subsidiary of Railsr (formerly known as Railsbank), have been subject to regulatory actions:

**Transactive Systems:** Though Transactive is not a bank, it has held e-money institution licenses in the UK and in the European Union. The company has worked with companies in high-risk sectors, including foreign exchange trading, a type of speculative investment known as contracts for difference (CFDs), and numerous companies in the crypto and virtual asset space, including Crypto.com. In early January, the Lithuanian central bank, the company's financial regulator in the EU, cited the scale and significant anti-money laundering failures and ordered the company not to take on new clients and to immediately cease providing services to existing clients in certain high-risk categories.

**PayrNet:** Also licensed as an e-money institution in Lithuania, PayrNet was a subsidiary of UK-based Railsr. Railsr itself has faced numerous challenges and went through a bankruptcy process in early 2023. In June of that same year, the Lithuania central bank revoked PayrNet's license and forced the entity into bankruptcy for "serious, systematic and multiple" violations of the country's payments laws and of AML/CFT requirements. At the time, PayrNet used the capabilities granted by its e-money license to provide services through some 90 intermediaries, but, according to its regulator, failed to conduct adequate due diligence, properly identify end clients, perform real-time or lookback transaction monitoring, report suspicious activity, or fulfill numerous other obligations required under the law.

**Solaris:** Unlike Transactive and PayrNet, Solaris is a fully licensed German bank, which leverages its license to provide BaaS capabilities. Solaris is the largest BaaS firm in Europe and works with household names like American Express, Samsung, and BP, but it also made an aggressive push to court business in the crypto industry. German industry publication *Handelsblatt* has reported that BaFin, the German banking regulator, was concerned enough about gaps in Solaris' controls, including related to anti-money laundering procedures, that it prohibited the bank from accepting any new clients without its approval. That decision followed an earlier mandate from BaFin that sent a special audit team from PwC to Solaris, stemming from compliance deficiencies surfaced in a 2020 examination.

## Are Banking-as-a-Service Models Sustainable?

Surely for all this trouble, banking-as-a-service must be a good *business*, right? For banks, it certainly *can* be, though that may be changing. For middleware platforms and for customer-facing fintechs that rely on BaaS, it is much more of an open question as to whether or not the economic models of their respective businesses are sustainable.

For many customer-facing fintechs, the economics were always uncertain. While some companies are mostly applying technology to long-standing business models, like non-bank lending, many are experimenting with new product structures and monetization strategies that have yet to be proven sustainable. Interchange-driven companies, whether consumer offerings like neobank Chime or business offerings like expense management and charge card startup Brex, have spent most of their existence in a climate where access to venture capital was easy, and "growth," measured in number of users or revenue, was the most important metric.

Access to plentiful venture capital (VC) cash fostered a fundraising and marketing spend arms race, as fintech startups sought to capture market share in all sorts of emerging categories, including neobanking, peer-to-peer payments, buy now pay later, spend management, business banking, and so forth. But, for many fintechs, the promised profits were slow to materialize. At the same time, fintechs are feeling the increasing regulatory pressure on their banking-as-a-service partners.

Whether or not a given fintech's bank partner received a public enforcement action, regulators are now sending a clear message, and banks are paying attention. How that increased regulatory pressure impacts the day-to-day relationship between a fintech and its banking-as-a-service partner could vary considerably, ranging from slower and more thorough reviews to being offboarded from their bank partner altogether. With their partners' expectations increasing, many fintechs have needed to hire and invest in beefing up compliance and control infrastructure. Realizing the risk that dependence on a single bank partner poses, fintechs have scrambled to line up backup bank partners, in case their primary bank is subject to a regulatory action or seeks to offboard them. All of these initiatives, though necessary, require time, money, and personnel to execute, resulting in a potentially significant outlay of resources for often already unprofitable fintechs to navigate.

For middleware providers, the sustainability of the business model may be an even greater question. Remember, the original premise for companies in this segment was to invest significant upfront resources in building technical connectivity and relationships with one or multiple bank partners, which is then monetized by scaling the number of customer-facing fintechs the middleware company serves. But, this is not really how things have turned out in the sector. Middleware providers have also taken a range of approaches around intermediating other aspects of the bank-fintech relationship, including, in some cases, helping to match fintechs with bank partners, facilitating the initial due diligence and onboarding process, and providing some elements of compliance functionality to their fintech and bank partners. The hope was to leverage technology and automation to achieve compliance at scale without ballooning personnel costs. Middleware platforms typically derive their revenue from setup and service fees paid by fintech clients, as well as from payments tied to interchange and deposits. But, middleware firms are feeling the fallout of reduced venture capital investments, especially in consumer fintech, and fintechs' reduced marketing spend as they pivot to profitability.

The result has been fewer new fintechs being founded and slower growth from existing companies, both of which translate to slower growth for middleware firms. At the same time, middleware firms are on the front lines of the fallout from increased regulatory action in banking-as-a-service. All middleware providers, but especially the firms that purported to take on compliance tasks for their fintech clients and bank partners, are facing sharply higher expectations for their compliance systems, practices, and staffing. Middleware firms also tend to face an inbuilt churn challenge. Their proposition is most useful for early stage fintechs looking to quickly and inexpensively launch a financial product. But, as is the nature of startups, many of those companies will fail over time, and thus no longer need a middleware provider's services. For the firms that make it and grow to a meaningfully large volume, once they have gained sufficient scale, they may be able to go directly to a partner bank and negotiate a better deal than working through their BaaS provider. The reality is that middleware providers are facing a perfect storm of slowing demand from fintechs, high rates of churn, and growing costs to meet heightened expectations from their bank partners. It is too early to say if the category, as we know it today, will disappear altogether. However, two middleware companies have already ceased to be standalone companies: Bond was acquired by core banking behemoth FIS, and Rize was acquired by regional bank Fifth Third. By early 2024, US middleware firms Unit, Treasury Prime, and Synctera were attempting to pivot from indirect models focused on selling to fintechs to an emphasis on selling software capabilities to banks to enable them to run their own BaaS programs.

Of the three parties, banks are the most well-positioned to navigate the current climate of uncertainty. As we noted in Chapter 1, even if the term banking-as-a-service is fairly new, the business model for banks is anything but. What has changed is the types of non-bank companies they partner with, the kinds of products and services being offered through them to end customers, and the rise of middleware platforms. The economics for a bank running a BaaS business model can be, but are not automatically, materially superior to a "typical" banking business. But the same forces impacting fintechs and middleware platforms are altering the considerations for banks. The reduction in VC investment in fintechs flows through to reduced demand for partner banks. Staffing and spending on compliance is increasing significantly at many banks in BaaS. Heightened due diligence and third-party risk management expectations change the cost structure for onboarding new fintech programs and effectively monitoring them once they are live. And some banks have actively chosen to "de-risk," by offboarding higher-risk programs like crypto firms or fintechs offering crypto-related features, cannabis businesses, or fintechs offering US consumer or business accounts to those outside of the US. These evolving factors all add up to slowing growth and increasing structural costs. These important shifts in the economics come at a time when the number of banks now competing for high-quality fintech clients has grown substantially compared to what it was 5 or 10 years ago. Again, the banking-as-a-service model itself is not going away, but there will be a period, possibly a painful one, of recalibration as banks adjust to the level of demand from fintechs vs. the amount of supply from BaaS banks.

## BaaS Headwinds Will Drive Market Recalibration

Almost every innovation comes with its challenges, and banking-as-a-service is surely no different. From an operational standpoint, banking-as-a-service models pose complex organizational and communications challenges, even more so when a middleware provider is in the mix. A single, relatively small bank can potentially support dozens of fintech programs with millions of customers and hundreds of millions in deposits and transaction volume—oftentimes dwarfing the size of a BaaS bank's "regular" business. To make matters more complicated, the products and services, customer types, and geographies served by a given bank's fintech clients can vary considerably, necessitating compliance programs appropriately tailored to risk levels. Those operational challenges have contributed to a growing number of regulatory actions faced by BaaS banks, with insufficient due diligence and inadequate third-party risk management being recurring themes. Finally, the sustainability of the economic models for the different participants in banking-as-a-service remains an open question. Many fintechs have long been dependent on recurring rounds of venture capital and have struggled to find viable pathways to profitability. Plummeting VC funding has translated to less demand for middleware platforms and banks for their services, right as compliance expectations and costs are increasing. This is not to say that banking-as-a-service is going to vanish overnight, but it will take some time to iterate current operating and economic models to find a sustainable market equilibrium.

## Endnotes

1  Federal Deposit Insurance Corporation (2023) Interagency Guidance on Third-Party Relationships: Risk Management, www.fdic.gov/news/financial-institution-letters/2023/fil23029.html (archived at https://perma.cc/D95B-XEH4)

2  Federal Deposit Insurance Corporation (2021) Conducting Due Diligence on Financial Technology Companies A Guide for Community Banks, www.fdic.gov/sites/default/files/2024-03/pr21075a.pdf (archived at https://perma.cc/RR36-XQHY)

3  Federal Deposit Insurance Corporation (2023) Interagency Guidance on Third-Party Relationships: Risk Management, www.fdic.gov/news/financial-institution-letters/2023/fil23029.html (archived at https://perma.cc/2M8J-LYH7)

**4**  Mikula, J. (2024) Evolve Hit with Fed Enforcement Action, But Why Did It Take This Long?, *Fintech Business Weekly*, fintechbusinessweekly.substack. com/p/evolve-hit-with-fed-enforcement-action (archived at https://perma.cc/ Y9WM-JKEB)

**5**  Kovacs, E. (2024) Evolve Bank Data Leaked After LockBit's 'Federal Reserve Hack', *Security Week*, www.securityweek.com/evolve-bank-data-leaked-after-lockbits-federal-reserve-hack/ (archived at https://perma.cc/CB3N-5RPZ)

**6**  Evolve Bank & Trust (2024) Cybersecurity Incident, www.getevolved.com/ about/news/cybersecurity-incident/ (archived at https://perma.cc/V2FC-J4XV)

**7**  Ibid.

**8**  Mikula, J. (2024) Evolve Hack Crisis: Russia-Linked Cybergang Leaks Records on Millions, *Fintech Business Weekly*, fintechbusinessweekly.substack. com/p/evolve-hack-crisis-russia-linked (archived at https://perma.cc/MYL2-ZLCQ)

**9**  Ibid.

**10**  Chakravarty, R. (2023) Metropolitan Commercial Bank Fined $29.5M by Fed, NYDFS, *Banking Dive*, www.bankingdive.com/news/metropolitan-commercial-bank-fined-30m-fed-nydfs-prepaid-card/697349/ (archived at https://perma.cc/ R7DQ-5FBA)

**11**  Chakravarty, R. (2024) Tennessee Bank Hit with FDIC Consent Order Over BaaS Business, *Banking Dive*, www.bankingdive.com/news/lineage-bank-tennessee-fdic-consent-order-baas-fintech-partner-synapse-synctera/708830/ (archived at https://perma.cc/HQK4-JDB6)

**12**  Vaske, R. et al. (2023) FDIC Consent Order with Cross River Bank Indicates Heightened Scrutiny of Bank-Fintech Partnerships, *Consumer Finance Monitor*, www.consumerfinancemonitor.com/2023/05/04/fdic-consent-order-with-cross-river-bank-indicates-heightened-scrutiny-of-bank-fintech-partnerships/ (archived at https:// perma.cc/5SN6-3CC8)

# 9

# US Case Studies: Synapse, Blue Ridge Bank, Goldman Sachs

CHAPTER OBJECTIVES

The United States arguably has the most prolific and diverse banking-as-a-service market. We have touched on some of the reasons why in previous chapters: The lack of new or alternate charter types, the abnormally large number of chartered institutions versus similar countries, and the requirement for fintechs to partner with banks to carry out regulated activities, like holding deposits or issuing payment cards. The BaaS market in the US is also quite diverse, with a variety of business models and types of banks in the space. In this chapter, we will explore three banks that are operating or have operated BaaS models through case studies: Synapse, Blue Ridge Bank, and Goldman Sachs.

## Synapse: From Middleware Innovator to Bankruptcy Meltdown

Perhaps no company better illustrates the recent arc of banking-as-a-service in the US than Synapse. Founded as SynapsePay in 2014, the company is widely credited as the first "middleware" intermediary to build a software-and-services layer on top of a partner bank, in a model that later companies like Unit, Treasury Prime, and Synctera would mimic. Synapse raised more than $50 million from marquee investors, like Andreessen Horowitz and Core Innovation Capital, and boasted a client roster that included leading names in fintech, like Mercury, Rho, Yotta, Cadre, Relay, GigWage, and Dave. But by April 2024, the company filed for Chapter 11 bankruptcy protection and attempted to sell substantially all of its assets to TabaPay, a payment infrastructure firm, for just $9.7 million.[1] When that sale fell through, Synapse collapsed into chaos, with dozens of fintech firms and hundreds of thousands of end users becoming collateral damage. As of June 2024, the bankruptcy case is ongoing, with many end users' funds frozen and no clear timeline on a resolution.[2]

As explained in depth in Chapter 6, the promise of middleware platforms like Synapse was twofold: For fintechs, middleware sought to provide a faster, easier, and less expensive path to market compared to working directly with a bank; for banks, middleware platforms promised cheap deposits and fee revenue, with the platform, rather than the bank, doing the heavy lifting of finding, onboarding, and managing fintech partners.

While other BaaS middleware platforms would mimic Synapse's original approach of providing a technical and program management layer on top of one or multiple bank partners, Synapse evolved its approach and structure in a fairly unique way over time. Synapse's initial bank partner was Evolve Bank & Trust, but recognizing the risk of having a single, critical point of failure, the company added additional bank partners over time, including Lineage Bank, AMG National Trust, and American Bank.

This decision wasn't unique to Synapse; other BaaS middleware providers also built networks of bank providers. What was unique to Synapse was its decision to secure licenses in its own right: Specifically, a broker-dealer license and state-issued lending licenses. Securing its own licenses, specifically the broker-dealer license, enabled Synapse to allow its customer-facing fintech clients to open brokerage accounts for their end users at Synapse itself, rather than opening traditional "checking" or demand deposit accounts at underlying bank partners. The brokerage accounts aren't really used for their intended purpose of holding and trading stocks, but rather as a stand-in for a traditional checking account. The brokerage accounts Synapse made available through its fintech clients came with a "cash management" feature, allowing them to function similarly to a traditional bank account, enabling end users to make deposits and payments via ACH, obtain a debit card linked to the account, and so forth. While, on the surface, this structure may be indistinguishable for a typical end user, it can come with additional risks in how funds are held, transferred, and insured. It is worth noting, though, the brokerage account with cash management capabilities structure isn't unique to Synapse. Incumbent brokerages, like Fidelity and TD Ameritrade, offer such accounts, and some customer-facing fintechs, like Brex and Robinhood, also make use of the structure. Synapse was unique in obtaining its broker-dealer license and incorporating the cash management account structure into its banking-as-a-service operating model.

Synapse would come to call its unique approach "modular" banking. In typical direct bank/fintech partnerships and those facilitated by BaaS middleware platforms, most of the features and capabilities of an end user's account would be tied to a single underlying bank. The structure was such that, even with a middleware provider and fintech sitting between an end user and the bank, those entities acted as service providers, and end users were entering agreements with and opening accounts at the underlying banks.

By contrast, Synapse's modular banking approach disaggregated the features and services associated with a single account across multiple bank partners. Account number issuance, BIN sponsorship, card issuing-processing, and funds custody could all be provided by discrete banks. With programs that offered brokerage cash management accounts through Synapse's broker-dealer license, customer-facing fintechs and end users typically only had agreements with Synapse itself; Synapse's bank partners provided supporting services and capabilities to Synapse, but had no direct relationship with Synapse's fintech clients or end users. This structure has exacerbated the problem of resolving Synapse's bankruptcy, conducting reconciliation between Synapse's records and funds held by its bank partners, and returning funds to end users.

While not inherently unworkable, in retrospect, Synapse's modular approach increasingly abstracted the relationship between end users and the underlying banks holding their funds and processing transactions, thereby increasing complexity and, with it, risk. Each individual bank supporting Synapse and its programs could only see a narrow slice of a given fintech's and end users' activities and relied on Synapse, as a broker-dealer and program manager, to ensure compliance with regulatory requirements, like KYC/KYB requirements and transaction monitoring. That's not to say that the banks partnering with Synapse had no legal or regulatory obligations, but more that ensuring their compliance with those obligations relied on their ability to supervise how Synapse operated its business.

In 2022, regulatory scrutiny on the banking-as-a-service sector began ramping up with Blue Ridge Bank's first consent order. And by 2023, the complexity of Synapse's model, shortcomings in its approach to risk management, and a dubious client base that included companies focused on crypto, DeFi (decentralized finance), small-dollar lending, remittance, and offering banking services to non-US citizens outside of the United States began to catch up with the company.[3]

In August 2023, potential issues with Synapse's relationship with Lineage Bank came to light, including Lineage's dependence on the deposits source through Synapse's fintech clients and questions about Lineage's ability to effectively oversee Synapse, its fintech clients, and their end users.[4] In February 2024, Lineage entered into a consent order with its primary federal regulator, the FDIC, which appears to stem in part from its relationship with Synapse.

In October 2023, long-simmering tensions with Synapse's first and arguably most important bank partner, Evolve Bank & Trust, and fintech client, Mercury, reached boiling point. Mercury, widely believed to be Synapse's largest client, informed the company it would not be renewing its partnership with Synapse and, instead, would work directly with Evolve. Around the same time, Evolve informed Synapse it believed the company was in breach of its contract and that it intended to terminate the relationship. In turn, Synapse claimed that FBO accounts, which hold pooled end user funds, at Evolve had a shortfall of over $13 million in missing customer funds, because of what Synapse claimed was an error on Evolve's part. Evolve responded by withholding a $16 million payment due to Synapse and demanding that Synapse increase the amount held in a reserve account at Evolve to $50 million, in order to protect the bank and end customers from any losses. The mounting financial pressure led to Synapse laying off around 40 per cent of its staff.

In December 2023, Synapse's troubles continued to multiply as one-time client Mercury claimed Synapse owed it as much as $30 million. Mercury not only filed a private arbitration claim but also sought to freeze Synapse's assets, arguing that the company was in "financial freefall," and that the freeze was necessary to preserve Mercury's chance of collecting should it prevail in its arbitration claim.[5] Synapse filed a counterclaim in arbitration, arguing that Mercury owed it as much as $36 million. Meanwhile, the situation with Evolve continued in the background, as Synapse sought to find a path to stabilize the company's finances.

In April 2024 Synapse filed for Chapter 11 bankruptcy protection as part of a proposed $9.7 million asset sale to payment infrastructure firm TabaPay. As a precondition of the TabaPay deal, Synapse needed to reach a settlement with Evolve Bank & Trust, which would require Evolve to cover any shortfall in end customer funds and to pay Synapse's bankruptcy estate $2 million, with each party releasing the other from any claims. But when the settlement between Evolve and Synapse fell apart, TabaPay walked away from the deal, leaving Synapse to collapse in spectacular fashion. As of late June 2024, a Chapter 11 trustee, former FDIC Chair Jelena McWilliams, was appointed to replace Synapse's management team. End user funds of approximately $265 million have been frozen since mid-May 2024, with a shortfall of approximately $85 million between what users are owed and what Synapse's bank partners believe they actually hold.[6]

The venture capital investors who put more than $50 million into Synapse have been wiped out and will see no return on their investment. Secured creditors, which include Silicon Valley Bank and TriplePoint, are unlikely to be fully repaid. Synapse's unsecured creditors are unlikely to see any of the money they are owed. And it is unclear when end users will regain access to their funds and, if there is a shortfall, who will be responsible for it.

Synapse itself will cease to exist, and the collateral damage from its failure seems likely to include a number of its fintech clients like Yotta and Juno. Synapse is hardly the only US banking-as-a-service middle-ware platform experiencing stress as banks and the market respond to decreased VC funding to fintechs and increased regulatory scrutiny of BaaS banks. Some platforms exited through acquisitions, like Rize, Bond, and Apto Payments. Other platforms, like Treasury Prime, Synctera, and Unit have struggled to pivot and redefine their offerings to match the changing market realities. Synapse, though ultimately not successful as a standalone business, did help define a new operating model and new era in banking-as-a-service.

### Blue Ridge Bank: How an Aggressive BaaS Strategy Leads to Regulatory Repercussions

Blue Ridge Bank, headquartered in Martinsville, Virginia, is fairly representative of the typical community bank that jumped into the banking-as-a-service game in recent years. The OCC-regulated bank was originally founded in 1894. As recently as the end of 2015, Blue Ridge had just $267 million in assets, putting it on the smaller end of community banks. But in the back half of the 2010s, Blue Ridge began growing aggressively, both organically and through merger and acquisition activity. From 2016 through 2020, Blue Ridge engaged in three M&A transactions, with fellow Virginia-area banks River Bancorp, Virginia Community Bancshares, and Bay Banks of Virginia.[7]

Blue Ridge also began pursuing a banking-as-a-service strategy in 2020, with the bank citing the potential for growth by gaining digital customers across the US without the need to add physical branches. Blue Ridge recognized the opportunity to leverage BaaS relationships to gather low-cost deposits and drive fee revenue, according to media coverage at the time.[8]

Blue Ridge offered a variety of BaaS capabilities, including holding insured deposits, card issuance, payments processing, and lending. Blue Ridge's strategy included partnering with middleware platforms Unit and Increase, as well as direct partnerships with fintechs. By the end of 2021, the bank was working through Unit and Increase and partnered with numerous fintechs on its own, including Upgrade, Kashable, Jaris, Aeldra, Grow Credit, MentorWorks, and Marlette (also known as Best Egg). Through middleware intermediary Unit, Blue Ridge supported programs that included AngelList, Mos, lance, Invoice2Go, and benepass.[9] Through Blue Ridge, platform partner Increase offered payments services used by fintechs like Ramp, Modern Treasury, and Gusto. By the end of the first quarter of 2022, Blue Ridge's BaaS program had generated over $20 million in loans, just shy of $330 million in deposits, and nearly $50 million in trust accounts.

But, by late 2022, Blue Ridge disclosed it had reached a wide-ranging formal agreement with its primary federal regulator, the Office of the Comptroller of the Currency (OCC). While the agreement does not explicitly specify that Blue Ridge's BaaS business gave rise to the action, the contents of the order make clear that that was the case. The agreement highlights a number of deficiencies at Blue Ridge, including in its approach to third-party risk management, anti-money laundering and Bank Secrecy Act compliance, customer and enhanced due diligence, suspicious activity monitoring and reporting, and information technology control. The agreement also required Blue Ridge to obtain OCC non-objection before onboarding new fintech partners or offering new products through existing third-party partners.

Blue Ridge failed to adequately remediate the problems highlighted in its 2022 formal agreement with the OCC, leading its regulator to take more severe action. In January 2024, Blue Ridge reached a consent order with the OCC related to the bank's unsafe and unsound banking practices and deficiencies in its Bank Secrecy Act/Anti-Money Laundering compliance program. The consent order reiterated and built upon the issues highlighted in Blue Ridge's 2022 formal agreement and required the bank to develop and submit for regulatory approval a written three-year strategic plan for the bank. The consent order deemed Blue Ridge to be in "troubled condition" and imposed punitive capital requirements on the bank, raising its total capital ratio to a minimum of 13 per cent and its leverage ratio to a minimum of 10 per cent.

Between its first and second enforcement actions, Blue Ridge undertook a change in management, bringing in experienced community banker William "Billy" Beale to replace former CEO Brian Plum. Beale's priority was to resolve the bank's regulatory issues, which he plans to do by returning to a focus on traditional community banking and growing deposits through those channels. As a result, Blue Ridge began "derisking" its BaaS program, by offboarding smaller fintech partners with low numbers of accounts or minimal deposits.[10] To meet the heightened capital requirements called for by its OCC consent order, Blue Ridge undertook a capital raise, finalizing a $150 million private placement in April 2024. The bank also leaned on brokered deposits to backfill its balance sheet as it offboarded fintech programs, with such deposits growing from $45 million at the end of 2022 to about $515 million at the end of 2023, causing Blue Ridge's cost of funds to spike substantially, from 0.48 per cent to 2.39 per cent.[11]

In many ways, Blue Ridge is representative of community banks that sought to capitalize on the banking-as-a-service and fintech goldrush period of approximately 2019–2022. It grew quickly through indirect relationships facilitated by middleware platforms Unit and Increase, as well as pursuing direct partnerships. But, the bank failed to scale the needed capabilities to effectively oversee its growing number of third-party programs and their end customers, ultimately resulting in regulatory action. This isn't to say that community banks cannot successfully pursue BaaS business models, but rather that doing so requires adequate investment in control-side infrastructure. If anything, Blue Ridge should serve as a cautionary tale for banks considering pursuing BaaS lines of business.

## Goldman Sachs: A White-Shoe Investment Bank Tries its Hand at BaaS

Goldman Sachs occupies quite a different position in the financial services ecosystem compared to other banks offering BaaS capabilities. Until relatively recently, Goldman was regulated as a broker-dealer, and its business primarily centered around investment banking (underwriting debt and equity offerings) and trading. In fact, Goldman Sachs wasn't even licensed as a traditional commercial bank until the 2008 global financial crisis, when it converted into a Fed-supervised bank holding company in order to calm markets by gaining access to the backstop of the Fed's discount window.

Goldman did little to leverage its new status as a licensed bank until approximately seven years later. The firm began laying the groundwork internally for what would become its consumer banking effort, Marcus, which would launch with an installment lending product in 2016 (*Full disclosure: The author worked at Goldman Sachs and was part of the team that launched the Marcus consumer bank*). Around the same time, the bank would also acquire the online deposit platform and customers of GE Capital Bank, bringing approximately $8 billion in deposits and $8 billion in brokered certificates of deposits to Goldman.[12] Goldman temporarily renamed the consumer-facing deposit platform as GS Bank, before it was folded into Marcus and became the brand's online savings platform about a year later.

Now, Goldman's efforts with GS Bank and Marcus were direct-to-consumer, branchless banking, but they would not be considered banking-as-a-service. However, they did lay the groundwork for one prong of the bank's attempt at a banking-as-a-service and embedded finance strategy. While Goldman pursued a number of partnerships within its consumer division, including offering small business loans to third-party sellers on Amazon and Walmart marketplaces and acquiring the General Motors credit card program, it is best known for its marquee partnership with Apple.

Goldman's partnership to power the Apple Card credit card, viewed by many as a failure in retrospect, was thought of as a huge win for the bank at the time.[13] There is legitimate debate if the Goldman/Apple partnership really constitutes banking-as-a-service, as the structure of the credit card partnership is comparable to long-standing co-brand credit card programs, including from banks that specialize in co-brand and private label business, like Synchrony and Barclays.

Although there is justifiable disagreement about whether or not Goldman and Apple's partnership on Apple Card constitutes banking-as-a-service, it is worth examining as an example of an establishment bank entering a new business line, consumer credit cards, with a new distribution channel in its partnership with Apple. For Apple, the collaboration marked a continuation of its efforts to leverage its large customer base to build a platform in financial services, which dates at least to the launch of Apple Pay in 2014. But, perhaps unlike other areas of Apple's business, for the credit card offering, Apple is highly reliant on an external partner, in this case Goldman Sachs, to make the business work: Goldman is the card issuer, principal member of the network scheme (in this case, Mastercard), is responsible for the underwriting, origination, servicing, and collections of consumers' accounts, funds consumers' borrowing via its balance sheet, and is ultimately responsible for compliance with applicable law and regulation.

When the Apple Card was announced in February 2019, Apple's CEO Tim Cook hailed it as a game changer, calling it "the most significant change in the credit card experience in 50 years."[14] The card did boast some novel features: Users apply through the Apple Wallet app in an elegant, streamlined experience; if approved, a digital version of a user's card is instantly provisioned into their Apple Wallet; when their physical card arrives, users activate it by holding their phone near the box it came in, rather than dialing some 1-800 phone number; and the physical card, made out of titanium and weighing some 15 grams, was one of the first from a major issuer not to include the 16-digit account number on the card itself. Rather than requiring a separate app, management of the card, including transactions, reviewing and paying the account balance, and customer service is handled directly through the Wallet app. And the card boasts some notable customer-friendly features, including zero fees (even late fees), a billing cycle that matches the calendar month, and a balance payment interface that encourages cardholders to minimize interest expense by paying more than the minimum balance due.

The card officially launched to the public in August 2019 and, at the time, was broadly considered to be a success. Regulatory filings Goldman made later that year reflected the bank had extended some $10 billion in credit lines and had $736 million in outstanding card balances as of the end of September 2019, just a couple of months after the card went live. In October that year, Apple's Tim Cook hailed it as the "most successful launch of a credit card in the United States ever." In addition to being integrated into the iPhone itself, the Apple Card boasted 3 per cent cashback on Apple purchases and 24-month 0 per cent financing on eligible Apple purchases, including iPhones.

Goldman and Apple would deepen their partnership in 2023, with the announcement that April that Apple Card users would be able to open high-yield savings accounts, with funds held at Goldman, directly through the Wallet app. Apple Card users have the option of automatically depositing cash back into the saving accounts and can make additional deposits from external sources to the accounts. By August 2023, about four months after launch, Goldman had gained some $10 billion in deposits through the Apple savings account.

Despite the apparent success, there were signs, even early on, of tension in the relationship between Apple and Goldman Sachs.[15] The Apple Card was announced at an Apple event, with executives from Goldman in the audience, rather than on stage. Apple aggressively marketed the card as being "Created by Apple, Not a Bank," despite the critical program functions carried out by Goldman.[16] The high-profile nature of both Apple and Goldman also invited criticism, even when it was misplaced. For instance, well-known software engineer and creator of programming language Ruby on Rails, David Heinemeier-Hanson, described Apple Card as a "sexist program" shortly after it launched, saying that he and his wife received substantially different credit limits from "Apple's black box algorithm."[17] The controversy Heinemeier-Hanson touched off spread and ultimately resulted in one of Goldman's regulators, the New York Department of Financial Services (NYDFS), investigating the bank. Ultimately, the NYDFS found that Goldman, which is responsible for the Apple Card's credit underwriting and fair lending compliance, did not illegally discriminate in how it handled consumers' applications. Similarly, shortly after the launch of the savings feature, reports proliferated of users depositing and then being unable to immediately withdraw funds, which is a fairly common fraud prevention technique, but resulted in negative coverage of Apple and Goldman.

Perhaps more importantly than the occasional PR dust-up is that the economics of the Apple Card program for Goldman weren't great. Estimates of Goldman's losses on the card program, both due to the investments needed but also from loan losses, reportedly exceeded $1 billion by January 2023. The level of credit risk Goldman took on Apple Card users was materially different than the little consumer lending the firm had done previously through its Marcus brand. While almost all of the personal loans issued through Marcus were to "prime" borrowers with credit scores above 660, more than a quarter of loans extended to Apple Card borrowers were to cardholders with credit scores *below* 660.[18] This key difference, and the young age of the card portfolio, helped drive charge-offs on the Apple Card portfolio to around 3 per cent, substantially higher than mainline card issuers like JPMorgan Chase or Bank of America.

Between the red ink and Goldman's wider retreat from consumer banking, reports surfaced by the end of 2023 that Goldman was looking for a way out of its partnership with Apple. As of May 2024, the Apple Card program remains with Goldman, but it is widely anticipated to shift to a new bank partner in the near future.

The challenges with the Goldman partnership may help explain why for its buy now, pay later offering, Apple Pay Later, the company sought to in-source as much of the program as possible, including underwriting and capital to fund the loans, though Apple still relies on Goldman for access to Mastercard's payment rails—though by late June 2024, Apple announced it would cease offering its own BNPL financing, instead relying on partners to offer such plans through Apple Pay. For its part, Goldman has largely withdrawn from the consumer banking business broadly, both under its Marcus brand and through BaaS-like partnerships, though it is expected to continue offering savings accounts in some capacity.

## Goldman's Second BaaS Strategy: Transaction Banking

The Apple partnership, born out of Goldman's consumer initiative, isn't Goldman's only foray into banking-as-a-service. Goldman set out to build a tech-forward, modern transaction banking platform, offering treasury management and payments capabilities for enterprises, beginning in 2018. The offering launched in 2020, with Goldman itself becoming the first user of the platform, which the bank dubbed TxB.

Because Goldman built the platform from scratch, it was able to prioritize application programming interface (API) development from day one, rather than making it an afterthought. Offering API access to its platform enables third parties to directly and programmatically interact with the capabilities TxB offers, including virtual account opening, making payments and checking payments status, and accessing real-time data on balances and transactions, for instance. Those third parties could be *direct* clients of Goldman, or they could be platform business themselves, leveraging TxB's capabilities to add features and functionality to their offering. For instance, Goldman partners with money movement platform Modern Treasury to enable joint customers to embed domestic and international payments into their products; procurement and spend management platform Coupa partners with TxB to enable its customers to make domestic, cross-border, and foreign exchange payments across 124 currencies and 167 countries; and payment facilitator Stripe partners with TxB to power its Stripe Treasury product, which enables platform businesses to offer their end users business bank accounts.

Still, like its consumer BaaS efforts, Goldman's push with transaction banking hasn't been without hiccups. Compared with smaller community banks that rapidly scaled BaaS programs, Goldman's progress has been fairly slow, with just a handful of public partnership announcements, though the measured pace shouldn't be too surprising, given Goldman's considerably larger regulatory profile compared to typical BaaS banks. Even with Goldman's more cautious approach, its efforts have attracted some push back from regulators. For instance, in late 2023, the *Financial Times* reported that the

Federal Reserve Board, one of Goldman's regulators, had raised issues with the bank, including around due diligence and monitoring higher-risk non-bank clients like those sourced through BaaS relationships.[19] The warning reportedly resulted in Goldman ceasing to sign riskier fintech clients.

Goldman Sachs has faced significant turmoil in recent years, with mounting losses in its consumer and platform solutions divisions eventually leading to investors running out of patience and forcing a change in strategy at the bank. Goldman's own consumer and co-brand credit card "platform" efforts are firmly in the rearview mirror. The transaction banking business, housed in the recently created "platform solutions" division, seems to be on firmer footing, though the leader of that division left her role in early 2024.

## US Banking-as-a-Service at a Crossroads

The three companies profiled in this chapter, though not clear-cut successes from a profitability or return on investment perspective, provide a window into the different types of entities engaged in banking-as-a-service (bank vs. middleware; large bank vs. small bank), the challenges of building and scaling such businesses, and the impact of heightened regulatory scrutiny on the industry. That said, as touched on in previous chapters, there are numerous examples of banks successfully executing banking-as-a-service strategies, including long-time players like The Bancorp Bank and Pathward, but also more recent entrants, like Coastal Community and nbkc. And a new crop of "BaaS native" banks, that combine the tech-first mentality of middleware startups with the benefits of holding a bank charter, are seeking to solve a core challenge faced by many older community banks: A dependency on legacy core banking software, like that provided by FIS, Fiserv, and Jack Henry. Firms like Column, Lead Bank, and Grasshopper have built their own technology from the ground up, rather than relying on third-party providers, providing them with greater flexibility and eliminating the need and added complexity of working through a BaaS middleware solution. At the same time, recognizing the opportunity and the demand from traditional community banks to offer BaaS capabilities, the traditional core providers are working to expand their offerings to include this. There are a lot of unknowns facing both US banks and fintechs, including regulation and enforcement, ever-changing consumer preferences, VC investment levels, and the macroeconomic environment, all of which will continue to shape which banking-as-a-service models are sustainable and which are not.

## Endnotes

**1** Mikula, J. (2024) Synapse Files for Bankruptcy, TabaPay to Acquire Assets & Affiliates, *Fintech Business Weekly*, fintechbusinessweekly.substack.com/p/synapse-files-for-bankruptcy-tabapay (archived at https://perma.cc/6J2G-ZL6K)

**2** Mikula, J. (2024) "Full Reconciliation... May Not Be Possible," Synapse Trustee Says, *Fintech Business Weekly*, fintechbusinessweekly.substack.com/p/full-reconciliation-may-not-be-possible (archived at https://perma.cc/652X-KGBX)

**3** Mikula, J. (2022) Evolve's Problematic Partners: Bankruptcies, Regulatory Actions, Abrupt Shutdowns, *Fintech Business Weekly*, fintechbusinessweekly. substack.com/p/evolves-problematic-partners-bankruptcies (archived at https://perma.cc/935U-G7ZX)

**4** Mikula, J. (2023) The Smallest Bank in Tennessee Grew Fast with BaaS. Why It May Give the Entire Industry a Hangover, *Fintech Business Weekly*, fintechbusinessweekly.substack.com/p/the-smallest-bank-in-tennessee-grew (archived at https://perma.cc/AC3D-LYPH)

**5** Mikula, J. (2023) Mercury Seeking $30M from Synapse, Emergency Court Filing Reveals, *Fintech Business Weekly*, fintechbusinessweekly.substack.com/p/mercury-seeking-30m-from-synapse (archived at https://perma.cc/PH37-6RER)

**6** Mikula, J. (2024) Synapse Trustee: $85M Gap vs. What Depositors Are Owed, *Fintech Business Weekly*, fintechbusinessweekly.substack.com/p/synapse-trustee-85m-gap-vs-what-depositors (archived at https://perma.cc/2BZ6-ENGA)

**7** Blue Ridge Bankshares (2022) Blue Ridge Bankshares, Inc. Announces Fourth Quarter and Full Year 2021 Results, www.blueridgebankshares.com/news/news-details/2022/Blue-Ridge-Bankshares-Inc.-Announces-Fourth-Quarter-and-Full-Year-2021-Results/default.aspx (archived at https://perma.cc/C57S-DC43)

**8** Schulte, K. (2022) Embedded Finance Community Banks Move into Banking as a Service, *Virginia Business*, www.virginiabusiness.com/article/embedded-finance (archived at https://perma.cc/6KWS-SZ7F)

**9**   Blue Ridge Bankshares (2022) Investor Presentation May 2022, s201.q4cdn.
       com/389310288/files/doc_presentations/2022/05/1/INVESTOR-
       PRESENTATION-Final-5-4-22.pdf (archived at https://perma.cc/H46S-NN34)

**10**  Seay, L. (2023) Blue Ridge Charts Return to Regulatory Compliance,
       Community Banking Focus, *S&P Global*, www.spglobal.com/
       marketintelligence/en/news-insights/latest-news-headlines/blue-ridge-charts-
       return-to-regulatory-compliance-community-banking-focus-77112701
       (archived at https://perma.cc/V65V-PF8D)

**11**  Mikula, J. (2024) Blue Ridge's Brokered Deposits Soar 1,000% As It
       Offboards Fintechs, *Fintech Business Weekly*, fintechbusinessweekly.substack.
       com/p/blue-ridges-brokered-deposits-soar (archived at https://perma.cc/2X63-
       RTYS)

**12**  Goldman Sachs (2015) Goldman Sachs Bank USA to Acquire the Online
       Deposit Platform and Assume the Deposits of GE Capital Bank, www.
       goldmansachs.com/media-relations/press-releases/current/announcement-
       13-aug-2015.html (archived at https://perma.cc/KSS2-CWWC)

**13**  Son, H. (2019) Goldman Sachs CEO says Apple Card is the Most Successful
       Credit Card Launch Ever, *CNBC*, www.cnbc.com/2019/10/15/goldman-sachs-
       ceo-says-apple-card-is-the-most-successful-credit-card-launch-ever.html
       (archived at https://perma.cc/6PN3-AETJ)

**14**  Horowitz, J. (2019) Tim Cook says Apple Card is a Game Changer. Experts
       Are Not So Sure, *CNN*, www.cnn.com/2019/03/25/tech/apple-credit-card/
       index.html (archived at https://perma.cc/7EW2-JM23)

**15**  LaCapra, L. and Ma, W. (2023) How the Partnership Between Apple and
       Goldman Sachs Soured, *The Information*, www.theinformation.com/articles/
       how-the-partnership-between-apple-and-goldman-soured (archived at https://
       perma.cc/TW5U-7GYU)

**16**  Ogden, M. (2019) Created by Apple, Not a Bank, *Credit Union Times*,
       www.cutimes.com/2019/03/28/created-by-apple-not-a-bank/ (archived at
       https://perma.cc/RP53-6AFF)

**17**  Vigdor, N. (2019) Apple Card Investigated After Gender Discrimination
       Complaints, *New York Times*, www.nytimes.com/2019/11/10/business/
       Apple-credit-card-investigation.html (archived at https://perma.cc/6YZ6-
       E7UN)

**18**  Son, H. (2022) Goldman's Apple Card Business Has a Surprising Subprime
       Problem, *CNBC*, www.cnbc.com/2022/09/12/goldmans-gs-apple-card-
       business-has-a-surprising-subprime-problem.html (archived at https://perma.
       cc/BA4D-JEBB)

**19**  Franklin, J. and Quinio, A. (2023) Fed Warned Goldman Sachs Over Risk and
       Compliance Oversight at Fintech Unit, *Financial Times*, www.ft.com/content/
       d17609f2-e693-4d41-95ea-602878abeccf (archived at https://perma.cc/
       RA98-YRAA)

# 10

# UK/EU Case Studies: Railsr, Griffin, Solaris

CHAPTER OBJECTIVES

Much of the earlier chapters of this book focus on banking-as-a-service in the US context, but BaaS and the use cases it enables, particularly embedded finance, are global phenomena. However, while BaaS exists in markets around the world, operating and business models in specific jurisdictions are strongly shaped by local regulatory and banking market factors. For example, in the United Kingdom and the European Union, numerous differences in the history and present of the financial services market, regulatory environment, license types available, and consumer habits and preferences make for substantial differences in banking-as-a-service models. In this chapter, we'll explore some of the factors shaping banking-as-a-service and fintech in the UK and EU and illustrate what BaaS looks like with case studies of three firms in the region: Griffin, Railsr, and Solaris.

There's one foundational difference between the US and European countries: The UK and EU countries tend to have substantially fewer banks and more concentrated banking markets than the US. In the UK, the "Big 5," HSBC, Barclays, Lloyds, NatWest (which includes RBS), and Standard Chartered, dominate the market. The five largest UK commercial banks hold just shy of 60 per cent of all commercial banking assets in the country.[1]

As of July 2023, the UK's Prudential Regulation Authority lists 336 institutions authorized to accept deposits, including banks and building societies.[2] With a population of about 67 million, that works out to approximately five chartered institutions per million people, compared to 28 chartered institutions per million people in the United States.

Highly concentrated banking sectors dominated by a few big names are the rule, not the exception, across EU countries. In the Netherlands, the five largest banks, which include ABN Amro, ING, and Rabobank, hold about 93 per cent of assets in the commercial banking system. In Ireland, the five largest banks hold about 86 per cent of commercial banking assets. And in Germany, the top five banks hold an astounding 94.3 per cent of assets.[3] While a high degree of asset concentration is the norm, the number of institutions compared to population size does vary substantially. For instance, the Netherlands has about five chartered banks per million people (including branches of foreign banks authorized to operate in the country), while Ireland has about 52 licensed institutions per million people (including not-for-profit credit unions and authorized foreign branches).

This is all to say, most markets in the UK and EU lack the type of "community banks" that are common banking-as-a-service partners in the US, owing to the US's unique dual state/federal banking system and historic restrictions on interstate branch banking. In the banking-as-a-service model, banks make up the "supply side," enabling their non-bank partners to leverage their licenses to distribute regulated products. While there are no doubt variations across the 44 countries that make up Europe, including the UK and the 27 that belong to the European Union, banking markets in these countries generally have fewer banks and are much more highly concentrated.

Another key difference impacting the dynamics of BaaS in the UK and EU: The relative ease of obtaining a license to engage in regulated activities, thereby reducing demand for BaaS providers. Since the 2008 global financial crisis, obtaining a de novo bank license in the US has become significantly more difficult, with an average of six new banks opening per year since 2010, compared to an average of 132 new banks forming per year from 2000 to 2009.⁴ Faced with the difficulty of obtaining a de novo license, many US fintechs, including those seeking to operate BaaS business models like Column or Lead Bank, have instead acquired existing banks. But bank M&A, especially so-called "charter strip" acquisitions, in which an institution is acquired primarily for its existing charter and repurposed for a new business model, has also faced increasing roadblocks in the US. By comparison, both customer-facing fintechs and firms seeking to offer BaaS capabilities have had a relatively easier time in the UK and EU. Examples of firms that obtained newly granted bank licenses in the UK and EU include consumer and SMB neobanks like Monzo, Starling, Revolut, bunq, and N26, and fully licensed banks operating BaaS or BaaS-like models, including ClearBank, Solaris, Griffin, and Banking Circle.

But it's not just that it can be easier to obtain a de novo bank license. The UK and EU offer a variety of other types of license types, including for e-money institutions, payments institutions, and payment initiation service providers.⁵ These alternate license types do not enable companies to hold customer deposits but do allow them to engage in a subset of activities that fully licensed banks can do. More importantly, they are typically faster to obtain than a bank license and have significantly lower capital requirements.

E-money institutions, or EMIs for short, are permitted to issue electronic money (e-money) and provide payments services. E-money is a digital representation of currency that can be used for making payments. Common use cases of EMI licenses include neobanking, offering prepaid cards, digital wallets, and peer-to-peer payments. E-money institutions are required to safeguard user funds, which they most commonly do by segregating them and holding them at an insured depository institution. EMIs are permitted to hold customer funds indefinitely and enjoy the benefit of "passporting," allowing a company to secure its license in a single country but operate across the EU. Although it is worth noting that, post-Brexit, UK firms seeking to operate in the EU need to obtain a license from an EU member state and vice-versa. EMIs are generally eligible to be principal members of Visa and Mastercard, thus enabling them to issue debit cards without relying on a bank partner.

Payments institutions, or PIs, can also provide payments services, but there are some key differences compared to EMIs. Payments institutions can only hold customer funds for a short period necessary to execute transactions, rather than indefinitely, as EMIs can. Primary use cases for PIs include credit transfers, direct debits, payment instrument acquisition or issuing, and remittance services. PIs cannot issue e-money, which is the primary difference from EMIs. The licensing process is typically simpler and minimum capital requirements lower than for e-money institutions. A payment institution can also "passport," or operate across the EU, after obtaining its license in an EU member country and appropriate permissions in the countries in which it wishes to operate.

Payment initiation service providers, or PISPs, arose in part from the UK and EU's efforts to encourage and codify open banking. PISPs are a specific type of payment institution and generally require being licensed as such. Like other payments institutions, properly licensed PISPs are eligible to operate across the EU on their home country licenses, once they've secured the necessary permissions to do so. Payment initiation services can connect to a user's bank account through open banking in order to initiate a payment on their behalf. A common use case for PISPs is e-commerce merchants wanting to offer account-to-account payments. Another example is automated financial management tools that leverage PISPs to automate money movement between accounts on a user's behalf.

The UK and most EU countries also offer non-bank consumer lending licenses. While it's possible for non-bank lenders to obtain their own licenses in the US as well, thereby eliminating the need to partner with a bank, as covered in Chapter 2, those licenses are issued on a state-by-state basis. Product features like minimum and maximum loan amounts, term, and interest rate also vary by US state, making a state lending license approach unpalatable for lenders that want to operate on a nationwide scale. But in the UK and EU, such lending licenses are granted at the national level, meaning non-bank lenders only need apply for a single license, have one rather than numerous regulators overseeing them, and can offer a single, consistent product across a given country.

Specific regulations governing consumer credit can vary substantially by country across the UK and the EU, as do consumer preferences and habits. The availability of consumer credit data and how it is used for underwriting also varies substantially by country. For instance, the UK consumer credit market fairly closely resembles the US: The same three major credit bureaus, Experian, Equifax, and Transunion, operate in the country, maintaining records of consumers' outstanding debts and repayment histories. Similar unsecured consumer credit products, used primarily to finance consumption spending, are available, including charge and credit cards, installment loans, and buy now, pay later. In general, UK consumers carry high levels of debt, especially compared to some other European countries. In 2022, household debt in the UK reached 146 per cent of net disposable income, though this metric includes mortgage debt; for the same year in the US, household debt was 102 per cent of net disposable income.[6]

While trends vary country to country, consumer credit for consumption—credit cards, personal loans and the like—tend to be significantly less popular in many EU countries, for both cultural and historical reasons as well as country-specific regulation. For instance, Germans have a reputation for fiscal discipline and for taking a dim view of debt. Cash remains the most popular payment method in the country, accounting for nearly 60 per cent of transactions, according to the Deutsche Bundesbank.[7] Germany's next door neighbor, the Netherlands, is also historically a debt-averse society, apart from mortgages, but favors debit cards to cash: 85 per cent of point-of-sale transactions were via debit card as of 2021, according to the Dutch central bank.[8] Country-specific regulations, particularly interest rate caps, can make consumer lending, especially to riskier segments, economically unviable, thereby limiting supply of credit. In EU countries with rate caps, which includes many of the largest member states, the caps tend to be lower than in the US, where many consumer lenders will charge as much as 36 per cent on an annualized basis. Rewards credit cards, a major driver of adoption and usage in the US, are less common and offer less generous rewards in the UK and EU, owing at least partially to lower credit card interchange rates.

Interchange rates for both credit and debit are capped in the UK and EU. Issuers can generally receive a maximum of 0.20 per cent on consumer debit transactions and 0.30 per cent for consumer credit transactions for intra-EU and intra-UK transactions, though rates may be higher for cards issued outside of the EU or UK.[9]

In addition to substantially eroding issuers' ability to fund card rewards, lower interchange also dramatically reduces a key revenue source for many fintechs. As discussed in Chapter 3, interchange is a primary revenue source for many US fintechs, as it is about seven times higher for debit and as much as nine times higher for credit transactions than in the UK and EU. Lower interchange rates mean fintech business models that depend on interchange as a revenue source are less attractive, helping to explain lower rates of VC funding and consumer fintech businesses in the UK and EU.

The UK and EU have a variety of factors shaping both supply of and demand for banking-as-a-service capabilities. They generally lack the US's history of community banks and tend to be dominated by a few large banks, which may not be capable of or interested in BaaS business models. The availability of and capabilities provided by alternate kinds of licenses, including e-money, payments institution, and lending licenses, reduces the need for fintechs to partner with banks. And lower demand for credit, interest rate caps, and lower interchange fees may reduce demand and limit the viability of some fintech business models, thereby reducing demand for BaaS capabilities.

This is all to say, while there certainly is a banking-as-a-service ecosystem in the UK and EU, including companies like Griffin, Solaris, and Railsr, the use cases, dynamics, and economics of the BaaS market differ considerably from the United States.

## Railsr: From Aggressive Growth to Bankruptcy

Railsr, formerly known as Railsbank, was an early pioneer of the banking-as-a-service model in the UK. The company was founded in 2016 by Nigel Verdon, who had previously served as CEO of international payments firm Currency Cloud, and Clive Mitchell, previously a direc-tor at PwC and the Chief Information Officer of a UK hospitality company. Railsr took advantage of the UK's e-money license to offer BaaS capabilities without the need to hold its own bank license or to partner with a bank, an approach that isn't possible in the US. Railsr had aggressive, global ambitions, seeking to become something akin to payments facilitator Stripe, but for banking: A single, seamless plat-form that could enable fintechs and brands to quickly and easily offer financial services around the world.

The UK's Financial Conduct Authority approved Railsr's applica-tion for an e-money license in the spring of 2018. Necessitated by the official exit of the UK from the European Union in January 2020, Railsr also secured an e-money license in Lithuania, enabling it to operate across the EU. Railsr expanded into Asia-Pacific, opening an office in Singapore in 2019, and launched its "Credit Card-as-a-Service" offering in the US, through its partnership with BaaS-focused bank Cross River. Railsr expanded into Australia through a partner-ship with fully licensed startup bank Volt. And Railsr beefed up its capabilities in its home market by acquiring the UK assets of Wirecard after the company's fraud scandal and subsequent collapse.

Through its own EMI licenses and its bank partnerships, Railsr's capabilities have included current (checking) accounts, open banking, ledger transfer, safeguarding of assets, BIN sponsorship, physical and virtual card issuance (prepaid, debit, credit), mobile wallets, account-to-account payments, cross-border and foreign exchange transactions, and select lending products. In 2022, Railsr boasted more than 250 customers, who, in turn, supported 5.5 million end-user accounts. Customers of Railsr have included UK earned wage access firm Wagestream, financial management app Plum, health rewards plat-form Paceline, expense management solution SimpledCard, spend and investment app Unifimoney, Crypto.com, and numerous others.

The company raised over $130 million in equity and, at one point, was valued at nearly $1 billion.[10] But, Railsr's dependency on third-party partners, specifically Volt, compliance issues in its EU operations, and difficulty digesting its acquisition of Wirecard's UK assets would catch up with the company, ultimately leading to a "pre-pack" bankruptcy process in which the company was acquired by a consortium of investors for about £414,000.[11]

Railsr's Australian bank partner, Volt, shut down its deposit-taking business in 2022 and forfeited its banking license, after failing to raise additional needed capital. The move left Railsr, which operated as Railspay in Australia, without a bank partner in the country. Railsr's e-money license to operate in the EU, issued by the central bank of Lithuania and held by its PayrNet subsidiary, was revoked in 2023, due to what the regulator described as "serious, systematic and multiple violations" of payments laws and anti-money laundering regulations.[12]

The issues highlighted by the Lithuanian central bank are reminiscent of some of the challenges and resulting regulatory actions against US banks in the banking-as-a-service space. The regulators found that Railsr, through its PayrNet entity, did not conduct adequate and, in some cases, any due diligence on intermediaries it worked with; did not control whom intermediaries provided services to, including how (or if) those intermediaries conducted necessary money laundering and terrorist financing checks; did not adequately perform transaction monitoring; and did not consistently report suspicious client operations, among numerous other alleged shortcomings. Lithuanian regulators eventually forced the subsidiary into bankruptcy.

Ultimately, the challenges posed by developments in Australia and the EU, the difficulty of incorporating its acquisition of Wirecard's UK assets, and its effort to launch in the US market proved too much for Railsr. After the bankruptcy and sale process, a new executive management team was appointed, and Railsr continues to operate in the UK.

If there is any lesson to learn from the Railsr case, it's arguably that, in BaaS, there are fewer economies of scale when expanding to distinct geographies, which come with their own regulatory requirements, licensing regimes, and economic and business models.

## Griffin: A Newly Founded, BaaS-Native Bank

Griffin, also based in the UK, was founded in 2017. As of spring 2024, Griffin has raised about $65 million in equity from investors like EQT Ventures, Notion Capital, and MassMutual Ventures. Griffin has pursued a notably different strategy than Railsr. Instead of obtaining an e-money license or serving only as a software layer that partners with licensed institutions, Griffin decided to pursue its own banking license. While obtaining a de novo bank license in the UK is arguably easier than in the US, it is typically still a years-long endeavor. Griffin submitted its application for a UK bank license in 2022, received permission to operate with restrictions in a process known as "mobilization" in the UK in March 2023, and launched as a fully operational bank in March 2024.

Griffin isn't the only fully licensed bank in the UK providing banking-as-a-service capabilities. Incumbent NatWest offers a platform dubbed Boxed, which supports digital wallets, card issuing, and lending products. NatWest also entered into a strategic partnership with Vodeno, a European software firm providing an API-based technology platform to enable businesses to embed financial products, including payments, deposits, point-of-sale credit, and merchant cash advances. While NatWest is one of the largest banks in the UK and benefits from deep experience and a strong balance sheet, it also has legacy technical infrastructure and competing priorities.

In contrast to a legacy firm like NatWest, Griffin operates what some are now calling a "headless" banking model, in which Griffin holds the bank license and manages its balance sheet, but distribution of products is *only* through third-party partners, either fintechs or brands offering embedded financial products. Griffin itself is not a customer-facing brand. This can also be thought of as a kind of wholesale/retail model, in which Griffin is a "wholesaler" of banking services to its fintech and brand clients, who, in turn, are "retailers" of financial services to end users. The approach is generally comparable to Column's in the US, though Column obtained its charter through an acquisition and thus does continue to operate a small retail operation, including a single bank branch. Like Column, Griffin is targeted to a developer audience. It describes itself as "API-first and developer focused" and offering "best-in-class technology." With clear documentation and a developer sandbox, builders can test Griffin's offerings immediately, without the need to complete any paperwork or sign NDAs.

As of spring 2024, Griffin's capabilities include customer onboarding (KYC/KYB processes, including AML and fraud checks), safeguarding accounts, which can be used to hold segregated funds for e-money and payments institutions, client money accounts, and access to UK payment rails that include Faster Payments, Bacs, and CHAPS. Griffin plans to add support for prepaid and debit physical and virtual cards and direct debits in the near future.

With Griffin only receiving full authorization from UK regulators in March 2024, how it will be received by the market remains to be seen. During its mobilization phase, the firm worked with a number of unspecified fintechs to validate its products and begin scaling its operations. Known customers include UK bulk payment platform Comma, which leverages Griffin's API-delivered KYB capabilities to streamline its onboarding process, and Hong Kong-based ProMEX, which built out a prototype of its carbon credit trading platform using Griffin's sandbox environment.

Griffin's founders have said that, now that the bank is fully operational, it will focus on providing services to firms in industries that have undergone "digital transformations" in recent years, but remain underserved by establishment banks.

## Solaris: The European Union's Leading BaaS Bank

Berlin-based Solaris, like the UK's Griffin, is a fully licensed bank, also referred to as a "credit institution" in Europe. In addition to its bank license, Solaris also holds e-money institution licenses in the EU and the UK. Solaris's German bank and Lithuanian e-money licenses enable it to offer financial services through the European Economic Area, and its UK e-money license enables it to offer corresponding services in the UK as well.

The company, previously known as Solarisbank, was founded in 2015 as part of German startup studio Finleap. Solaris officially launched in early 2016, upon securing its bank license from Germany's banking regulator, BaFin. As of spring 2024, Solaris has raised a whopping €481 million in equity from investors that include Finleap, ABN AMRO's Digital Impact Fund, SBI Group, Visa, Samsung Catalyst Fund, and numerous others. As of 2022, the company was valued at about $1.6 billion.[13] Solaris most recently raised funds in early 2024 to facilitate the onboarding of the credit card program of ADAC, a European automobile association, as well as to strengthen its core capital and continue investments in its banking platform.

Solaris offers capabilities across digital banking, payments, lending, and identity, including deposits and current accounts, payment cards, buy now pay later, consumer loans, and KYC. Like the UK's Griffin and US's Column, Solaris could be considered a "headless" bank, in that it doesn't directly serve end users, but rather only works with fintechs or brands that use Solaris's capabilities and charter to offer regulated products to their customers. Unlike legacy banks trying their hand at BaaS, similarly to the UK's Griffin, Solaris was purpose-built from scratch as an API-first financial institution. Its infrastructure is entirely cloud-based, it enables clients to manage customer accounts and data in real time, and it simplifies how clients use its data for analysis and decision making. Solaris boasts more than 90 partners, including household names like Samsung and American Express, as well as fintech startups like Clanq, Finom, Vivid Money, and Tomorrow.

Solaris has also pursued higher-risk clients in the cryptocurrency industry. The company has worked with crypto firms that include Coinbase and Seychelles-based Huobi, for instance. Solaris's work with such clients may have helped attract regulatory scrutiny. In 2020, the German bank regulator, BaFin, required Solaris to be supervised by a special auditor, a role ultimately filled by audit firm PwC. And in January 2023, the company announced it would be required to seek permission from BaFin before onboarding any new business relationships. Solaris hasn't been the only German fintech to run into issues; Berlin-based fully licensed neobank N26 has also faced scrutiny and restrictions from BaFin. The need to seek regulatory permission before onboarding new BaaS customers is reminiscent of similar regulatory restrictions on US banks that have run into trouble. In March 2024, BaFin fined Solaris €6.5 million for failing to report suspicious transactions in a timely manner. Solaris "has systemically submitted suspicious money laundering reports late," BaFin concluded.[14]

Solaris has, no doubt, run into some growing pains with regard to its regulatory issues. Still, such setbacks are not uncommon in *any* bank, let alone a newly formed one operating a relatively novel business model. Solaris's full bank charter, robust technology stack, and impressive stable of customers suggest the company is well-positioned to continue as a top BaaS provider in Europe.

## UK and EU BaaS Shaped by Regional Differences

The wider forces that have and continue to shape banking-as-a-service in the US, including levels of venture capital funding, the health of the fintech ecosystem, and macroeconomic conditions equally impact the UK and EU. But there are also significant differences that drive the UK and EU's unique BaaS ecosystem: Banking markets with a markedly different history than the US, including substantially fewer chartered institutions and greater concentration, the existence of e-money, payment institution, and payment initiation service provider licenses, key differences in regulation, and different needs and preferences of consumers.

The institutions examined here, Railsr, Griffin, and Solaris, offer a snapshot of BaaS approaches in the UK and EU, but they are far from the only providers. Incumbents, including NatWest and Société Générale, which acquired technology platform Treezor in 2019, also are exploring BaaS and embedded finance as distribution channels. Other startups in the space include tokyo, ClearBank, weavr, and Swan. Though the BaaS market in the UK and EU hasn't been without turbulence, it hasn't seen nearly as severe a regulatory or economic fallout as in the US, and is well-positioned to continue developing to take advantage of the market opportunity.

# Endnotes

**1**  World Bank Group (n.d.) Global Financial Development, databank.worldbank. org/source/global-financial-development/Series/GFDD.OI.06 (archived at https://perma.cc/38XV-B5R8)

**2**  Bank of England (n.d.) Institutions in the UK Banking Sector, www. bankofengland.co.uk/statistics/data-collection/institutions-in-the-uk-banking-sector (archived at https://perma.cc/5GZ7-8Z9V)

**3**  World Bank Group (n.d.) Global Financial Development, databank.worldbank. org/source/global-financial-development/Series/GFDD.OI.06 (archived at https://perma.cc/N4YX-DN6X)

**4**  Adams, R. and Gramlich, J. (2014) Where Are All the New Banks? The Role of Regulatory Burden in New Charter Creation, *Finance and Economics Discussion Series of Federal Reserve Board*, www.federalreserve.gov/econresdata/feds/2014/ files/2014113pap.pdf (archived at https://perma.cc/Q5ZF-78LB)

**5**  PSP Lab (2021) What Is an E-Money Institution UK?, psplab.com/kb/ what-is-e-money-institution-uk/ (archived at https://perma.cc/47RJ-HDKE)

**6**  OECD (2024) Household Debt, data.oecd.org/hha/household-debt.htm (archived at https://perma.cc/J56N-SFKQ)

**7**  Deutsche Bundesbank (2022) Payment Behaviour in Germany in 2021, www. bundesbank.de/en/press/press-releases/payment-behaviour-in-germany-in-2021-894120 (archived at https://perma.cc/WL26-ZXG6)

**8**  DeNederlandscheBank (2021) Point-of-Sale Payments in 2021, www.dnb.nl/ media/jzvoftlz/point-of-sale-payments-in-2021.pdf (archived at https://perma. cc/5C9V-HH9P)

**9**  Visa (2024) Interchange Fees, www.visa.co.uk/about-visa/visa-in-europe/ fees-and-interchange.html (archived at https://perma.cc/G4FG-GZTZ)

**10**  Lunden, I. (2023) Railsr, the UK Embedded Fintech Once Valued at Nearly $1B, Goes into Bankruptcy Protection under New Consortium Owner, *TechCrunch*, techcrunch.com/2023/03/09/railsr-off-the-rails-embedded-finance/ (archived at https://perma.cc/7YNA-TZ96)

**11**  Hurley, J. (2023) Railsr Sold for £414,000 to "Related Parties" in Pre-Pack Deal, *The Times*, www.thetimes.com/business-money/money/article/railsr-sold-for-414-000-to-related-parties-in-pre-pack-deal-mr9qzmk3r (archived at https://perma.cc/TCN8-RXGV)

**12**  Mikula, J. (2023) Off the Rails: Bankrupt Railsr's E-Money Entity Shutdown, Criminal Charges Possible, *Fintech Business Weekly*, fintechbusinessweekly. substack.com/p/off-the-rails-bankrupt-railsrs-e (archived at https://perma. cc/4Z6P-C395)

**13**   Lunden, I. (2023) Solaris Raises $42M at a Flat $1.6B Valuation to Expand in Embedded Finance After a Rough 2022, *TechCrunch*, techcrunch. com/2023/07/11/solaris-embedded-finance-42-million/ (archived at https:// perma.cc/W98K-BPZN)

**14**   Houlihan, A. (2024) Bafin Fines German Fintech Solaris SE €6.5M for Late Filing STRs, *AML Intelligence*, www.amlintelligence.com/2024/03/news-bafin-fines-german-fintech-solaris-se-e6-5m-for-late-filing-strs/ (archived at https:// perma.cc/A6VH-ZPFT)

# 11

# Latin America Case Studies: Dock, Pomelo

CHAPTER OBJECTIVES

In this chapter, we'll review key attributes and similarities and differences compared to other markets of the two largest countries in Latin America: Brazil and Mexico. We'll also learn how those characteristics have shaped the fintech market and demand for banking-as-a-service and take a look at two regional leaders in the space: Dock and Pomelo.

Like the UK and European Union, the banking market, regulatory and licensing structure, demographics, and consumer preferences in Latin America are both diverse, across the region, and unique, particularly in comparison with the United States. Latin America encompasses the region from Mexico to the tip of Argentina and Chile. Nearly 660 million people live across 33 countries, with a wide variety of historic, linguistic, cultural, and legal roots and traditions. Many venture investors focus on the two largest markets in Latin America, by both population and size of their economies: Mexico and Brazil. As venture funding flows, so too does new company formation and, often, innovation.

## Mexico: A Vibrant Market with Regulatory Headwinds

Despite being neighbors with strongly interlinked economies, including in the financial sector, Mexico's banking market looks and operates quite differently than the United States'. Mexico's banking sector is historically highly concentrated, with about 50 commercial banks, of which just six control about 75 per cent of the banking system's assets: BBVA Bancomer, Santander, CitiBanamex, Banorte, HSBC, and Scotiabank. The country's banking sector has strong links to Spain, as both BBVA and Santander are headquartered in the country; Banamex is part of US-based Citigroup; and British bank HSBC's footprint in the country came via its acquisition of Bital in 2002. Mexico also has relatively fewer branches than the United States, with about 12.8 branches per 100,000 adults, compared to nearly 27.2 branches per 100,000 in the US.[1]

In addition to large commercial banks, other types of banking and financial services licenses exist in the country, including Sociedades Financieras Populares (SOFIPOs), which are intended to serve low-income individuals and micro-, small-, and medium-sized enterprises (somewhat comparable to community banks or credit unions in the US); Sociedades Financieras de Objeto Múltiple (SOFOMs), which are non-banks that may be regulated or non-regulated and provide services like lending, leasing, and factoring; and Sociedades Financieras de Objeto Limitado (SOFOLs), which are non-banks that specialize in mortgage and real-estate financing.[2]

The relatively small number of banks, high degree of concentration in the sector, and outsized market power that incumbents are able to exercise may contribute to the paucity of new bank formation in the country, though established players have worked to extend their reach and promote access and inclusion in the formal financial sector through the launch of digital-only efforts. For instance, in early 2024, Banorte launched its own digital-only bank, Bineo, and Santander plans to expand its digital-only brand, Openbank, to Mexico in the back half of 2024.

Despite its well-developed establishment financial sector, banking and credit penetration in Mexico is substantially below not only the

United States, but also peers in Latin America. Nearly half of Mexicans over 15 are unbanked, compared to about 16 per cent unbanked in Brazil and about 5 per cent in the US.[3] Likewise, access to credit is constrained, as demonstrated by the country's 34 per cent private credit-to-GDP ratio; the same measure is about 72 per cent in Brazil and over 215 per cent in the US.[4]

Perhaps unsurprisingly, given its high rate of unbanked and low credit penetration, is the extremely high preference for cash in Mexico compared with the US or peer group economies in Latin America. Prior to the Covid-19 pandemic, as much as 90 per cent of the population preferred to use cash as their primary means of payment, though this has since declined somewhat to about 82 per cent in 2022.[5] Cash preference remains elevated even when consumers also have access to card and electronic payment methods. By comparison, in Brazil, cash use continues to decline, especially since the introduction and rapid adoption of the country's instant payment system, Pix. Since the introduction of Pix in 2020, cash withdrawals at ATMs and bank branches have dropped some 25 per cent.[6] In 2023, estimates suggest about 30 per cent of point-of-sale transactions in Brazil were in cash. In the US, cash usage has been steadily declining, with cash being used for about 18 per cent of all transactions in 2022.[7]

Why the radical difference in bank account and credit penetration and cash usage in Mexico? Significantly higher rates of employment in the "informal" economy, tax avoidance, lack of trust in the financial system and banks, and high fees and poor customer service all serve as disincentives, especially to lower-income households, to participate in the formal banking sector. Analysis indicates 60 per cent of Mexican workers have informal jobs, meaning they lack employment protections and benefits, like social security.

Workers who are not formally employed may be paid in cash or otherwise lack documentation of their income, leading to a desire to avoid the actual or perceived surveillance that comes from using the formal banking system and resulting possible costs or penalties from the tax authorities. Trust in the banking system in Latin America broadly, including in Mexico, is considerably lower than in the United States, owing to the region's history of financial instability, currency crises and inflation, and bank failures. Mexico's highly concentrated banking sector lacks competitive pressure, contributing to high fees and poor service. Notably, around 30 per cent of Mexican banks' revenue is derived from punitive fee income, compared to just 4 per cent in the US banking sector.[8]

In addition to the above, there are also specific factors on the credit side contributing to significantly diminished access. One major challenge is a lack of data necessary to underwrite Mexican borrowers. The proportion of the population covered by the main national credit reporting agency, Buró de Crédito, is significantly lower than developed economies. If coverage of Mexican consumers is poor, data necessary to underwrite small businesses is even more difficult to come by. Mexican consumers also exhibit materially different repayment behavior than the US, with substantially higher delinquency and default rates. This may owe in part to scarcer data, making it more difficult to underwrite consumers, and actual or perceived lower consequences for non-payment.

There are a handful of other key differences worth touching on. Unlike the US, where the central bank has a dual mandate to ensure price stability and promote full employment, Mexico's central bank, Banxico, only focuses on managing inflation, stemming from the country's struggle with high rates of inflation and currency devaluation in the 1990s. Given its proximity to and interlinkages with the US economy, changes in Mexico's interest rate tend to closely mirror the US's rate, though, owing to structurally higher inflation, Mexico's nominal interest rate tends to be materially higher than the US's.

When it comes to setting interchange rates, a key source of revenue in fintech and banking-as-a-service business models, unlike most countries, where the card schemes set the rates themselves, the Mexican bank association set these rates until the early 2000s. Recognizing market problems, including high concentration of issuers and acquirers, limited use of payment cards, and limited network development, Banxico began to regulate credit and debit interchange rates, which currently have a weighted average of about 1.53 per cent and 1.15 per cent, respectively. While higher than interchange rates in the EU, these rates are lower than those in the United States, where, as discussed before, all credit cards and debit cards issued by banks with less than $10 billion in assets are not capped by regulation. In addition to global card schemes, like Visa and Mastercard, Mexico also has two domestic schemes, PROSA and EGlobal, though, in late 2023, Visa reached a definitive agreement to acquire a majority stake in PROSA.

Recognizing the lack of competition in the Mexican banking sector and the negative impact on financial access and inclusion, particularly for lower-income households and micro and small businesses, the Mexican government passed the Ley para Regular las Instituciones de Tecnología Financiera, popularly known as the "Fintech Law," in 2018. Explicit goals in passing the law included:[9]

- Promoting financial inclusion
- Providing legal security to technological financial services users
- Triggering greater competition in the financial services market
- Increasing the number of participants in the financial sector
- Preventing money laundering activities through electronic means
- Regulating the transactions with digital assets in Mexico

The far-reaching law touches on numerous areas, including open banking and digital assets, as well as defining two new types of licensed Financial Technology Institutions (FTIs) in Mexico: Institución de Fondeo Colectivo (IFCs), which are permitted to carry out debt and equity crowdfunding activities; and Institución de Fondos de Pago Electrónico (IFPEs), which are roughly comparable to e-money institutions in the UK and EU.[10] The impacts and success of the law have been uneven. Mexico boasts a vibrant fintech ecosystem, with about $1.7 billion in venture investments into fintech companies in 2021 and nearly 800 fintech companies operating in the country as of 2023. But, overcoming consumer preferences, especially for cash and in-person transactions, remains a challenge. Despite the challenges, Mexican fintech firms continue to make inroads across a variety of product categories. Though one of the most successful "fintechs," e-money institution Spin, is owned by and distributed through the omnipresent Mexican convenience store Oxxo, which speaks to the need for physical touchpoints to facilitate cash-in and cash-out transactions.

When it comes to banking-as-a-service operating models specifically, Mexico has proven to be a somewhat difficult market to navigate. In the period when the Fintech Law was first going into effect, numerous firms were allowed to operate on a "transitory" basis, while they sought licensing under the new law, including firms that were operating BaaS-like models. But ultimately, several companies, including those using their licenses to provide services to other, customer-facing firms, were denied licenses, causing significant challenges in the sector.[11] Deposit and debit BaaS programs particularly faced skepticism from regulators concerned about disaggregating customer-facing firms from where users' funds are actually held, though there are IFPEs seeking to provide BaaS-like capabilities for deposits and debit card issuing.

There are more differences and nuances to the establishment banking market, regulatory considerations, fintech ecosystem, and consumer preferences and behavior than can reasonably be unpacked here. In some ways, Mexico looks more like the UK and EU, with a highly concentrated banking sector that has shown little interest in powering BaaS business models, as the risk is often perceived to outweigh the benefits. On the other hand, Mexico faces a host of idiosyncratic factors, particularly its high rate of informal employment and cash use and low rates of bank account penetration and access to credit. So while there are certainly unmet needs that represent potential products and markets BaaS could help serve, particularly bridging the gap between cash and digital payments and access to credit, there are also significant challenges and barriers to doing so.

## Brazil: Counting on BaaS to Expand Financial Access and Inclusion

Like Mexico, the banking sector in Brazil historically has been highly concentrated. The five largest banks by assets account for just shy of

80 per cent of assets in the country.[12] Those five banks, in order of asset size, are: Itaú Unibanco, Banco do Brasil, Banco Bradesco, Caixa Econômica Federal, and Santander Brasil. In total, Brazil boasts 16 public banks, 104 private banks, and 71 banks controlled by foreign capital, for a total of 191 banks.[13] The number of bank branches in Brazil peaked in 2017 at over 21,000, but has since begun declining. As of 2022, there were around 17,000 bank branches in the country, or about 17.1 branches per 100,000 adults, which is higher than Mexico but below the United States.[14] That the number of branches began declining after 2017 is at least partially a reflection of the growth of digital distribution, with startups like NuBank quickly growing, and new payment mechanisms, like the central bank-operated real-time payment network Pix.

The Brazilian regulatory establishment consists of four key regulators: CVM, for securities; the Central Bank, which oversees prudential and financial institution supervision; SUSEP, for insurance; and PREVIC, for pensions. Brazilian regulators distinguish between a number of types of financial institutions, including Bancos Comerciais (commercial banks), Bancos de Investimento (investment banks), Sociedades de Poupança ou Empréstimos (savings banks), Financeiras (credit, financing, and investment companies), and Corretoras (brokerage firms), among other types of entities. Brazilian regulation also allows for payments institutions, including issuers of electronic currency, issuers of post-paid instruments, and "enrollers," which are payments entities that enroll a user to accept forms of payment issued by payments institutions without themselves managing the payment account. Payments institutions include entities that are roughly comparable to e-money institutions in other jurisdictions.

Despite its incumbent banking system sharing some commonalities with Mexico, Brazil boasts substantially higher rates of bank account adoption and credit penetration. About 84 per cent of Brazilians over 15 have an account at a financial institution or mobile money provider.[15] And domestic credit to the private sector reached nearly 72 per cent of GDP in 2022, behind the US but substantially ahead of Mexico.[16] This may owe, at least in part, to relatively higher levels of formal employment, with recent data suggesting about 66 per cent of those working are doing so in formal arrangements.[17] This compares favorably to Mexico. A substantially larger proportion of the population is also covered by credit bureaus in the country, with the World Bank estimating slightly over 80 per cent of adults were listed with current information on debts and repayments as of 2019.

Interchange rates in Brazil are regulated. Bank-issued debit cards are capped at a maximum 0.5 per cent interchange. Prepaid cards, which function similarly but are more commonly issued by fintechs in Brazil, are capped at a maximum of 0.7 per cent.[18] As of early 2024, interchange on credit cards is not capped, though regulators have expressed that they are pursuing an approach to encourage debit cards to be used for payments, while credit cards are used for borrowing, and have said they would consider a cap on credit card interchange. One major wildcard in Brazil that is a non-issue in Mexico is the country's wildly popular instant payment network, Pix. By just two and a half years after launching, over 140 million individuals, or about 80 per cent of the adult population, had used the service.[19] Some contributors to Pix's success include Brazilian regulators requiring banks to support it, competitive pricing compared to alternatives, and a simple QR code-based user experience. While the primary use case has been in peer-to-peer payments, there are growing signs of Pix displacing cash and cards in consumer-to-business transactions as well.

Brazilian regulators are keen to promote access and inclusion and see potential in banking-as-a-service, sometimes also referred to as "fintech-as-a-service" in the country, to help achieve those goals. Like Mexico, incumbent banks have been less than eager to make the regulated capabilities their licenses authorize available to third parties. New entities licensed as payment institutions, like Dock and Pomelo, have arisen to fill the gap. Dock leverages its infrastructure to provide payments capabilities to firms like Adyen, PayPal, caju, Getnet, and numerous others. Argentina-based Pomelo, which is also authorized as a payment institution in Brazil, partners with companies that include e-commerce marketplace Rappi, neobank Stori, and crypto exchange Bitso. The Brazilian regulatory regime does not specifically address banking- or fintech-as-a-service, though, acknowledging the growing importance of the model, the Brazilian central bank plans to introduce a BaaS-specific regulatory framework in 2024.

On the BaaS supply side, Brazil arguably has somewhat more favorable conditions as compared to those in Mexico, as entities holding payments institutions licenses can support third parties' operations. On the demand side, Brazil has higher rates of employment in the formal economy, bank account adoption, credit bureau coverage, and credit use, despite its banking sector remaining highly concentrated. While down from its 2021 highs, venture funding to fintechs in Brazil remains robust. As of early 2024, Brazil boasted over 1,600 fintechs, though some have struggled as economic and VC fundraising conditions have evolved. While there are certainly similarities between the two largest economies in Latin America when it comes to banking, fintech, and BaaS, there are also meaningful differences across establishment and startup players, approaches to regulation, and consumer habits and preferences that must be taken into account in evaluating the current and future opportunities for banking-as-a-service in these two markets.

## Visa-Backed Dock Has Regional Ambitions

São Paulo, Brazil-based Dock has emerged as a leader in the banking-as-a-service space, not just in its home country, but throughout much of Latin America. The company operates not only in Brazil, but also Chile, Argentina, Peru, Ecuador, Colombia, Panama, Guatemala, and Mexico. Originally known as Conductor when it was founded in 2014, early on, the company's potential caught the interest of a critical strategic investor: Payments behemoth Visa, which led Dock's 2018 funding round, investing an undisclosed amount at the time. Since then, Dock has raised a mammoth $280 million from investors that include Viking Global Investors, Lightrock, and Silver Lake Waterman.

Dock, licensed as a payment institution in Brazil, offers a fairly full stack of capabilities: Payments APIs, including access to Pix, debit and credit card issuing and processing, merchant acquiring and payments capture, end customer onboarding, transaction monitoring and fraud prevention, and multi-channel customer communications, among other features. Dock further extends its offering through partnerships with Amazon AWS, consulting firm Jaú Partners, IT services provider Homine Technologia, payment solutions firm Retail Payment Ecosystem, and others. In addition to those mentioned earlier, Dock counts names like payments service dLocal, banking and payments infrastructure provider fiserv, and e-wallet and point-of-sale provider Mercado Pago as clients.

Dock has supplemented its capabilities and geographic footprint through strategic acquisitions. In 2021, it completed its acquisition of Mexican fintech Cacao Paycard. Cacao, founded in 2017, operated as an issuer and payment processor that, in turn, supported customer-facing fintechs like Albo, Oyster, Kapital, Clip, and Bnext. Cacao's operations predated the 2018 passage of Mexico's Fintech Law. After the law went into effect, Cacao was permitted to continue operating under a "transitory" basis, while it sought authorization from the Mexican banking regulator, the CNBV. Cacao's application to operate as an IFPE, however, was ultimately denied, which resulted in its fintech clients needing to immediately cease taking on new end users. Dock's acquisition of Cacao came with its debit and credit card infrastructure and over 50 customer-facing fintechs. After the acquisition of Cacao, Dock refocused the business on payment processing. The same year, Dock acquired Brazilian banking-as-a-service provider BPP. BPP, a licensed payment institution in Brazil, came with direct connections to Brazil's interbank payments systems, SPB and SPI, card issuing, merchant acquiring, digital accounts, and instant payment service Pix.

As of early 2024, Dock boasts some 70 million active end user accounts across approximately 400 customers and handles around 8 billion transactions per year worth over 1 trillion reais (about $200 million).

## Pomelo Taps into Crypto Demand in Inflation-Plagued Argentina

Like Dock, Argentina-based Pomelo has expanded from its home country to other major Latin American markets. In addition to Argentina, it has a presence in Brazil, Mexico, Colombia, Chile, and Peru. Pomelo, founded in 2021, has raised over $100 million from investors that include Index Ventures, Sequoia Capital, and Tiger Global Management.

In its home country of Argentina, Pomelo operates as a payments service and is not authorized by the central bank to operate as a "financial entity." In early 2023, the company achieved the milestone of securing authorization from Brazilian regulators to operate as a payments institution in the country, enabling it to issue e-money and post-paid instruments.

Pomelo's cloud platform enables its clients to issue debit, credit, prepaid, and corporate cards, process payments, and manage programs on both Visa and Mastercard networks. Use cases include lending, cash management for investing platforms, just-in-time funding, expense management, remittances, buy now pay later, payment facilitation, and more. Pomelo even enables payment cards to be linked to crypto accounts, which is a particularly attractive feature in some Latin American markets, especially Argentina, that have struggled with high rates of inflation and seen an increase in interest in cryptocurrencies. The feature, leveraged by Pomelo clients Ripio and Bitso, enables users to connect a crypto wallet to their card to facilitate seamless spending directly from their crypto funds. In addition to core card issuing and management capabilities, Pomelo supports tokenization, for use with digital wallets like Apple and Google Pay, KYC/KYB identity verification, and card production and shipping.

Pomelo works with over 100 companies across Latin America. In addition to the clients mentioned earlier in this chapter, Pomelo counts firms like global financial app Nomad, international payments platform Global66, and commodity tokenization platform Agrotoken among its customers.

## BaaS Can Play Key Role in Financial Inclusion in LatAm

Latin America, led by the larger anchor economies of Brazil and Mexico, undoubtedly represents an enticing opportunity for fintechs, banking-as-a-service platforms, and their VC investors. Like the UK and EU, some jurisdictions in Latin America, including both Brazil and Mexico, have introduced new license types that are easier, faster, and less expensive to obtain than a traditional banking license. Both Brazil and Mexico historically have highly concentrated banking sectors dominated by a few large players that have left many consumers, especially lower-income ones, without access to basic banking services and credit. Those households represent a true greenfield opportunity for fintechs, enabled by banking-as-a-service operating models.

That isn't to say there are no challenges, however. Particularly in Mexico, the rate of unbanked consumers has remained high, despite the best efforts of the government, establishment banks, and upstart fintechs alike. An uncertain political and regulatory environment also introduces risk: Despite the passage of Mexico's Fintech Law, firms have experienced delays in receiving a decision, and some have had license applications unexpectedly declined. Differences in licensing and regulatory requirements makes operating across Latin America more cumbersome in the much more highly integrated EU. Still, as success stories like Dock and Pomelo exemplify, the banking-as-a-service model has immense potential in Latin America, both as business in their own right, as well as the customer-facing firms they make possible.

## Endnotes

**1** World Bank Group (n.d.) International Monetary Fund Financial Access Survey, data.worldbank.org/indicator/FB.CBK.BRCH.P5 (archived at https://perma.cc/GYW8-YFG9)

**2** Reeves, C. (2023) Exploring Mexico's Financial Landscape: A Comparison of SOFOM, SOFOL, and SOFIPO, *Premier Banking Consultancy*, banklicense.pro/exploring-mexicos-financial-landscape-a-comparison-of-sofom-sofol-and-sofipo/ (archived at https://perma.cc/7WY6-D38A)

**3**  World Bank Group (n.d.) Global Findex Database, data.worldbank.org/ indicator/FX.OWN.TOTL.ZS (archived at https://perma.cc/4DMP-3V3V)

**4**  World Bank Group (n.d.) International Monetary Fund International Financial Statistics, data.worldbank.org/indicator/FS.AST.PRVT.GD.ZS (archived at https://perma.cc/GE7D-DL6V)

**5**  Guerra, J. (2023) How Long Will Cash Dominate in Mexico?, *Mexico Business News*, mexicobusiness.news/finance/news/how-long-will-cash-dominate-mexico (archived at https://perma.cc/U3UW-TPBZ)

**6**  International Monetary Fund (2023) Pix: Brazil's Successful Instant Payment System, www.elibrary.imf.org/view/journals/002/2023/289/article-A004-en. xml (archived at https://perma.cc/E6JL-FK3M)

**7**  The Federal Reserve (2023) Findings from the Diary of Consumer Payment Choice, www.frbservices.org/news/fed360/issues/061523/cash-2023-diary-consumer-payment-choice (archived at https://perma.cc/9LB8-VRNX)

**8**  International Monetary Fund (2022) Mexico: Financial Sector Assessment Program—Financial System Stability Assessment, www.elibrary.imf.org/view/ journals/002/2022/335/article-A001-en.xml (archived at https://perma.cc/ A7MH-523Q)

**9**  Valderram, C. and Salvador, A. (2023) Fintech Laws and Regulations Mexico 2023–2024, *ICLG*, iclg.com/practice-areas/fintech-laws-and-regulations/ mexico (archived at https://perma.cc/AB2U-XWBZ)

**10**  González, C. and Ruíz, C. (2021) Secondary Fintech Regulations Related to E-money Institutions (IFPEs), *White & Case*, www.whitecase.com/insight-alert/secondary-fintech-regulations-related-e-money-institutions-ifpes (archived at https://perma.cc/K2YJ-4EVY)

**11**  Mikula, J. (2022) Mexico Passed a "Fintech Law," but Regulatory Headaches Remain, *Fintech Business Weekly*, fintechbusinessweekly.substack.com/p/ mexico-passed-a-fintech-law-but-regulatory (archived at https://perma.cc/ G5K4-Y2LM)

**12**  World Bank (2024) 5-Bank Asset Concentration for Brazil, Retrieved from FRED, fred.stlouisfed.org/series/DDOI06BRA156NWDB (archived at https://perma.cc/VM4V-CEMC)

**13**  International Monetary Fund (2005) Banco Central do Brasil's Foreign Exchange System, www.elibrary.imf.org/display/book/9781589064232/ ch08.xml (archived at https://perma.cc/7T8D-PHQN)

**14**  World Bank Group (n.d.) International Monetary Fund Financial Access Survey, data.worldbank.org/indicator/FB.CBK.BRCH.P5 (archived at https://perma.cc/GP74-6EVU)

**15**  World Bank Group (n.d.) Global Findex Database, data.worldbank.org/ indicator/FX.OWN.TOTL.ZS (archived at https://perma.cc/69QN-DRAC)

**16**  World Bank Group (n.d.) International Monetary Fund International Financial Statistics, data.worldbank.org/indicator/FS.AST.PRVT.GD.ZS (archived at https://perma.cc/C9EP-UJP4)

**17**  Sanyal, R. (n.d.) COVID-19 Impact: Brazil's Labour Market Puzzle, *CEIC Data*, info.ceicdata.com/covid-19-brazils-labour-market-puzzle (archived at https://perma.cc/X64N-MZVA)

**18**  Versiani, I. and Ayres, M. (2022) Brazil's Central Bank Caps Prepaid Card Interchange Fees; Fintech Stocks Fall, *Reuters*, www.reuters.com/business/finance/brazils-central-bank-limit-prepaid-card-interchange-fee-setback-fintechs-2022-09-26/ (archived at https://perma.cc/5VA7-M865)

**19**  Brandt, C. (2024) Pix: The Latest Updates on Brazil's Leading Instant Payment Scheme, *European Payments Council*, www.europeanpaymentscouncil.eu/news-insights/insight/pix-latest-updates-brazils-leading-instant-payment-scheme (archived at https://perma.cc/XC79-Q266)

# 12

# Asia-Pacific Case Studies: Standard Chartered, Nium, Airwallex

CHAPTER OBJECTIVES

In this chapter, we'll take a look at the establishment banking systems and key demographics of Indonesia, Singapore, and Australia, including how key attributes of each have influenced the development of fintech and banking-as-a-service. We'll also examine banking-as-a-service providers that operate in the region: UK-headquartered bank Standard Chartered, and regional upstarts Nium and Airwallex.

The Asia-Pacific (APAC) region, depending on exactly how one defines it, is home to some 39 countries that, together, comprise more than half the world's population. Countries in the region run the gamut from tiny island nations to behemoths like China and India. There are also dramatically different historical legacies, contemporary foreign policy postures, and economic interdependencies across the region and between countries in it and the rest of the world, especially Western, developed economies like the US and UK. So it should be no surprise that economic conditions and the banking systems in APAC countries vary substantially. For instance, Australia has near-100 per cent banking penetration, whereas only 55 per cent of adults in Indonesia have access to a bank account.[1]

These differences help inform how establishment banks, fintech startups, and banking-as-a-service have evolved in individual countries and in the region at large. Venture capital funding to fintech firms in the region has largely followed the pattern in other regions, spiking dramatically to over $50 billion in 2021 and 2022, before dropping substantially.[2] But looking at funding to the region overall obscures that some countries, especially larger or more developed fintech markets, like India, Indonesia, and Australia, have captured a greater share of VC dollars, compared to smaller and less wealthy countries.

## Indonesia: Leaning on Fintech for Financial Inclusion

Indonesia, composed of some 17,000 islands with nearly 280 million people, is the fourth most populous country. In comparison to other countries discussed in previous chapters, Indonesia's banking system has some unique elements. While there are approximately 120 commercial banks in the country, the sector is dominated by state-owned institutions. The three largest state-owned banks in the country, Bank Mandiri, Bank Rakyat Indonesia, and Bank Negara Indonesia, combined, hold $335 billion of assets, as of 2023.[3] By comparison, in 2023 the largest privately owned institution, Bank Central Asia, held about $90 billion in assets. The heavy involvement of the Indonesian state in the banking sector goes all the way back to the 1997 Asian Financial Crisis, in which the banking sector in the country basically collapsed amid a currency crash and the realization that many banks' lending portfolios held poorly underwritten or non-performing loans. The Indonesian government stepped in to rescue, recapitalize, and reform the sector, with the impacts being felt to this day.

Regional governments across Indonesia also play a significant role in the banking sector dating back to the 1960s, through their owner-ship of regional development banks. As the name suggests, these primarily focus on providing capital for municipal projects that private banks otherwise would not provide, though some have subsidiaries known as Bank Perkreditan Rakyat, or People's Credit Banks, which serve local populations with basic banking and credit services.

There is also a substantial presence of foreign banks that have license to operate in Indonesia, reflecting the country's regional ties to nearby countries and historical ties to Europe. Foreign, privately held banks operating in Indonesia include ABN Amro, American Express, Barclays, BNP Paribas, Citibank, DBS Bank, Bank of America, JPMorgan Chase, and Standard Chartered. Indonesia, as a majority Muslim country, also boasts a small but growing presence of Islamic banking services that comply with religious requirements laid out in the Qur'an.

In aggregate, Indonesia boasts 15.8 bank branches per 100,000 adults, though inclusion in the formal financial system still lags, with only about 55 per cent of adults 15 or older having an account at a financial institution or mobile money provider.[4,5] Access to credit in the country is also significantly constrained, with a private credit-to-GDP ratio of 35 per cent.[6]

While traditional bank account penetration is low compared to developed economies, use of e-wallets is widespread. Such digital wallets are governed by Indonesia's Payment Systems Regulation, which was updated in 2020 to account for changes in the rapidly growing sector. The regulations provide for two broad licensing categories: Payment service providers, which offer capabilities to process transactions for end users, including e-wallets, e-money issuers, and issuers of debit and credit cards; and payment service infrastructure providers, which include backend capabilities, such as clearing, switching, and settlement providers.

Dominant e-wallet providers in the country include ride-hailing firm Gojek, which offers a standalone payment app, GoPay, China-based Ant Financial's DANA e-wallet, and state-owned platform LinkAja. There are an estimated 310 million e-wallets in use in Indonesia, with consumers often using more than one provider. E-wallets carry a fixed transaction cost of 0.7 per cent, which is set by the central bank.[7] The fee is lower than the typical 1 per cent cost to accept debit card payments in the country and is split among the parties facilitating the e-wallet transaction, which helps to explain its widespread use. The ability to be licensed as a payment service or infrastructure provider and the existing widespread use of e-wallets may reduce the need for banking-as-a-service capabilities compared to other countries, as e-wallets provide a pathway for financial inclusion without the need or complexity of a banking-as-a-service structure. Banks in Indonesia that operate partner banking models include Bank Jago, which partners with Gojek, Seabank, which operates the Shopee e-commerce platform, Hana Bank, which partners with popular messaging app Line, and Standard Chartered, which partners with Bukalapak and is profiled below.

### Standard Chartered Nexus: Proving Banks Can Innovate

Standard Chartered has a history stretching back 170 years that spans multiple continents, making it a somewhat unlikely candidate to be an early adopter of innovative banking models, including banking-as-a-service. The name Standard Chartered comes from the merger in 1969 of the Chartered Bank of India, Australia, and China, which was originally organized under a charter from Queen Victoria, and the Standard Bank of British South Africa. Fast forward to 2024, and the bank, though headquartered in London, is heavily focused on markets in Asia, Africa, and the Middle East, with operations in 53 markets worldwide. Standard Chartered has long prioritized innovation, with examples ranging from implementing the first ATM in Asia to launching digitally native banks in Hong Kong and Singapore. Areas of focus in emerging tech include blockchain, generative AI, and, yes, banking-as-a-service.

Standard Chartered's banking-as-a-service offering, branded as nexus, offers a "white-label plug and play" solution enabling third parties to offer current and saving accounts, debit cards, and lending products under their own name. Standard Chartered pitches nexus as a way for existing platforms, like social media, e-commerce, and ride hailing, to add embedded capabilities. The bank's BaaS capabilities are available in 30 markets across Asia, Africa, and the Middle East where it has existing retail operations.

Standard Chartered has two high-profile success stories in the massive Indonesia market: E-commerce platforms Bukalapak and Sociolla. Bukalapak, used by some 110 million consumers and

20 million businesses, is akin to a combination of Amazon and an Asian-style superapp. In addition to the kinds of products you would expect to find on an e-commerce site, Bukalapak also enables users to top up their mobile phone credit, pay electric, water, and internet bills, summon a courier, and even get health insurance. Bukalapak leverages Standard Chartered's nexus BaaS capabilities to power its BukaTabungan digital banking service. Powered by nexus, BukaTabungan allows for fully digital account opening by leveraging Indonesia's biometrics identity program, E-KTP. The account requires no minimum balance and has no administration fee, promoting the financial inclusion of lower-income households in the banking system.

Similarly, in 2020 Standard Chartered partnered with beauty and personal care e-commerce platform Sociolla. The partnership enables Sociolla's users to access products like savings accounts, credit cards, and loans under its own brand name. The two partnerships showcase somewhat distinct use cases for Standard Chartered's BaaS capabilities: While Bukalapak, as a superapp, lends itself to being used as an everyday bank account, vertical shopping platform Sociolla is an ideal example of where credit, in the form of buy now, pay later-style financing, can be deployed successfully.

Standard Chartered is a notable outlier when it comes to establishment institutions operating at the forefront of banking innovation. In many of the bank's markets, including Indonesia, there are large portions of the population that have historically been unbanked. But, realizing these consumers and small business may be unlikely to walk into a bank branch to open an account, Standard Chartered, through its nexus BaaS offering, is meeting these users where they are: Superapps like Bukalapak and shopping destinations like Sociolla.

## Singapore: An Island Financial Powerhouse

Singapore, a city-state of nearly six million people, has leaned into a growing role as a financial services hub in Asia, capitalizing on Hong Kong falling out of favor with expats and foreign companies amid mainland China's growing control over the former British territory.

There are over 150 deposit-taking institutions, which include full banks, merchant banks, wholesale banks, and finance companies. The banking sector in aggregate holds assets of nearly $2 trillion, which is over four times the size of the Singaporean economy. The banking sector is highly concentrated, with three Singapore-headquartered banks, DBS, Overseas-Chinese Banking Corp., and United Overseas Bank, holding more than half the sector's assets.[8] Foreign banks with a significant presence in Singapore include Standard Chartered, Bank of America, CIMB Bank, Citibank, HSBC, JPMorgan Chase, and others.

Singapore has relatively few physical bank branches, at just seven branches per 100,000. The prevalence of branches has been declining in the country for some time, though even as far back as 2004, there were only approximately 12 branches per 100,000, which is significantly lower than other developed economies.[9] That said, the lack of branches, in Singapore's case, is not correlated with a lower rate of bank account penetration. The country boasts near-universal banking access, with nearly 99 per cent of the population over 15 having a bank or mobile money account.[10] Likewise, Singapore has well-developed credit markets, with a private credit-to-GDP ratio of about 130 per cent.[11]

The Monetary Authority of Singapore, known by its acronym MAS, is widely viewed as being innovation-friendly and has worked to develop infrastructure and policies to support the banking and fintech ecosystem in the country. For instance, MAS offers digital licenses for both full and wholesale banks. MAS also operates a fintech "regulatory sandbox," which enables companies to experiment with new products and services in a live environment but within a defined space and duration. The sandbox is intended to allow firms to test products with the supervision of regulators and, if successful, exit the sandbox and comply with all applicable legal and regulatory requirements.

In addition to traditional banking licenses, MAS also offers a category of licensing for what it terms payment service providers. Within this category, MAS offers a standard payment institution license, major payment institution license, and money-changing license. The regulatory regime recognizes seven types of payments services, including account issuance, domestic money transfer, cross-border money transfer, merchant acquiring, e-money issuance, money-changing service, and digital payment token service (crypto). In Singapore, interchange rates are not regulated by the government, with card schemes like Visa and Mastercard setting applicable rates based on market conditions. Interchange fees can average 1.8 per cent of a transaction or higher, with the bulk of the fee going to card issuers. Higher interchange rates may provide more attractive opportunities for fintech business models reliant on interchange and, in turn, help attract venture capital investment. Examples of companies offering banking-as-a-service capabilities in Singapore include Rapyd, Matchmove, and Nium, all of which are licensed as major payment institutions in the country.

### Nium: Powering Startups Around the Globe

Singapore-based Nium is, in some ways, the opposite of Standard Chartered. Founded in 2014 as InstaReM with a focus on remittances, the company rebranded to Nium in 2019 to reflect its growing offerings. Nium is venture backed and has raised nearly $300 million in equity to date, from investors that include Vertex Ventures, Silicon Valley Bank, and Temasek Holdings. Unlike Standard Chartered, Nium is not a bank. In Singapore, the company holds a major payment institution license. Nium supports various capabilities across over 35 markets through both licenses the company itself holds and through partnerships. For example, in the United States, Nium partners with Column Bank and Community Federal Savings Bank to enable it to operate in the country.

Capabilities that Nium offers include opening global multi-currency accounts for end users, foreign exchange, physical and virtual card issuing, and disbursements. Use cases include applications like payroll, travel providers, and spend management platforms. Given Nium's substantial global footprint, it has achieved significant traction with platforms that need to operate on a global basis in areas like B2B payments and remote staffing. For instance, Nium client

Deel is a global HR platform that simplifies the process of hiring, employing, and paying staffers that reside outside of a company's home market. Deel handles the complexities and logistics of complying with country-specific labor, employment, and tax law by serving as the employer of record. In order to process payroll and remit taxes across more than 100 countries, Deel needs access to local country currencies and payment rails. That is what Nium provides, through its own licenses, partnerships, and technology platform.

Another example of the potential of Nium's expansive reach is its client Treviso, a Brazilian-based financial institution focused on foreign exchange contracts, and commercial, financial and tourism exchange. The latency of international payments and foreign exchange has been a major pain point for Treviso and its clients. International transactions, especially if they need to be routed through US dollars and the US financial system, historically have been slow, expensive, and opaque. Treviso leveraged Nium to digitize and more efficiently scale its operations, including by enabling real-time settlement in certain currency corridors. Faster settlement improves the end customer experience and can help improve capital efficiency.

KBank, a 70-year-old financial institution in Bangkok, Thailand, also partners with Nium to solve challenges facing their customers. For example, KBank leverages Nium in its international trade products to improve the quality and speed of international payments, remittance, and foreign exchange capabilities. The partnership enables KBank's customers to make real-time payments to 30 countries across Asia-Pacific and Europe, a substantial improvement over legacy bank remittance services.

Nium's global ambitions are notable and have garnered comparisons to fintech behemoth Stripe. But Stripe's primary line of business, merchant acquiring, is substantially less complicated, both from an operational and a legal/compliance perspective, than holding end user funds, card issuing, and disbursing payments. Nium's partnership with global brands like Payoneer, Deel, and Visa-owned CurrencyCloud are a testament to how far Nium has progressed in achieving its vision.

## Australia: An Unlikely Financial Innovator

Australia also holds outsized importance in the region's financial and banking market. Comparatively small, at about 26 million people, the country is both well-integrated into regional economies and has strong links with Western countries, particularly the United Kingdom and United States. There are about 95 banks in Australia, according to the Australian Banking Association, though the sector is highly concentrated.[12] In 2023, assets of authorized depository institutions totaled some AUD $5.3 trillion, or about USD $3.5 trillion. The four largest banks, the Commonwealth Bank of Australia, Westpac Banking Corporation, National Australia Bank, and Australia and New Zealand Banking Group, held approximately 72 per cent market share. In addition to authorized depository institutions, Australia charters credit unions and friendly societies, which offer savings and investment products. Foreign banks also have a significant presence in the country, with institutions like Bank of America, JPMorgan Chase, ABN Amro, Union Bank of India, Bank of China, MUFG, and numerous others operating in the country.

The presence of physical bank branches in Australia, like many other developed countries, has been declining. As of 2021, the country had about 24 branches per 100,000 adults.[13] With almost 99 per cent of banking interactions taking place digitally, the demand for physical branch infrastructure has declined substantially. The decline in branches has not impacted the rate at which Australians are able to access financial services, as 100 per cent of adults over 15 have access to banking or mobile money accounts.[14] Likewise, credit markets in the country are well developed, with a private credit-to-GDP ratio of 133 per cent.[15]

In addition to deposit-taking institutions, the Australian Prudential Regulatory Authority also offers a financial services license, which allows institutions to offer investment management services, and a credit license, which allows institutions to offer consumer and commercial credit, including credit cards. Interchange in the country is regulated, with transactions that are subject to a fixed-fee cap charging AUD $0.10 for debit and prepaid card transactions, while those governed by a percentage-based rate cap may charge up to 0.20 per cent. Although the Australian market is already well banked, that doesn't mean there hasn't been demand for banking-as-a-service capabilities, particularly to support embedded finance use cases. Both incumbents, like big-four bank Westpac, and new entrants, like Airwallex, enable third parties to add capabilities to hold funds, issue cards, and make payments.

### Airwallex: A Global, Multi-Currency Platform

Like Nium, Australia-founded and Singapore-based Airwallex, founded in 2015, was originally conceived of as a solution to complex, slow, expensive cross-border payments. Also like Nium, Airwallex is not a bank but instead operates through e-money and payments licenses and partnerships with regulated financial institutions. Nium partners with banks like JPMorgan Chase, Barclays, DBS, and Standard Chartered. It has expanded its capabilities from its origins in payments and foreign exchange to include global multi-currency accounts, expense management, bill pay, treasury management, and card issuing. The company has raised over $900 million of capital from investors that include Tencent, Salesforce Capital, and Sequoia.

While Airwallex may have originally built its multi-country infrastructure to offer products and services to end users under its own name, it also leverages its platform to offer banking-as-a-service capabilities. Airwallex enables third-party partners to offer local accounts in 22 currencies, receive and make payments in 150 countries, issue payment cards in 36 markets, and to offer credit products. Airwallex offers pre-built components and handles some compliance functions, like KYC and KYB checks, simplifying the process for third parties to build on its platform.

Airwallex boasts over 100,000 companies that use its services, though not all of those leverage its banking-as-a-service capabilities. Airwallex boasts major fintechs like US expense management and charge card startup Brex, accounting platform Xero, and Chinese fast fashion retailer Shein as clients. Companies like Stake, TradeBridge, and volopay make use of Airwallex's BaaS platform to embed its capabilities in their offerings. Stake, a trading and investing platform, leverages Airwallex to enable users to pay in, hold funds, and pay out across numerous currencies. TradeBridge, which operates in the e-commerce, healthcare, and corporate sectors, uses Airwallex to offer embedded multi-currency wallets. And spend management startup volopay leverages Airwallex to seamlessly issue white-label virtual and physical prepaid cards.

Airwallex's operations, though, have, in some markets, raised some of the questions and scrutiny other BaaS platforms have faced. For instance, in the US market, where Airwallex partners with Evolve Bank & Trust, scammers have allegedly used its platform to facilitate "pig butchering" crypto scams and money laundering activities.[16] The company has also been accused of seeking to find ways to circumvent Hong Kong's strict money laundering laws to make it easier for customers to sign up there.[17] Bank partners Citibank and the National Australian Bank ceased providing services to Airwallex customers because of red flags around its customers, the abrupt resignation of Airwallex's compliance chief, and patterns of risky transactions.[18] As of mid-2024, it is unclear how widespread and significant the problems may be, versus being the growing pains of a rapidly expanding company.

## Potential for BaaS in the Region Remains High

The history and contemporary realities on the ground in Asia-Pacific countries have strongly shaped how banking-as-a-service has developed in the region. Like Europe and Latin America, many APAC countries offer non-bank licenses, like e-money or payment institution charters, which may lessen the demand for BaaS capabilities. At the same time, establishment banks, as demonstrated by Standard Chartered, have demonstrated an understanding of how consumers and businesses, especially those that may have been unbanked in the past, shop for and interact with financial services through non-financial platforms, like Bukalapak and Gojek. That said, as Airwallex demonstrates, BaaS in the region is susceptible to the same kinds of risks seen in other jurisdictions, especially around KYC/KYB and anti-money laundering compliance. But the sheer scale of the opportunity, due both to the number of people and the relatively lower level of bank and credit penetration in APAC countries, means the upside for banking-as-a-service in the region remains huge.

## Endnotes

**1** World Bank Group (n.d.) Global Findex Database, data.worldbank.org/indicator/FX.OWN.TOTL.ZS (archived at https://perma.cc/T5YK-KQP4)

**2** KPMG (2023) Fintech Funding in ASPAC Very Soft; H1'23 Sees Lowest Level in Almost 10 Years, kpmg.com/xx/en/home/insights/2023/07/pulse-of-fintech-h1-2023-aspac.html (archived at https://perma.cc/27SY-AYME)

**3** Guild, J. (2024) The Rise of Indonesia's Banks, *The Diplomat*, thediplomat.com/2024/03/the-rise-of-indonesias-banks/ (archived at https://perma.cc/AW9F-G8V6)

**4** World Bank Group (n.d.) International Monetary Fund Financial Access Survey, data.worldbank.org/indicator/FB.CBK.BRCH.P5 (archived at https://perma.cc/JN5T-WR6U)

**5** World Bank Group (n.d.) Global Findex Database, data.worldbank.org/indicator/FX.OWN.TOTL.ZS (archived at https://perma.cc/ET6V-TEEA)

**6** World Bank Group (n.d.) International Monetary Fund International Financial Statistics, data.worldbank.org/indicator/FS.AST.PRVT.GD.ZS (archived at https://perma.cc/RNQ9-RDXR)

**7** Potkin, F. (2019) Indonesia Plans Fixed Fees for E-Wallet Transactions: Sources, *Reuters*, www.reuters.com/article/us-indonesia-ewallets/indonesia-plans-fixed-fees-for-e-wallet-transactions-sources-idUSKBN1YZ06Y/ (archived at https://perma.cc/Y76D-XACY)

**8** Yamagucchi, Y. and Taqi, M. (2023) Asia-Pacific's 50 Largest Banks by Assets, 2023, *S&P Global*, www.spglobal.com/marketintelligence/en/news-insights/research/asia-pacifics-50-largest-banks-by-assets-2023 (archived at https://perma.cc/95W7-5UX3)

**9** World Bank Group (n.d.) International Monetary Fund Financial Access Survey, data.worldbank.org/indicator/FB.CBK.BRCH.P5 (archived at https://perma.cc/YY37-3FE7)

**10** World Bank Group (n.d.) Global Findex Database, data.worldbank.org/indicator/FX.OWN.TOTL.ZS (archived at https://perma.cc/PBY3-7MU8)

**11**  World Bank Group (n.d.) International Monetary Fund International Financial Statistics, data.worldbank.org/indicator/FS.AST.PRVT.GD.ZS (archived at https://perma.cc/A2B3-VWH3)

**12**  Australian Banking Association (2023) Banking by Numbers: 2023, www.ausbanking.org.au/insight/banking-by-numbers (archived at https://perma.cc/UC5W-ME74)

**13**  World Bank Group (n.d.) International Monetary Fund Financial Access Survey, data.worldbank.org/indicator/FB.CBK.BRCH.P5 (archived at https://perma.cc/9E4F-PKRF)

**14**  World Bank Group (n.d.) Global Findex Database, data.worldbank.org/indicator/FX.OWN.TOTL.ZS (archived at https://perma.cc/9SLR-2D2V)

**15**  World Bank Group (n.d.) International Monetary Fund International Financial Statistics, data.worldbank.org/indicator/FS.AST.PRVT.GD.ZS (archived at https://perma.cc/C286-U8PE)

**16**  Mikula, J. (2024) Feds Freeze $5m at Evolve in "Pig Butchering" Crypto Fraud, Money Laundering Case, *Fintech Business Weekly*, fintechbusinessweekly.substack.com/p/feds-freeze-5m-at-evolve-in-pig-butchering (archived at https://perma.cc/W86F-TCKL)

**17**  Baird, L. and Shapiro, J. (2024) Airwallex Sought Way Around Hong Kong Anti-Money Laundering Rules, *Australian Financial Review*, www.afr.com/companies/financial-services/airwallex-sought-way-around-hong-kong-anti-money-laundering-rules-20240103-p5euuy (archived at https://perma.cc/3LGN-F76A)

**18**  Grieve, C. (2021) 'Denied': NAB, Citi Pulled Banking Services from Fintech Unicorn Airwallex Over Risk Fears, *The Sydney Morning Herald*, www.smh.com.au/business/banking-and-finance/denied-nab-citi-pulled-banking-services-from-fintech-unicorn-airwallex-over-risk-fears-20210413-p57iv9.html (archived at https://perma.cc/4FJQ-GUKR)

# 13

# Africa Case Studies: Ukheshe, Jumo, OnePipe

---

CHAPTER OBJECTIVES

In this chapter, we'll undertake an overview of the basic demographics, banking systems, and regulations and how they've shaped fintech and banking-as-a-service in three markets in Africa: South Africa, Nigeria, and Kenya. We'll also take a look at three companies operating in the space: Ukheshe, Jumo, and OnePipe.

---

It's impossible to boil down the continent of Africa, comprising over a billion people living in 54 distinct countries across more than 11 million square miles, into a handful of neat case studies. Levels of economic development, banking systems and infrastructure, and cultural history and consumer preferences vary substantially across the continent. There are, however, some common themes and challenges that form barriers to inclusion in formal financial systems, including lower levels of wealth and income, uneven access to internet and mobile phone infrastructure, and even a lack of basic identity credentialing in some places.

Still, the challenges in extending access to financial services are surmountable; for instance, high rates of adoption of mobile money solutions like M-PESA, which require only a simple mobile phone with SMS capabilities, demonstrate the ingenuity necessary to find novel solutions to difficult problems. Like with telecommunications infrastructure before it, many countries in Africa have the opportunity to leapfrog legacy approaches to banking long used in developed markets, like physical, branch-based distribution, and pursue more modern, innovative distribution models, including through banking-as-a-service and embedded finance.

## South Africa: The Continent's Largest Economy

South Africa, the largest African economy by GDP, has relatively few banks for an economy of its size. The country has just 17 local banks, plus an additional 46 branches or representative offices of foreign banks, for a total of 63 institutions, as of 2022. In addition to typical commercial banks, South Africa also licenses mutual and co-operative banks, which are owned by their members and are somewhat comparable to credit unions in the US and building societies in the UK context. South Africa also allows foreign banks to establish representative offices, which are not allowed to carry out full banking activities, and branch offices, which are permitted to conduct full banking operations.

As is the case in many parts of the world, the banking sector in South Africa is highly concentrated. The "big four," composed of Standard Bank Group, FirstRand, Absa Group, and NedBank Group, hold nearly all banking assets in the country.[1] In addition to large, establishment banks, South Africa boasts a number of fully licensed digital-only banks, like TymeBank and Bank Zero. The country has a relatively small branch network, with just eight branches per 100,000 people, less than a third compared to the US.[2] But despite comparatively thin branch density, banking adoption in South Africa is robust, with about 90 per cent of people over 15 years of age owning a bank or mobile money account.[3] Likewise, credit markets in the country are generally well developed, with an overall private credit-to-GDP ratio of about 92 per cent, though this has contracted in recent years from a high of 142 per cent in 2007.[4]

Although the concept of e-money exists in South Africa, only registered banks may issue it, which is a notable difference compared to other profiled countries. There is no dedicated "fintech license," though the Financial Sector Conduct Authority, a regulator in the country, has a department dedicated to fintech that offers firms guidance on regulation, a regulatory sandbox to test products and services, and an innovation accelerator program. Despite high banking penetration, cash is still a primary form of payment, with 86 per cent of South Africans saying they frequently use cash, and physical currency still accounting for about 73 per cent of in-person transactions.[5] When cards are used, how interchanged rates are determined varies based on the type of transaction. For ATM, cashback at point-of-sale, debit, and credit card transactions, interchange rates are determined by the South African Reserve Bank, the country's central bank. Depending on the type of transaction, debit card interchange is typically between 0.35 per cent and 0.55 per cent, and credit card interchange typically ranges from 1.40 per cent to 1.90 per cent.[6]

Despite being the continent's largest economy, South Africa came in third in total venture funding in 2023, with about $600 million invested in South African startups across all sectors (not just fintech), though the numbers vary depending on what source you look at. Top sub-sectors within fintech include payments and investing. The combination of a lack of a standalone fintech or e-money license and a highly concentrated establishment banking sector that is dominated by a small number of players may be responsible for relatively lower levels of fintech development and adoption in the country. One of the leading examples of a new, digital-only institution, TymeBank, is a fully licensed bank, rather than relying on a non-bank license or a banking-as-a-service operating model.

### Ukheshe: Developing New Capabilities to Meet Local Challenges

South Africa-based Ukheshe originally sought to solve a common problem in the country: How to pay someone without using cash, if they don't have a bank account? The company's cofounders, Clayton Hayward and Mike Smits, leveraged their backgrounds in telecommunications and financial operations to try to solve that problem. But as the company built and explored that problem space, as is so often the case, it discovered underlying structural reasons that contribute to high rates of unbanked households in South Africa and throughout the continent, like those mentioned in this chapter's introduction. Ultimately, the company pivoted to focus on building what would become its Eclipse platform, simplifying how companies work with financial institutions to embed payments into their products and services by offering payments, core banking, and compliance in a single, API-enabled platform. The company, founded in 2018, has raised $42 million in capital to date from investors that include Development Partners International and Fireball Capital. Ukheshe has also participated in Mastercard's Start Path program, in 2020, and subsequently became one of Mastercard's 29 global Engage partners.

Ukheshe has leveraged strategic acquisitions as part of its growth strategy. In 2020, the company acquired digital payments platform Oltio, which supported Mastercard's QR-based payment service, Masterpass. The Oltio acquisition served as the foundation for Ukheshe's QR Scan to Pay capability. And in 2024, the company announced its acquisition of EFT Corporation from Loita Transaction Services. The purchase of EFT Corporation comes with its pan-African payment solutions and switching infrastructure, which power digital payments in 35 African markets and for over 100 processors and banks. EFT Corporation continues to operate as a standalone brand, but, as part of Ukheshe, enables additional use cases for both companies' existing customers.

Through its acquisitions and in-house development, Ukheshe's Eclipse platform has grown to offer a broad set of capabilities, including fully digital KYC, QR code-based payments, tap to pay on point of sale or mobile phone, physical and virtual card issuing, cross-border payments and remittances, and more. The platform supports top ups (cash in) and cash out through numerous channels, including EFT, retail, cash agents, card, and wallet to wallet. Use cases include person-to-person and person-to-merchant payments, digital wallets, point-of-sale acceptance, and payroll. Ukheshe also offers adjacent capabilities, such as phone top ups, utility payments, bill payments, transport vouchers, and insurance. Clients and partners include Nedbank, Standard Bank, Capitec Bank, Diamond Trust Bank, Mastercard, Chipper, vodacom, and numerous others. Ukheshe has expanded from its home country of South Africa to offer capabilities in a total of eight countries, including Kenya, Zimbabwe, Ghana, and Mauritius.

## Kenya: A Vibrant Regional Leader

Kenya is the seventh largest economy in Africa, by GDP, and has emerged as a vibrant regional leader, including in banking and financial services. According to the Central Bank of Kenya, there are 43 commercial banks and mortgage finance institutions in the country, which includes three publicly owned institutions: Consolidated Bank of Kenya, Development Bank of Kenya, and National Bank of Kenya. Of the 40 privately owned institutions, 25 are locally controlled, and 15 are majority foreign-owned. The overall Kenyan banking sector has approximately $50 billion in assets, with just two institutions, Equity Bank Group and KCB Group, accounting for approximately half the assets. The Kenyan central bank also authorizes e-money institutions and payment service providers. E-money institutions are required to ring fence and safeguard customer funds and to maintain good risk management practices, among other requirements.

In addition to privately owned institutions, the Kenya Post Office Savings Bank, referred to locally as Postbank, is authorized to operate through separate legislation and is not overseen by the country's central bank. Due to its unique operating authority, interest income savers earn from funds at Postbank are exempt from tax. Other types of licensed financial services entities include foreign exchange bureaus, remittance providers, savings and credit cooperatives, and credit reference bureaus.

The number of physical bank branches in Kenya peaked in 2015, at 5.6 branches per 100,000, and declined to just 4.4 branches per 100,000 by 2023.[7] However, thanks in large part to the ubiquity of Kenya-based M-PESA mobile phone-based money transfer service, about 87 per cent of adults over 15 own a bank or mobile money account.[8] M-PESA was founded in Kenya in 2007 and allows users to store funds and send payments via PIN-secured SMS messages. The other mobile money operators, which include Airtel Money and Telkom Kenya, have a de minimis market share. Since its launch, M-PESA has expanded to Ethiopia, South Africa, Afghanistan, Egypt, Ghana, Lesotho, the Democratic Republic of Congo, Mozambique, and Tanzania. M-PESA boasts over 38 million users in Kenya, for a penetration rate of an astounding 76 per cent.[9] Access to credit, however, remains substantially constrained in the country, which has a private credit-to-GDP ratio of just 31.5 per cent.[10]

Like South Africa, cash remains the dominant payment method in Kenya, especially for in-person and smaller transactions. An estimated 84 per cent of survey respondents reported using cash at physical points of sale in 2023, though this was a 5 per cent point decline compared to 2019. Transaction fees for making payments via mobile wallets and bank-to-bank transfers, including M-PESA, have, in some cases, discouraged adoption of these channels while driving users to prefer cash. As of 2022, interchange rates in Kenya are not regulated, which enables market participants (the acquiring bank, issuing bank, and networks) to set prices. Relatively high interchange costs, especially for Visa-issued cards, serve as a disincentive for merchants to accept card payments, especially for smaller-sized transactions.

Kenya, despite being the seventh-largest African country by GDP, led the pack in terms of VC investment, with startups across all sectors taking in some $800 million in 2023, though numbers varied by source. The early success of M-PESA, which predates contemporary fintech, may help explain the country's outsized fundraising performance. Leading Kenyan fintechs include Tala and Branch, both focused on microlending, comparison platform PesaBazaar, and savings and credit service Jumo. Recognizing the potential for improved access and inclusion—and the revenue opportunities—Kenyan banks have become increasingly willing to partner with fintech firms and to offer APIs for third parties to build on.

*Jumo: Enabling Savings and Lending Products*

Jumo, based in Kenya, offers two main products, Core and Unify, which enable banks and mobile money providers to offer lending and savings products more quickly and easily. The company, founded in 2015, is primarily focused on building and selling software solutions to financial institutions, rather than holding its own license and operating a banking-as-a-service platform itself. Through early 2024, Jumo has raised an impressive $320 million in equity capital and counts top-tier firms like Goldman Sachs and Fidelity as investors. Jumo partners with local institutions like Ecobank, Mansa Bank, Telenor, MTN, and Tigo, which leverage its software platform to offer lending and savings products to their users. In addition to its home market of Kenya, Jumo also actively serves companies in Ghana, Tanzania, Uganda, Zambia, Côte d'Ivoire, and South Africa, with operations in Nairobi, Cape Town, Porto, and London.

Examples of products customers of Jumo leverage the platform to offer include loans like VitKash, QUIKLOAN, XpressLoan, and Ahomka, offered by mobile network MTN in conjunction with partners Mansa Bank, Letshego, Ecobank, and Absa. Savings products include Timiza Akiba and Kasaka Savings, offered by Airtel and MTN, respectively, with Absa Bank. According to Jumo, through partnerships with its clients, it serves over 25 million consumers and small businesses, and it has disbursed over 186 million loans worth in excess of $6 billion.

For example, in Tanzania, Timiza Akiba is a savings product offered by mobile phone service Airtel in partnership with Letshego bank, which, in turn, leverages Jumo's software platform. It is one of a multitude of financial capabilities the mobile operator offers, which include Kamilisha (comparable to overdraft credit), Airtel Money (digital wallet), Timiza (loans), Afya Bima (insurance), and remittances. The Timiza Akiba savings product is no-fee and encourages users to save by providing a bonus as a reward for saving. The minimum deposit to open an account is just TSH 100, which is equivalent to about USD $0.04. An example on the lending side is Kopa Cash, which is also offered by mobile operator Airtel and built on Jumo's platform. Kopa Cash is a short-term unsecured loan repayable in 7 to 30 days, with fees ranging from 4 per cent to 10 per cent of principal lent.

As a pure software play, Jumo is more comparable to a core banking platform, like those offered in the US by stalwarts like FIS and Fiserv, than the approach of banking-as-a-service intermediaries, like Unit or Treasury Prime, which historically have primarily focused on selling to and serving customer-facing fintechs as clients. Given the widespread adoption of mobile money solutions in Kenya, with trailblazer M-PESA holding 76 per cent market share of mobile wallets, Jumo is well-positioned to aid firms in extending their capabilities with new products and features, rather than going head-to-head with established players.

## Nigeria: A Growing Fintech Ecosystem

Nigeria ranks between South Africa and Kenya, coming in at Africa's fourth-largest economy by GDP. The Central Bank of Nigeria supervises 26 commercial banks in the country. In aggregate, Nigerian banks held approximately N107 trillion, equivalent to about $80 billion, in assets, as of November 2023.[11] The banking sector is somewhat less concentrated than other African countries, with the top five institutions holding approximately 70 per cent of the banking system's assets.[12] Those five largest banks are: Access Bank, Zenith Bank, First Bank of Nigeria Holdings, United Bank for Africa, and Guaranty Trust Bank. In addition to commercial banks, the central bank also charters merchant banks, microfinance banks, and development banks. Beyond banking licensing, there are defined non-bank licenses for activities and business models that include payment service providers, payment terminal service providers, mobile money operators, switching and processing, and payment solution service providers. Mobile money operators, which about 20 non-bank firms hold licenses for, are eligible to issue electronic wallets and process fund transfers and payments, making them somewhat comparable to e-money institution licenses in other countries.

As is the case with the other countries profiled, bank branches are relatively scarce in Nigeria, with about 4.3 branches per 100,000 adults, which is a decline of about a third since 2010.[13] Financial inclusion is significantly lower in Nigeria than in South Africa or Kenya, with only about 54 per cent of adults over 15 owning a bank or mobile money account, though the metric has been improving.[14] Credit is also extremely hard to come by, as demonstrated by the country's 14 per cent private credit-to-GDP ratio.[15]

Though declining, cash remains the dominant payment method in Nigeria, especially at physical points of sale. As recently as 2019, prior to the Covid-19 pandemic, cash accounted for over 90 per cent of transaction volume. That dropped sharply in 2020, as concerns about physical cash as a vector for the pandemic spread, and cash plummeted to around 70 per cent of transactions and has continued its slide since then. Lost cash transaction volume has largely shifted to digital wallets and debit cards, with the two combined accounting for about 25 per cent of point-of-sale transactions in 2022. The Nigerian central bank regulates interchange on card transactions, with a rate of 0.40 per cent on credit, debit, and prepaid transactions, up to a maximum of N1,300 (about $1) on most transactions and a rate of 0.85 per cent, up to a maximum of N3,200 (about $2.40), on travel and entertainment merchants.[16] Additional fees that go to the payment services terminal provider or the payment terminal services aggregator, rather than the card issuer, are also allowed.

Nigeria, the continent's fourth-largest economy, also ranked fourth in VC investment, with Nigerian companies across all sectors raising about $400 million in 2023. Nigeria has a vibrant fintech ecosystem, including well-known companies like payments and remittance firm Flutterwave, payment processor Paystack (acquired by Stripe), and licensed microfinance institution Kuda Bank. There are a number of firms that provide BaaS-like capabilities, by making their infrastructure available via API, including OnePipe, Flutterwave, and Okra.

## OnePipe: Enabling Fintechs and Embedded Finance

Nigeria's OnePipe is an embedded finance and banking-as-a-service platform that simplifies how businesses integrate banking partners' capabilities into their offerings. Founded in 2018, the company has raised about $13 million from investors that include Atlantica Ventures, Tribe Capital, and V&R Associates. OnePipe has also participated in the prestigious Techstars accelerator program. On the bank side, OnePipe helps its partners monetize their existing capabilities by providing an intermediary technology platform to connect banks with customer-facing fintechs. OnePipe works with banks like Fidelity Bank Nigeria, Heritage Bank, and Polaris Bank. OnePipe enables use cases that include virtual accounts for payments, account-to-account transfers and direct debits, embedded wallets, subscription management, and white-label bank accounts. Businesses that have integrated OnePipe's capabilities include local airline Air Peace, agriculture supply chain platform Winich Farms, and embedded lending platform Migo. Customers of OnePipe leverage the platform for capabilities like in-store and online payments processing, collecting recurring payments, and payroll and salary lending.

For instance Migo, the lending platform, sought to use OnePipe to streamline its borrowers' repayment experience. Migo leverages OnePipe's platform and its underlying partner bank APIs to create an embedded account for borrowers and automate the movement of funds, creating a low-friction, convenient repayment experience. The accounts Migo creates for repayment can even be used by borrowers as their primary transactional account. The partnership is a win-win, in that it provides end users a better, lower-cost experience and simplifies operations and improves repayment behavior for Migo.

Another OnePipe customer, Releaf, was looking to streamline operations in its agricultural sourcing operations. The company sources and procures produce from more than 1,800 small farmers in Nigeria, which, historically, it had paid in cash. But the dependence on cash was both an operational bottleneck and risk for the company. Using cash also had drawbacks for the farmers, namely, that it made it more difficult to participate in the formal banking sector and to take advantage of savings and credit offerings. Releaf leveraged OnePipe's platform to build a branded digital bank account, the Releaf Wallet. Farmers are able to sign up for an account by calling a designated shortcode number, without the need to visit a bank branch or complete any paperwork. Once they are up and running, farmers can use the accounts to withdraw cash as needed at nearby agents, build a banking history that enables access to credit, save more effectively, and buy discounted mobile phone credit.

Like Kenya-based Jumo, OnePipe is primarily a software play, in that the company itself is not a bank nor holds e-money or payments licenses. However, Jumo is focused primarily on selling software to banks and mobile money operators, whereas OnePipe, while it has partnerships with licensed banks, sees its market primarily as selling to fintechs and other businesses looking to embed financial capabilities into their products and services.

## Potential for Fintech and BaaS in Africa Remains High

There are numerous barriers to financial inclusion in Africa, ranging from living too far from a bank branch to lacking necessary identity credentials to open an account. Even for those who fulfill the basic prerequisites, it can be challenging for financial institutions with the higher fixed costs that go hand in hand with legacy approaches to serve generally lower-income and lower-wealth customers in an economically feasible manner. Technology, including banking-as-a-service and the embedded finance use cases it enables, is helping to tackle these issues. Modern infrastructure can help lower the cost to serve customers, making it more economically attractive to extend inclusion in the formal financial sector to those previously shut out. Digital distribution, both by banks directly and through third-party partners, makes it possible to reach customers where they are and present contextually relevant solutions, rather than forcing them to come into a bank branch. Africa has long been an innovator in financial services, and stakeholders' adoption of and experimentation with BaaS will, no doubt, take account of local market conditions and be tailored to solve local market challenges.

# Endnotes

**1**  World Bank Group (n.d.) Global Financial Development, databank.worldbank. org/source/global-financial-development/Series/GFDD.OI.06 (archived at https://perma.cc/ZY25-89P2)

**2**  World Bank Group (n.d.) International Monetary Fund Financial Access Survey, data.worldbank.org/indicator/FB.CBK.BRCH.P5 (archived at https:// perma.cc/65Z9-BS4X)

**3**  World Bank Group (n.d.) Global Findex Database, data.worldbank.org/ indicator/FX.OWN.TOTL.ZS (archived at https://perma.cc/5VES-5CFL)

**4**  World Bank Group (n.d.) International Monetary Fund International Financial Statistics, data.worldbank.org/indicator/FS.AST.PRVT.GD.ZS (archived at https://perma.cc/6D7B-XTAY)

**5**  Cash Matters (2023) The Value of Cash and Payment Choice in South Africa, www.cashmatters.org/blog/the-value-of-cash-and-payment-choice-in-south-africa (archived at https://perma.cc/7E8Y-CRTW)

**6**  Goga, S. (2014) Interchange Determination: An Assessment of the Regulation of Interchange in South African in Light of International Developments, The Competition Commission, www.compcom.co.za/wp-content/uploads/2014/09/ Interchange-determination.pdf (archived at https://perma.cc/6MEY-AUMC)

**7**  World Bank Group (n.d.) International Monetary Fund Financial Access Survey, data.worldbank.org/indicator/FB.CBK.BRCH.P5 (archived at https:// perma.cc/M8Z8-RHNT)

**8**  World Bank Group (n.d.) Global Findex Database, data.worldbank.org/ indicator/FX.OWN.TOTL.ZS (archived at https://perma.cc/PQB7-J27Y)

**9**  Abuya, K. (2023) Despite Kenya's Central Bank Backing, Mobile Money Rivals Are No Match for M-PESA, Tecchcabal, techcabal.com/2023/06/26/ kenya-mobile-money-rivals-are-no-match-for-m-pesa/ (archived at https:// perma.cc/B474-AFGD)

**10**  World Bank Group (n.d.) International Monetary Fund International Financial Statistics, data.worldbank.org/indicator/FS.AST.PRVT.GD.ZS (archived at https://perma.cc/5EEP-TDS5)

**11**  Vanguard (2024) Banks Grow Total Assets By 50% N107.3trn, www. vanguardngr.com/2024/02/banks-grow-total-assets-by-50-n107-3trn/ (archived at https://perma.cc/SZ55-7EBF)

**12**  World Bank Group (n.d.) Global Financial Development, databank.worldbank. org/source/global-financial-development/Series/GFDD.OI.06 (archived at https://perma.cc/T3YB-V7LV)

**13**  World Bank Group (n.d.) International Monetary Fund Financial Access Survey, data.worldbank.org/indicator/FB.CBK.BRCH.P5 (archived at https://perma.cc/VQK6-VGRC)

**14**  World Bank Group (n.d.) International Monetary Fund International Financial
Statistics, data.worldbank.org/indicator/FS.AST.PRVT.GD.ZSboth (archived at
https://perma.cc/9DEA-CSTF)

**15**  World Bank Group (n.d.) Global Findex Database, data.worldbank.org/
indicator/FX.OWN.TOTL.ZS (archived at https://perma.cc/D3DN-E5QG)

**16**  Hayashi, F. (2022) Public Authority Involvement in Payment Card Markets:
Various Countries, Federal Reserve Bank of Kansas City, www.kansascityfed.
org/documents/9022/PublicAuthorityInvolvementPaymentCardMarkets_
VariousCountries_August2022Update.pdf (archived at https://perma.
cc/7S4R-BG77)

# 14

# Middle East Case Studies: United Payment, QNB, NymCard

CHAPTER OBJECTIVES

In this chapter, we'll profile three distinct countries in the region: Turkey, Qatar, and the United Arab Emirates. We'll review key attributes of each country, including demographics, the banking system, and regulation, and discuss how these shape fintech and banking-as-a-service. We'll also take a look at a banking-as-a-service provider in each country: United Payment, QNB, and NymCard.

The Middle East region, at least by typical Western definition, encompasses the Arabian Peninsula, Egypt, Turkey, Iran, and Iraq. Over 370 million people live across more than 2.7 million square miles. Sometimes referred to as the "Cradle of Civilization," the Middle East has a complicated geopolitical past and present, which, while well beyond the scope of this book, certainly informs the region's financial services landscape. The region has historical ties to the UK and Europe, as well as contemporary commercial links around the world, as a major exporter of oil and natural gas. Some countries in the Middle East have experienced significant out migration, primarily to Europe, while others, especially oil-rich Gulf states, have sizable inflows of foreign workers, primarily from Pakistan, India, and other South Asian countries. Cognizant of the global imperative to lower carbon emissions, oil-producing countries in the

Middle East have worked to diversify their economies, by investing both at home and abroad. Several Middle Eastern countries, including the United Arab Emirates and Qatar, have worked to establish themselves as financial hubs in the region. And Turkey, which spans both Europe and Asia, also plays a critical role in providing financial services in the region.

## Turkey: A Bridge Between East and West

Turkey is often thought of as a "bridge" between Europe and Asia. On the European side, it borders Greece and Bulgaria, while, on the Asian side, it borders Syria, Iraq, Iran, Armenia, and Georgia. Turkey is generally considered to be part of the Middle East, though definitions of the region vary. The Turkish population numbers approximately 85 million as of 2022. The Turkish economy has grown massively, if somewhat unevenly, since the turn of the century. In 2000, Turkish GDP measured about $275 billion, but, by 2022, that had grown to over $900 billion. However, the Turkish economy does face some challenges that directly impact the banking sector, namely, inflation. For much of 2000–2020, annual inflation ran between 5 and 10 per cent, which is already high by developed economy standards. But in the post-pandemic period, Turkey has suffered with inflation as high as 80 per cent on a year-over-year basis.[1] In an effort to fight that inflation, the country quickly raised its key interest rate from 8.5 per cent in early 2023 to 50 per cent by the spring of 2024.[2]

As of 2023, there are approximately 60 banks that operate in Turkey, which includes domestic public (state-owned) and private commercial banks, foreign banks that operate in Turkey, and development and investment banks.[3] The country, in which nearly 100 per cent of the population identifies as Muslim, also has a number of public and private Islamic banks, which comply with Sharia's prohibition on charging interest. Like many other countries, the Turkish banking sector is dominated by a small number of firms. The "big four," Türkiye Cumhuriyeti Ziraat Bankası (Ziraat Bank), Türkiye

Vakıflar Bankası T.A.O. (VakifBank), Türkiye İş Bankası (İşbank), and Türkiye Halk Bankası (Halkbank), combined, account for about $382 billion, or just over half of the banking system's total assets of approximately $730 billion.[4] Three of the four largest banks by assets are state-owned. Foreign banks operating in the country include Dutch bank ING, UK-based HSBC, Citibank, JPMorgan Chase, Qatar-based QNB (profiled below), and a handful of others.

In addition to various types of banks, Turkey also offers an e-money license, which can enable firms to issue electronic money, offer payments services, provide digital wallets, conduct currency exchange, and offer acquiring services, including processing card transactions. As of 2024, there are approximately 60 licensed e-money institutions. In 2021, Turkey also introduced legislation to provide clarity by directly speaking to the banking-as-a-service model, using the terminology "service model banking" and defining the two key actors as the "service bank" and "interface provider."[5] The country's central bank also introduced an Open Banking Gateway, which can be used to facilitate payments services, in late 2022.[6] Interchange rates, a key component of many fintech and BaaS business models, are calculated according to a formula set by the Competition Authority and carried out by the Interbank Card Center, an industry consortium that is partially owned by the Turkish central bank. As of 2024, credit card transactions carry a maximum interchange rate of 3.36 per cent and debit transactions allow interchange up to 0.67 per cent.[7] Fintech investment in the country, while much lower than other geographies on an absolute dollar basis, has been increasing. The country saw just $12 million of venture investments into fintech firms in 2016, but that had grown to $64 million by 2021. Payments firms dominate the startup landscape, with 216 payments-focused firms operating in the country.

The Turkish banking sector, like many other developing countries, has leaned heavily into digital distribution, particularly with the introduction of 2013's Law on Payment and Securities Settlement Systems, Payment Services and Electronic Money Institutions. Regulation issued in May 2021 that governs remote customer acquisition made obtaining a customer's wet signature redundant, which has helped to pave the way for digital-only account opening processes. Physical branch density in the country peaked at about 20 branches per 100,000 adults in 2013 and has steadily declined since then, reaching about 15 branches per 100,000 in 2021.[8] Still, inclusion in the formal financial system lags behind other more developed economies, with less than 60 per cent of adults having access to a bank account.[9] Access to credit, measured by domestic credit as a percentage of GDP, had been consistently improving since the early 2000s and reached about 75 per cent in 2020, but has since contracted significantly as interest rose sharply to combat inflation. By 2022, the domestic credit-to-GDP ratio had dropped to just 55 per cent.[10]

### United Payment: A Turkish Fintech Powerhouse

United Payment was originally founded in Istanbul in 2010 with a business model focused on operating physical self-service kiosks which consumers could use to carry out basic financial transactions like buying mobile phone credit. The original offering didn't resonate, but the company pivoted to building financial and payments infrastructure and, in 2015, obtained its e-money and payment services licenses in Turkey. In 2019, the company took an undisclosed amount of external capital from Finberg, a Turkish fund manager that has also invested in numerous other Turkish and regional fintechs, including e-wallet startup Hayhay and supplier financing platform Figopara. Oyak Asset Management Venture Capital also invested an unknown amount into the company in 2021. While United Payment describes itself as offering "fintech-as-a-service" rather than "banking-as-a-service," as the company itself does not hold a bank license, its role in providing infrastructure to other firms, who, in turn, use it to build customer-facing products is functionally the same thing.

United Payment boasts capabilities that include physical and virtual card issuing, white-label consumer and business digital wallets, international payments, merchant acquiring and point-of-sale solutions, physical cash management through its "smart safe," and branded self-serve kiosks that can be used for bill payment or cash withdrawal. In addition to supporting Visa and Mastercard networks, United Payment also issues cards compatible with Turkey's local card scheme, TROY.

United Payment's capabilities support a wide variety of use cases, including branded debit cards and wallets, customized e-commerce checkout solutions, foreign exchange and remittances, domestic and international payments, buy now pay later, and more. White-labeled digital wallets can be used to hold and transfer funds, make payments, and can even be linked to virtual and physical payment cards or linked to credit instruments, like BNPL. United Payment also supports digital marketplace and retail platforms through its escrow feature, which enables end users to safely transact on such platforms without fear of being scammed. Clients building on United Payment's infrastructure don't need to obtain their own licenses, and the company handles the complexity of legal and regulatory compliance, technical integrations, payment operations, fraud, and so forth, making it straightforward to integrate financial features in their offerings.

United Payment's clients include major names in fintech, like Wise (formerly TransferWise), Remitly, TransferGo, and dLocal, as well as major consumer brands like Unilever, Samsung, BMW, and Pepsi. Through its partnerships, United Payment supports approximately 15 million end users with a total annual transaction volume exceeding $3.4 billion. Through its collaboration with industry partners, United Payment's reach covers 91 countries and 54 currencies. And, importantly for a region with uneven access to formal financial services, it is not required that end users have a bank account to use the platform.

In May 2024, the company announced that it became the first Turkish fintech to secure an e-money license in nearby Azerbaijan, as it seeks to solidify its position as a regional financial services provider. The company also holds an e-money license and operates in Georgia. United Payment has regional offices in Romania and the UK, though it does not hold licenses to operate in those countries as of 2024.

## Qatar: A Tiny Gulf Nation that Punches Above its Weight

Qatar, a British protectorate from 1961 until the country gained independence in 1971, consists of a thumb-shaped peninsula jutting from Saudi Arabia, with a landmass of less than 5,000 square miles. The country has grown substantially since 2020, both in terms of GDP and population, as it allowed the entrance of large numbers of foreign workers. In 2005, Qatar had a population of fewer than 850,000 people, which ballooned to more than 2.75 million by 2020. The migrant workforce in the country is estimated at some 2 million people, representing nearly 95 per cent of the country's workforce. As it has allowed foreign migrants to enter the country to work, Qatar has also seen its GDP grow significantly. In 2000, Qatar's GDP was a little under $18 billion, and it had soared to just over $235 billion by 2022. The large foreign workforce introduces interesting challenges and needs in the financial sector, including access to financial services and high demand for remittance products. In sharp contrast to Turkey, inflation rates in Qatar historically have been significantly more muted, spiking to 15 per cent during the 2008 Global Financial Crisis and 5 per cent during the post-Covid era, but otherwise hovering between 1 per cent and 4 per cent.

There are just 18 licensed banks in Qatar, which includes domestic- and foreign-based banks, as well as Islamic banks. The Qatar National Bank, known as QNB, is by far the largest bank in the country by assets, with over $320 billion in assets as of 2022.[11] QNB has a market share of nearly 60 per cent, as measured by assets. Foreign banks that operate in Qatar include Barclays, HSBC, Standard Chartered, and BNP Paribas. The number of physical branches in Qatar on a per capita basis has been steadily declining since the early 2000s. In 2004, the country had 21.5 branches per 100,000 adults. By 2021, that had declined to 8.5 per 100,000.[12] Despite the declining number of branches, about two-thirds of adults in Qatar have access to a bank account.[13] On an aggregate basis, access to credit is fairly widespread, as measured by a domestic credit-to-GDP ratio of just over 100 per cent in 2022.[14] However, given Qatar's outside immigrant population, credit availability is uneven.

In addition to the traditional banking sector, Qatar introduced regulations in 2021 to formally regulate and supervise payment service providers. The scope of the regulation includes e-money issuance, merchant acquiring, domestic funds transfers, and other related activities, like owning and operating ATMs. The country has made a concerted effort to foster innovation and development in its financial sector, including through the Qatar Fintech Hub (QFTH), which offers support services such as mentorship and startup incubation. Focus areas for fintech in the country include digital payments, Islamic finance, and SMB financing. Qatar also offers a regulatory sandbox, which enables fintechs to test new products and services in a controlled environment. The country's fintech hub also is a venture investor itself, providing capital investments to firms both in Qatar and the surrounding region. An estimated 800 firms spanning fintech, but also IT, tax, investment, and related consulting firms are registered with the country's Qatar Financial Centre. Recent venture investing trends across all sectors, not just fintech, mirror those in other countries, with a spike in investing activity during 2021–2022 and sharp drop off in 2023. On an absolute basis, venture investments in the country in 2023 totaled about $12 million.

Although Qatar lacks banking-as-a-service-specific regulation, the Qatari central bank has struck an innovation-friendly posture. In addition to permitting e-money licensing, the central bank has also developed regulations and guidelines intended to foster innovation, including for electronic KYC (e-KYC), open banking, and cloud computing.

### QNB: A Tech-Forward 60-Year-Old Bank

QNB, known as Qatar National Bank until 2004, was originally founded in 1964. The bank is half owned by the Qatar Investment Authority, with the balance owned publicly and traded via the Qatar Stock Exchange. The bank has and continues to play a key role in supporting the economy and development of Qatar. QNB not only dominates in its home country, with nearly 60 per cent market share by assets, but also abroad. QNB, through its International Network, has a strong presence throughout the Gulf countries, with operations in Saudi Arabia, Kuwait, Oman, and the UAE, as well as elsewhere in the Middle East, Africa, Asia, and Europe. Including Qatar, QNB International Network has an operating presence in 28 countries.

QNB has supported major development projects in Qatar and abroad, such as the Hamad International Airport, natural gas projects in Ras Laffan, the towers housing the Qatar Financial Centre headquarters, and the Shard Tower in London.

QNB is a full-service bank that serves retail, business, and corporate clients. Its spectrum of retail consumer products includes deposit accounts, prepaid, debit, and credit cards, loans, insurance, wealth management, asset management, and private banking. For small and medium enterprises, QNB offers a similar span of deposit, spending, and borrowing products, as well as merchant and e-acquiring. For corporates, QNB has full-featured, global transaction banking, structured and project finance, and support for international trade transactions.

The bank prioritizes innovation through a number of initiatives across four key themes: Marketplaces and platforms, robotics and automation, AI and data analytics, and APIs and open banking. In June 2022, the bank announced the launch of its open banking platform, the first such platform for a Qatari bank and one of the first in the region. QNB also operates its own fintech accelerator program. Note that while in the US market, "open banking" generally refers to the ability to move account data via API, in QNB's case, it is using the term to refer to a broader set of capabilities. QNB's open banking platform enables third-party partners to integrate the bank's core financial services, including both accessing customer data and facilitating payments. The open banking platform is part of QNB's strategy to collaborate with non-bank partners to drive innovation, efficiencies, and a superior user experience. In 2024, QNB launched its open banking API for corporate clients, also a first in the country. The API enables corporate clients to access data and initiate payments programmatically, including through integrations with other applications they use to manage their businesses, such as enterprise resource planning platforms.

An example of a third-party partner that leverages QNB's capabilities is Qatari digital wallet Ooredoo. In addition to home internet, TV, entertainment services, and mobile phone plans, Ooredoo offers a digital wallet. The wallet offers a broad set of functionalities, including international transfers and the ability to top up mobile phone credit in 80 countries, key capabilities for Qatar's large foreign workforce. Ooredoo also enables users to transfer money to and from local bank accounts, mobile wallets, or as cash for pickup around the world, through its integration with remittance service Moneygram. Ooredoo even offers capabilities designed for merchants, like payment gateway services that allow e-commerce sites to accept digital payments for services. Services like Ooredoo exemplify the potential of the banking-as-a-service model, both to serve consumers' needs and also as important distribution channels for financial institutions.

## United Arab Emirates: Diversifying its Economy Through Innovation

The United Arab Emirates, often referred to simply as the UAE, is composed of seven emirates: Abu Dhabi, Ajman, Fujairah, Sharjah, Dubai, Ras al-Khaimah, and Umm al-Quw. Altogether, the UAE spans over 32,000 square miles. Like Qatar, the UAE has seen both its population and GDP increase sharply since around 2000, driven in part by large numbers of foreign workers. In 2000, the UAE was home to about 3.275 million people. By 2020, the number of inhabitants grew to exceed 9.25 million. Estimates put the share of Emirati citizens at less than 12 per cent of the total, while the remainder are foreigners, primarily immigrants from nearby South Asian countries. Likewise, GDP grew from just over $100 billion in 2000 to over $500 billion in 2022. While Abu Dhabi is the capital of the UAE, the country's largest city is Dubai, though both cities are home to a number of major financial institutions.

There are over 50 banks operating in the UAE, including domestic- and foreign-based banks, investment banks, and Islamic banks. The largest banks in the UAE include First Abu Dhabi Bank, with over $300 billion in assets, Emirates NBD Bank, with over $200 billion in assets, and Abu Dhabi Commercial Bank, with about $130 billion in assets. Combined, the three account for more than half of the banking sector's total assets.[15] Foreign banks from neighboring countries include financial institutions headquartered in Bahrain, Iraq, Jordan, Iran, Oman, and Pakistan. European banks like BNP Paribas, HSBC, NatWest, and Standard Chartered also have a presence, as do American firms Citibank and American Express. The UAE also offers e-money licensing, with three regulatory entities, the Central Bank of the UAE, the Financial Services Regulatory Authority, and the Dubai Financial Services Authority, authorized to issue e-money licenses.[16] Regulations allow for the operation of payment institutions and payment services providers, which can offer digital wallets, money transmission, payment processing, payment accounts, and stored value services.

As is the case with other countries in the region, the density of bank branches has been declining for some time. In 2004, the UAE had about 15 branches per 100,000 adults. As its population has increased, that ratio has declined, and by 2021, the country had just 7.6 branches per 100,000 adults.[17] Still, penetration of banking services is comparatively high, with over 85 per cent of the population aged 15 or older having access to a bank or mobile money account.[18] Access to credit, as measured by the domestic credit-to-GDP ratio, has been less even, particularly through the pandemic period. In 2020, the ratio was about 90 per cent but dropped to 66 per cent by 2022.[19]

The UAE, like other regional powers, has sought to diversify its economy, including by supporting innovation in the financial services and fintech sector. Government-supported initiatives include the Dubai Future Accelerators program and the Abu Dhabi Global Market Regulatory Lab, for instance. The Central Bank of the UAE also offers a regulatory sandbox and tailored framework, enabling new firms to test new products and services in a controlled environment. Key focus areas have included peer-to-peer payments, digital payments, wealth advising and management, blockchain and crypto, and Islamic finance. There are estimated to be at least 71 fintech firms operating in the UAE, with overall venture investment in the country (not just fintech) reaching nearly $1.2 billion in 2022.

While other countries in the region have taken a regulator-driven approach to some aspects of financial innovation, including open banking, the UAE has favored a more market-led approach, in which regulators have focused on giving guidance and letting market actors sort out implementation. Establishment banks haven't shied away from developing external APIs, and newer players, like NymCard, have created a modern flexible platform to meet the needs of both consumers and businesses in the UAE as well as abroad.

### NymCard: Providing Regional Fintechs with BaaS Infrastructure

Dubai-based NymCard was founded in 2018 with the goal of building a state-of-the-art technology stack to power fintech and embedded finance solutions for both consumers and businesses in the Middle East/North Africa region.[20] The company announced it had raised an additional $22.5 million round of financing in June 2022, bringing its total funding raised to over $35 million.[21] Investors include Shorooq Partners, OTF Jasoor Ventures, and VentureSouq. In addition to its home market of the UAE, NymCard also has a presence in regional hubs in Cairo, Egypt, and Riyadh, Saudi Arabia.

In 2020, NymCard secured its in-principle approval from the Financial Services Regulatory Authority to transfer and hold money, carry out currency exchange, and issue payments instruments with stored value. This enables NymCard to offer a variety of services, including BIN sponsorship, cross-border payments, virtual IBANs, treasury management, and program management, including built-in risk mitigation and customizable controls. Program management capabilities mean companies building on NymCard's platform can take advantage of its team of internal legal and compliance experts to ensure they meet the requirements of sponsored banks, card schemes, and other stakeholders. NymCard achieves broad reach through partnerships with Visa, Mastercard, and Western Union, as well as support for wallets like Apple Pay and Google Pay.

Product support includes prepaid card, credit cards, and multi-currency accounts. NymCard's custom-built credit card technology stack enables those building on it to have extremely granular control over product and account characteristics, including business rules, fees, and branding. Capabilities include credit decisioning, leveraging credit bureaus for external scoring and in-house modeling, dynamically configurable business rules, account servicing, and delinquency management functions, including seamless integration with collection agencies.

In 2023, NymCard announced the acquisition of Spotii, a buy-now-pay-later firm previously acquired by Australian BNPL firm Zip. Spotii came with a footprint of over 1,500 merchant partners and more than one million end users across Saudi Arabia, the UAE, and Bahrain. The acquisition expanded NymCard's capabilities to include Spotii's risk engine and underwriting experience, enabling NymCard's clients to offer their end users credit-on-demand products. These capabilities and products support a wide variety of potential use cases, including neobanking, corporate cards, gift cards, youth banking, travel cards, and payroll cards.

NymCard boasts over 300 fintech clients on its platform, including Saudi-based Pemo, Wally, and Lamha. Pemo offers expense management, corporate cards, invoicing, payments, and accounting automation solutions. Wally began as an expense tracking and personal financial management tool, before pivoting to a ChatGPT-powered personal finance app. And Lamha offers a corporate expense tracking and automation tool that allows companies to easily understand where they are spending, track against budget, and generate financial reports and KPIs. In late 2023, NymCard struck a partnership with Qatar-based CWallet. CWallet operates a digital wallet that enables users to receive direct deposit of salary payments, conduct both online and offline payments, and conduct foreign exchange and remittance transactions. The partnership between the two companies enables CWallet to issue branded prepaid cards to its users in Qatar.

## Regulatory Clarity Supports BaaS in the Region

The Middle East boasts a vibrant and growing banking and fintech sector. In many ways, the region has been able to progress more quickly, thanks to relatively streamlined and unified regulatory structures, than some developed Western markets, especially the United States. The Middle East has also benefited from being able to observe different market structures and regulatory approaches in the UK and

Europe, including initiatives like e-money and payments institution licensing and open banking regulation, in order to learn from what worked and what didn't work in those markets. One must be careful about not painting with too broad a brush, as the economic, banking, regulatory, and political realities can vary substantially from country to country. But as the cases of Turkey, Qatar, and the United Arab Emirates make clear, the potential for fintech and banking-as-a-service in the region is bright.

## Endnotes

1   Trading Economics (2024) Turkey Inflation Rate, tradingeconomics.com/turkey/inflation-cpi (archived at https://perma.cc/D5GK-4ZZB)

2   Trading Economics (2024) Turkey Interest Rate, tradingeconomics.com/turkey/interest-rate (archived at https://perma.cc/V5DT-Q2UV)

3   The Banks Association of Turkey (2024) Statistical Reports, www.tbb.org.tr/en/banks-and-banking-sector-information/statistical-reports/20 (archived at https://perma.cc/EV9L-4V5F)

4   The Banks Association of Turkey (2024) Statistical Reports, www.tbb.org.tr/en/banks-and-banking-sector-information/statistical-reports/20 (archived at https://perma.cc/H2QX-7U2X)

5   Canpolat, Y. (2023) The Future of Banking? A Look into Türkiye's Regulation on Banking as a Service Business Model, mondaq, www.mondaq.com/turkey/fin-tech/1297570/the-future-of-banking-a-look-into-t%C3%BCrkiyes-regulation-on-banking-as-a-service-business-model (archived at https://perma.cc/2Q5K-SJ7R)

6   Duncan, E. (2022) Turkey Launches Open Banking Infrastructure, Open Banking Expo, www.openbankingexpo.com/news/turkey-launches-open-banking-infrastructure/ (archived at https://perma.cc/H4FB-A9EP)

7   Bankalararasi Kart Merkezi (2024) Inter-Member Interchange Commissions, bkm.com.tr/en/useful-information/commissions-and-fees/interbank-interchange-commissions/ (archived at https://perma.cc/TH8S-S3P8)

8   World Bank Group (n.d.) International Monetary Fund Financial Access Survey, data.worldbank.org/indicator/FB.CBK.BRCH.P5 (archived at https://perma.cc/99BG-M6QU)

9   World Bank Group (n.d.) Global Findex Database, data.worldbank.org/indicator/FX.OWN.TOTL.ZS (archived at https://perma.cc/Y3Y8-LGJW)

**10**   World Bank Group (n.d.) International Monetary Fund International Financial Statistics, data.worldbank.org/indicator/FS.AST.PRVT.GD.ZS (archived at https://perma.cc/J4PV-B54B)

**11**   Jimenea, A. and Taqi, M. (2023) Middle East and Africa's 30 Largest Banks by Assets, 2023, S&P Global, www.spglobal.com/marketintelligence/en/news-insights/research/middle-east-and-africas-30-largest-banks-by-assets-2023 (archived at https://perma.cc/6VKK-MB9R)

**12**   World Bank Group (n.d.) International Monetary Fund Financial Access Survey, data.worldbank.org/indicator/FB.CBK.BRCH.P5 (archived at https://perma.cc/FG69-CMXK)

**13**   World Bank Group (n.d.) Global Findex Database, data.worldbank.org/indicator/FX.OWN.TOTL.ZS (archived at https://perma.cc/3HGT-FQ9F)

**14**   World Bank Group (n.d.) International Monetary Fund International Financial Statistics, data.worldbank.org/indicator/FS.AST.PRVT.GD.ZS (archived at https://perma.cc/VS8Z-R4VM)

**15**   Jimenea, A. and Taqi, M. (2023) Middle East and Africa's 30 Largest Banks by Assets, 2023, S&P Global, www.spglobal.com/marketintelligence/en/news-insights/research/middle-east-and-africas-30-largest-banks-by-assets-2023 (archived at https://perma.cc/6NQD-WTLW)

**16**   10 Leaves (n.d.) Electronic Money Institution (EMI) Licenses in the DIFC, 10leaves.ae/publications/difc/electronic-money-institution-licenses-in-the-difc (archived at https://perma.cc/Q5MJ-64B4)

**17**   World Bank Group (n.d.) International Monetary Fund Financial Access Survey, data.worldbank.org/indicator/FB.CBK.BRCH.P5 (archived at https://perma.cc/7KNB-TEUW)

**18**   World Bank Group (n.d.) Global Findex Database, data.worldbank.org/indicator/FX.OWN.TOTL.ZS (archived at https://perma.cc/VEF5-9W5E)

**19**   World Bank Group (n.d.) International Monetary Fund International Financial Statistics, data.worldbank.org/indicator/FS.AST.PRVT.GD.ZS (archived at https://perma.cc/274Q-6NU8)

**20**   NymCard (2024) Who We Are, nymcard.com/who_we_are (archived at https://perma.cc/9XHE-734V)

**21**   Fintech Futures (2022) MENA's BaaS Provider NymCard Raises $22.5m Funding, www.fintechfutures.com/2022/06/menas-baas-provider-nymcard-raises-22-5m-funding/ (archived at https://perma.cc/D66C-3T2Z)

# 15

# Where Does Banking-as-a-Service Go from Here?

The term "banking-as-a-service" may be new, but the idea of a non-bank firm working with a chartered institution isn't. The explosion of interest in the topic and new approaches in the model have their roots in the birth of "fintech," which began around 2010 but reached new heights as venture capital funding to startups in the space exploded in the early years of the Covid-19 pandemic. At one point, it's estimated that one out of every five VC dollars was being invested into a fintech startup.[1]

But as should be clear by now, how banking-as-a-service has evolved, and where it will go from here, will be heavily shaped by local realities, including the history and present of banking markets, how legislation and regulation shape permitted activities and business models, demographics, consumers' and businesses' financial needs, availability of venture funding, and how technology itself evolves. These factors will influence the "supply" side, of what institutions are able and willing to support BaaS operating models, and the "demand" side of what companies need such services to support their businesses. Where BaaS goes from here will be determined by the intersection of supply and demand in individual markets.

## United States: Is BaaS Past its Peak?

As is often the case in banking and beyond, the United States is a unique market. Its "dual" state and federal banking system, its large number of licensed banks, lack of any kind of e-money or payments institution license, lack of a national non-bank lending license, and substantially higher rate of debit card interchange make it difficult to compare fintech, in general, and banking-as-a-service, specifically in the US to other markets. These and other factors support high levels of both supply of and demand for BaaS capabilities.

But while BaaS exploded in popularity as funding to new fintech firms spiked around 2020, that growth does not appear to be sustainable. Banks and customer-facing fintechs engaging in BaaS-powered business models have not always taken the necessary steps to ensure they are operating in a responsible, compliant manner. The disorderly bankruptcy of middleware platform Synapse, which saw hundreds of thousands of everyday consumers and businesses lose access to their funds for weeks, laid bare the worst-case scenario. Going forward, BaaS is likely to be shaped by forces that include regulatory backlash to excesses in the sector, reduced levels of VC funding, questions about the viability of certain business models, and the rise of "API-native" or "headless" banking.

**Regulatory backlash:** As covered in Chapter 8, BaaS isn't without operational challenges. Many of the banks that partner with fintechs in the US are small and may lack the resources or sophistication to properly manage sprawling partnerships. The issues haven't escaped regulatory attention. Since Blue Ridge Bank's first enforcement action in 2022, numerous other banks have been subject to regulatory action stemming from their BaaS activities and fintech partnerships. While some in industry have decried the lack of a clear "rule book" about how to meet regulators' expectations, beyond already-issued guidance, one is unlikely to be forthcoming. The regulatory backlash, coming from all three federal banking regulators, the OCC, the FDIC, and the FRB, is likely to persist, and other entities, like the CFPB or state banking regulators, may get involved as well. The upshot is increasing costs for all actors in the banking-as-a-service ecosystem: Banks, middleware firms, and customer-facing fintechs, as they work to achieve compliance and meet regulators' expectations. Some banks that only recently entered the space may choose to exit and refocus on their core businesses. Likewise, middleware intermediaries, like Unit, Treasury

Prime, and Synctera, are attempting to pivot from a business model focused on selling services to fintechs to a model of selling software to banks, putting them in competition with other new entrants and legacy core providers, like FIS and Fiserv. In the near- to-mid-term, heightened regulatory scrutiny is likely to reduce the supply of BaaS services and increase the expense and difficulty of working with a partner bank.

The June 2024 Russian hack of Evolve Bank & Trust, one of the most significant BaaS banks in the US, adds a new dimension of uncertainty. As of the end of June 2024, the full extent of the impact on Evolve and its sprawling collection of fintech programs is not known, but is believed to be significant.[2] The incident calls into question the "move fast and break things" mentality of some, though certainly not all, in fintech. There has long been a culture clash between "bankers," who tend to focus on risk mitigation, and the technologists that dominate non-bank fintech companies, who tend to prioritize innovation driven by a test-and-learn approach over perfection. Banking-as-a-service represents the intersection of these two mindsets. For the approach to succeed and endure, bankers and fintechs will need to build a mutual understanding in such a way that there is room for innovation and experimentation, while ensuring risks are adequately understood and controlled for.

**Reduced venture capital funding:** Funding to fintech startups reached a gargantuan $121.1 billion globally in 2021.[3] By 2023, it had dropped by more than 60 per cent to $46.3 billion. By 2024, funding levels appeared to stabilize around their pre-pandemic levels. On the one hand, the more sober funding climate should lead to more rational investing decisions. However, less funding for new fintech formation or growth of existing companies translates to lower demand for BaaS capabilities. Funding levels have reverted to the mean, but it may take longer for reduced demand for BaaS capabilities to flow through to BaaS intermediaries and banks.

**Business model viability:** A major driver of the appeal of BaaS for US banks was the outsized financial returns that banks like The Bancorp or Pathward, which have been in the space for quite some time, were able to generate. As more banks looked to enter the space, middleware firms sought to simplify the process of tech-driven startups working with risk-and-compliance focused banks. But with the peak of the trend in the US seemingly behind us, there are questions about the viability of certain business models, both for customer-facing fintech firms and middleware intermediaries. The middleware space has already seen consolidation, with Rize, Apto Payments, and Bond being acquired and the failure of Synapse. Whether or not those remaining are viable as standalone businesses is an open question.

**Rise of "headless" banking:** As we touched on in Chapter 6, there are multiple approaches to BaaS in the US. The popularity of middleware firms sought to solve one of the challenges of working with community banks: That their technology stacks are often from legacy core providers and are difficult to integrate. A new crop of banks sought to solve that problem at the source, rather than by creating a new layer on top of an antiquated system. Banks like Column, Lead, and Cross River have built "API-first" or "headless" banking solutions, in which much or all of their banking business is operated through partnerships facilitated by allowing third parties to integrate directly with their tech stacks. One can also think of this as a sort of wholesale/retail model, in which the bank provides the core capabilities of banking to its partners, which, in turn, build specific products to retail to their end customers. This approach, still in its infancy, has the potential to disrupt both middleware firms and legacy partner banks with outdated technology.

There's no question that BaaS in the US has experienced a period of pronounced turmoil. But the model of fintechs partnering with banks is unlikely to go anywhere. Absent the creation of some new type of national licenses, like the e-money and payments institution charters available in many other countries, fintech firms in the US will continue to be dependent on banks if they wish to offer regulated products and services, including holding deposits, issuing payment cards, and offering credit.

## The UK and the EU: Measured Adoption Likely to Continue

Other developed markets, particularly those in the UK and the EU, have largely avoided the excesses seen in BaaS in the US. While the specifics vary country to country, the existence of alternate license types, like those for e-money and payments institutions, have reduced the need for fintech firms to rely on banks and BaaS. Significantly lower interchange rates make business models dependent on interchange as a revenue stream relatively less appealing than in the US. Demand for credit in some EU countries, owing to regulatory constraints and cultural differences, also tends to be significantly lower. VC funding in these regions didn't spike as dramatically as it did in the US, meaning growth in the sector was more controlled. Stronger and more unified regulatory oversight also likely contributed to less-risky approaches in the region. That isn't to say there haven't been any problems. Railsr and Transactive Systems, for example, experienced similar problems and regulatory responses as those seen in the US. How BaaS evolves going forward is likely to be shaped by demand from fintech firms and for embedded finance use cases.

Like in the US, venture funding to fintechs in the UK and the EU has declined from peaks seen in the 2021–2022 period. Less funding will equate to fewer new firms being founded that may need BaaS capabilities and slower growth for existing firms. Embedded finance, in which non-financial companies complement their product offering by adding financial features, like payments and credit, is likely to be the primary demand channel for BaaS providers, both "headless banks," like Griffin and Solaris, as well as firms operating on e-money licenses, like Swan. Examples of such embedded finance use cases include accounting and invoicing platforms that offer businesses the ability to directly collect payments or e-commerce platforms that enable sellers access to financing as part of their offerings. Development in these areas is likely to continue at a measured pace.

## The Rest of the World Offers More Greenfield Opportunity

The most meaningful market for banking-as-a-service may be in the developing world. There's more greenfield opportunity, as access to basic banking services and credit still lag behind many developed countries. Banking-as-a-service has the potential to help boost access and inclusion in formal financial systems and, with that, overall economic development. But the success of fintech, in general, and BaaS models, specifically, isn't a sure thing and will be shaped by a number of country-specific factors, including regulatory and licensing approaches, reactions from incumbent financial institutions, access to VC funding, and local market customs and preferences.

**Regulatory and licensing approaches:** It's difficult to boil down the specifics of dozens of countries' regulatory and licensing approaches into a single neat conclusion, but it is possible to draw some common threads. Alternate license types, like frameworks for e-money and payments institutions, make it simpler for fintechs to operate without the need for BaaS capabilities. Interchange and lending rate caps may make payments and credit business models more or less attractive in a given country. The existence of alternate payment systems, like Pix in Brazil, may reduce the need for card-based payments altogether. Regulatory attitudes toward BaaS also vary substantially. For instance, in Mexico, despite the passage of its Fintech Law, BaaS operating models have been met with skepticism from regulators, introducing uncertainty to the approach, whereas other markets, like Turkey, have specifically acknowledged the model and codified expectations in regulation. Many developing countries explicitly encourage innovation in the financial sector and offer support, like regulatory "sandboxes," that provide safe harbor for firms experimenting with new approaches. How BaaS and its use cases evolve in any given market will be heavily influenced by how it is viewed by regulators.

**Reactions from incumbents:** The need for and availability of BaaS has and will continue to be influenced by how incumbent financial institutions respond to changing market conditions. For example, some "legacy" banks, like Standard Chartered in South East Asia and QNB in the Middle East, have taken a tech-forward approach, capitalizing on their strong history and balance sheets in their respective markets. Other banks have pursued strategies that see them competing head-to-head with fintechs by offering their own direct-to-consumer digital services, like Santander's Openbank in Mexico. In other countries, established banks have used their clout and political power to influence regulatory responses to emerging models in ways that favor incumbents. The risk-vs.-reward calculation for an existing bank developing a BaaS business line will vary not only by country, but even among institutions within a given country. How established banks respond to the opportunities and threats presented by BaaS will run the gamut.

**Access to VC funding:** Venture capital funding has been and will continue to be a key ingredient in how BaaS develops. VC funding is critical on the demand side, as most fintech startups that use BaaS services and many BaaS providers are VC-funded startups. Access to such funding is incredibly uneven and can be hard to come by in smaller and less-developed markets. For instance, while Brazil and Mexico have developed robust fintech ecosystems, smaller markets in LatAm are often overlooked by investors. Likewise in South East Asia, huge markets like India or Indonesia have been reasonably successful at attracting investment, while smaller neighbors struggle to do so. The venture capital model depends on investors achieving a small number of outsized returns to compensate for investments that don't pan out. Earning those outsized returns is dependent on having a large enough "total addressable market." Size of population but also income and wealth are important inputs into the calculation of how big a given market is and implicitly preferences larger and wealthier countries.

**Local market characteristics and preferences:** Idiosyncratic behavior can also have a significant impact on the viability of BaaS in a given country. As we saw in the case of Mexico, many consumers and businesses still have a strong preference for cash, which may attenuate demand for digital-only services that are users of BaaS infrastructure. Markets like Argentina or Turkey, that historically suffer from high inflation, may have unique customer demands and use cases. Markets in Africa, like Kenya, which have a long history and deep penetration of "mobile money" solutions, like M-PESA, may have unique competitive dynamics that shape demand for BaaS. Availability of complementary technology and data, like credit bureau coverage and open banking connectivity, can influence the viability of credit products. So while it is difficult to boil "local characteristics" down to a single takeaway, it is easy to say that demand for and the viability of BaaS in a given country will be heavily influenced by these kinds of preferences and characteristics.

## Fintech and Banking Aren't "Winner Take All" Markets

There is no single answer to the question "where does banking-as-a-service go from here?" While there are common themes and challenges, the trajectory will vary country to country, market to market. If there is one universal, inexorable trend, it is the decline of the importance of the physical bank branch. In-person interactions for financial services are unlikely to entirely disappear anytime soon. For less frequent and more complicated transactions, like buying a home or planning for retirement, some consumers are likely to prefer a human touch, no matter how sophisticated digital channels become.

Indeed, this is already happening, as we saw from declining branch numbers on an absolute and per capita basis in both developed and still-developing countries. How digital distribution will evolve and what it will look like in the future remains an open question. And there may be more than one "right" answer, as different segments of consumers and businesses have different preferences. Incumbent banks, new "headless" banks, upstart fintechs, and non-bank firms that embed financial capabilities in their offerings, are all likely to be puzzle pieces that fit together in order to meet users' financial needs going forward.

## Endnotes

1   Wilhelm, A. (2022) Is It Time to Worry about Fintech Valuations?, *TechCrunch*, techcrunch.com/2022/02/23/is-it-time-to-worry-about-fintech-valuations/ (archived at https://perma.cc/G4BV-LT5J)

2   Mikula, J. (2024) Evolve Hack Crisis: Russia-Linked Cybergang Leaks Records on Millions, *Fintech Business Weekly*, fintechbusinessweekly.substack.com/p/ evolve-hack-crisis-russia-linked (archived at https://perma.cc/EH9H-25GK)

3   KPMG (2023) Pulse of Fintech H2'23, assets.kpmg.com/content/dam/kpmg/xx/ pdf/2024/02/pulse-of-fintech-h2-2023.pdf (archived at https://perma.cc/AGW6-U2GG)

# ABBREVIATIONS AND DEFINITIONS

**Acquirer (merchant acquirer):** The financial institution or bank that enables a merchant to accept debit and credit card payments.

**Anti-money laundering (AML):** Legislation, rules, and regulations designed to prevent the use of the financial system to move or store funds generated from criminal activity.

**Application programming interface (API):** The method by which two or more computer systems interact to exchange information.

**Automated Clearing House (ACH):** Dominant US payment system for electronic bank-to-bank transfers.

**Bank identification number (BIN):** The first four to six digits of a payment card number, which typically identify the card network, card type, and issuing bank.

**Bank Secrecy Act (BSA):** Legislation that establishes program, record keeping, and reporting requirements for US financial institutions; amended substantially by the PATRIOT Act.

**BIN Sponsor:** The bank of record that sponsors a given card program.

**Buy now, pay later (BNPL):** A type of short-term financing that enables a borrower to spread the cost of purchase over a number of installments, most commonly consisting of a down payment and three subsequent payments.

**Customer Due Diligence and Enhanced Due Diligence (CDD/EDD):** Requirements and processes by which financial institutions onboard and monitor customers.

**Electronic Funds Transfer (EFT):** Electronic payments.

**Electronic Funds Transfer Act (EFTA):** Legislation designed to protect consumers in the US when making electronic payments, including through EFTs, ACH, card payments, and ATMs.

**Embedded finance:** The distribution of financial services, like payments or loans, by non-financial firms, often digitally.

**Embedded fintech:** The integration of fintech services into financial institutions' products sets, including their websites and mobile apps.

**Equal Credit Opportunity Act (ECOA):** Legislation prohibiting unlawful discrimination in credit transactions in the US.

**Fair Credit Reporting Act (FCRA):** The US federal law that regulates the collection and use of consumer credit data.

**Federal Deposit Insurance Corporation (FDIC):** A US federal banking regulator, which oversees state-chartered non-member banks and is responsible for administering deposit insurance.

**Federal Reserve Board:** The governing body of the US central bank, which is responsible for setting interest rate policy, but also maintains payment systems, like FedACH and FedWire, as well as being responsible for overseeing state-chartered member banks.

**Interchange:** The largest component of the merchant discount rate, which merchants pay to accept cards. Paid to the issuing bank.

**Issuer (and issuer-processor):** The bank or financial institution associated with a payment card. An issuer-processor is typically a third-party provider that helps process card transactions by connecting an issuing bank to card schemes, like Visa and Mastercard.

**Know-Your-Customer/Know-Your-Business (KYC/KYB):** Requirements for financial institutions to document and monitor their consumer and business customers.

**Marketplace lending:** A model in which a non-bank firm originates loans and often sells some or all of the associate loans or loan receivables.

**Merchant Discount Rate (MDR):** The cost, as a percentage of a transaction, that a merchant pays to accept card payments. Composed of interchange, card scheme fees, acquirer markup, and potentially other ancillary fees.

**Middleware provider:** A technology intermediary that connects a non-bank firm with a financial institution for the purpose of offering regulated financial services products, like deposit accounts or payment cards.

**Money Services Business (MSB):** A type of non-bank financial firm that offers regulated financial products, like international remittances or check cashing.

**Money Transmission License (MTL):** In the US, state-issued licenses for non-bank businesses that operate business involved with money movement, like peer-to-peer payments or remittance services.

**Net Interest Income (NII):** A banking metric that measures a firm's interest income less its interest expense.

**Net Interest Margin (NIM):** A banking metric that measures a firm's interest income less its interest expense as a percentage.

**Office of the Comptroller of the Currency (OCC):** The federal US agency responsible for chartering and overseeing national banks.

**Payment Gateway:** A service that facilitates a merchant accepting payments by connecting point-of-sale to a payment processor. Often bundled together with processing capabilities.

**Program Manager:** A non-bank company that contracts with an issuer, typically a bank, to establish, market, and run a card program.

**Rent-A-Bank or Rent-A-Charter:** A colloquial term for the arrangement in which non-banks partner with banks to offer regulated products. Often considered pejorative.

**Suspicious Activity Report (SAR):** Reports that regulated entities are required to file when they detect unusual or suspicious customer transactions.

**Truth In Lending Act (TILA):** A US law that protects consumers from inaccurate and unfair credit practices.

**Unfair, Deceptive, and Abusive Acts and Practices (UDAAP):** A broad authority for bank regulators to police the business practices and products of regulated entities.

# INDEX

# Looking for another book?

Explore our award-winning
books from global business
experts in Finance and
Banking

Scan the code to browse

www.koganpage.com/finance

# More books from Kogan Page

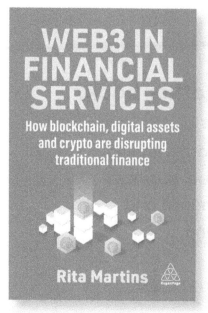

ISBN: 9781398615717

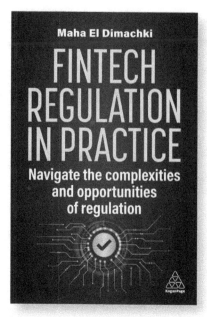

ISBN: 9781398615694

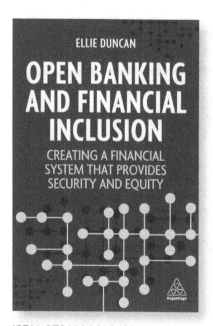

ISBN: 9781398612402

ISBN: 9781398613874

**www.koganpage.com**

www.ingramcontent.com/pod-product-compliance
Lightning Source LLC
Jackson TN
JSHW050808271224
76012JS00016B/28